DIXIE BE DAMNED

300 Years of Insurrection in the American South

DIXIE BE DAMNED

300 Years of Insurrection in the American South

Neal Shirley and Saralee Stafford

AK PRESS
EDINBURGH · OAKLAND · BALTIMORE

To our families who taught us to be proud of where we're from; to our friends who gave us their unending support, critique, advice, and patience; to all those who wear the mask, and those with whom we've shared the streets and occupations of the last few years; to all the lives who filled these pages with their words and deeds and passion for freedom, who are the very reason we took pause to write and the reason we still fight. This book belongs to y'all.

Dixie Be Damned: 300 Years of Insurrection in the American South

Text anti-copyright @ 2015 Saralee Stafford and Neal Shirley. This text may be freely reproduced for non-commercial purposes. Please inform the authors and publisher at the address below of any such use.

This edition © 2015 AK Press (Oakland, Edinburgh, Baltimore).

ISBN: 978-1-84935-207-9 | eBook ISBN: 978-1-84935-208-6
Library of Congress Control Number: 2014958842

AK Press   AK Press
674-A 23rd Street   PO Box 12766
Oakland, CA 94612   Edinburgh EH8 9YE
USA   Scotland
www.akpress.org   www.akuk.com
akpress@akpress.org   ak@akedin.demon.co.uk

The above addresses would be delighted to provide you with the latest AK Press distribution catalog, which features the several thousand books, pamphlets, zines, audio and video products, and stylish apparel published and/or distributed by AK Press. Alternatively, visit our websites for the complete catalog, latest news, and secure ordering.

Cover design by Neal Shirley
Interior Design by Margaret Killjoy | birdsbeforethestorm.net
Printed in the USA on acid-free paper.

CONTENTS

If I could do it, I'd do no writing at all here. It would be photographs; the rest would be fragments of cloth, bits of cotton, lumps of earth, records of speech, pieces of wood and iron, phials of odors, plates of food and of excrement.... A piece of the body torn out by the roots might be more to the point. As it is, though, I'll do what little I can in writing. Only it will be very little. I'm not capable of it; and if I were, you would not go near it at all. For if you did, you would hardly bear to live.

—James Agee, *Let Us Now Praise Famous Men*

"Living in the South often means slipping out of temporal joint, a peculiar phenomenon that I find both nourishes and wounds. To identify a person as a southerner suggests not only that her history is inescapable and formative but that it is also impossibly present. Southerners live uneasily at the nexus between myth and reality, watching the mishmash amalgam of sorrow, humility, honor, graciousness, and renegade defiance play out against a backdrop of profligate physical beauty."

—Sally Mann, *Deep South*

"Social Democracy thought fit to assign to the working class the role of the redeemer of future generations, in this way cutting the sinews of its greatest strength. This training made the working class forget both its hatred and its spirit of sacrifice, for both are nourished by the image of enslaved ancestors rather than that of liberated grandchildren."

—Walter Benjamin,
Theses on the Philosophy of History

"I would like to write the history of this prison, with all the political investments of the body that it gathers together in its closed architecture. Why? Simply because I am interested in the past? No, if one means by that writing a history of the past in terms of the present. Yes, if one means writing a history of the present."

—Michel Foucault, *Discipline and Punish*

AN INTRODUCTION

THIS BOOK IS THE PRODUCT OF SEVERAL YEARS OF LOVING LABOR AND TWO lifetimes' worth of conversations and reflections. It was written in the spaces between. Between debates over interpretation and research; between assemblies, marches, and riots; between work shifts and too little sleep; between bouts of crisis and caring for those we love; between fights and healing; between prison visits and noise demos; between the world we live in and the anger we feel toward that world. We are neither professional authors or academics, nor professionals of any other kind; in all of these endeavors we take solace in the creative power of experimentation and the slowly acquired knowledge that comes with it. This book has been no different.

Dixie Be Damned is not a "people's history" of the South or a compilation of politically removed academic articles about rebellions in the region. This is an experiment in reading and writing history from the perspective of two anarchists who grew up in this region. We wanted to see if sharing these stories would help illuminate why the past feels so inextricably present when we find ourselves in conflict with forces that would have us forget our histories.

While this project has been deeply researched, edited, and toiled over, it is anything but objective. Objectivity is a myth, designed to attract readers with the allure of a linear and clean narrative that presents itself as an authoritative and authentic past. This objectivity protects the status quo by presenting it as natural and inevitable. Yet it has not been easy for historians to craft a story of the South that accomplishes this task of sanitizing our past. When a storyteller's reverence for the Old South and "southern heritage" cannot avoid the obvious stains of racism and misogyny, the story switches to a carefully crafted narrative of progress—one that omits any thread of liberatory violence or conflict that challenges the social peace.

We fully admit that we too are storytellers. We wrote this book not to present Truth to the reader but to highlight those moments of revolt in which we have found inspiration and courage, from which we draw the possibility for a different historical understanding, and consequently a different understanding of our current struggles. The selected narratives that emerge in these pages are not an attempt to paint the entire history of this vast region in one new, singular light—that would be a dogmatic, futile, and ultimately authoritarian project. It is always the danger of writing history that, in the inevitable selection of certain episodes that highlight a specific perspective, one risks imposing a vulgar and one-dimensional view of the world. We are open to the possibility that the "historical project" is an inherently authoritarian endeavor but remain committed to digesting and learning from the many revolts and struggles that have been hidden from us. We grow tired of reading the historical analyses of those whose desires differ so starkly from our own.

We are indeed partisans, but of revolt and freedom, not of a specific cause or group or ideology per se, and we have no intention of deifying the protagonists of this book. Like our comrades today, the rebels and insurrectionaries in these pages were not heroes or villains but humans, and while we choose to focus on their liberatory practices in this text, we would remind the reader that many of the people within held attitudes that we would now find contemptuous. In many of the struggles we discuss, from slave rebellions to wildcats and prison riots, terrible things were done by people with whom we would likely have claimed affinity. For us, the center of gravity in this text is not the character of the individuals involved but the moments of rebellion and rupture, and what we can learn from them.

Writing and Reading This Book

Each of this book's seven chapters highlights a unique conflict or tension in a specific region and time period of the American South. These episodes were chosen both spontaneously and strategically. In part they represent to us a set of dynamics and responses to conditions that illuminate larger transitions in history that we found relevant to the anarchist project, as well as the broader desire to read history unconstrained from professionalism and political platforms. Mostly, though, these episodes were chosen because they found us. Our writing process was not solely spent researching in historical archives and online databases: this project was a part of our lives long before we began writing three years ago. The methodology of our research fought with the alchemy of our memories; we might come across a story in a book, but it is the ways in which it weaved itself with our own experience and knowledge of place that brought it to these pages.

We'd like to share one example of the kind of family stories that motivated this book: One of our great-great-great grandfathers, Hugh Sprinkle, was an established moonshiner and distributor before the Civil War in Yadkin County, North Carolina. When conscription came to the Yadkin Valley—the foothills of the Appalachian Mountains—Hugh Sprinkle, along with many other non-slaveholding small farmers, chose to go underground rather than fight for the Confederacy. They left their families, friends, and homes, and hoped to return at the end of the war. Hugh and his friends holed up together in the Deep Creek Quaker meeting house, a one-room log structure, before they moved on to the next safe house. Within days, they were tracked down by the Home Guard, who discovered their hiding spot after a local gave the deserters out. When the Guard came to apprehend them, a shootout ensued, at the end of which two of Sprinkle's friends and two Guardsmen were dead. The Home Guard arrested Sprinkle and put him on trial for the shooting, at which point he was forced to choose between going to war for the Confederacy or hanging. Between two deaths, he chose the battlefield. Against all odds, and partly because he became a prisoner of war within his first year of service, he survived the war. He returned home in the summer of 1865 after being forced to pledge his allegiance to the Union and lived out the remainder of his life on their small farm in the valley. Our ancestors would continue to make shine, some above ground and some underground, facing repression and imprisonment into the early twentieth century.

This is not the story of a proud Confederate veteran returning to a wife and daughter who would go on to found a local chapter of the Daughters of the Confederacy; this is the brutal reality of our ancestors, in all their shame and pride. Hugh was lucky to survive and continue making whiskey with his family, savvily using their grain crops in a world before federal alcohol regulation. Maybe Hugh didn't have the courage of the others who kept resisting after being captured. But a deeper reading of his capture at Harpers Ferry—the river town in West Virginia that John Brown's raid attempted to seize a decade prior—by the Yankees can be interpreted as a desperate act of resistance, a statement that he would rather rot in a prisoner of war camp than continue to sacrifice on the battlefield for slavers and planters.

In this one moment, in the midst of a shootout between deserters and guards over 150 years ago, there are multiple overlapping conflicts that reveal historical forces whose legacies we are still reckoning with today: the development of whiteness as a subjectivity through the creation of a policing force, conflict over the legitimacy of violence to defend or refuse an identity, collaboration with the state to avoid punishment, and the enclosure of commons through the hunting down of individuals that refuse to integrate into the war to save slavery.

Beyond any one specific story, the memories and experiences that fueled this writing are diffuse and myriad: listening to our families tell the same stories while sifting through selections of our great aunt's southern history books; walking into a tiny bookshop on Jekyll Island when we were covered in sand and mosquito bites; seeing yarrow in abandoned fields, wondering if they were descendants of the same flowers that were used to stop the bleeding of fugitives and deserters; watching from the windows of the restaurants where we work, as tobacco mills get refurbished into mixed-use lofts and tech start-ups, while we serve food to the architects of this "new" South; listening to the sound of catfish frying on a grandparent's back porch; watching parents fight over their rival college football teams, with signs in the yard that say "a house divided"; our pain and confusion about a grandmother never talking about growing up in a segregated town because she was white and didn't have to; falling asleep to the sound of gunshots on the battlelines of gentrification in our neighborhoods; defacing Confederate monuments; being made fun of for having too much or not enough of a southern accent; watching parents dance in drunken tears to "The Night They Drove Old Dixie Down" until two in the morning; hearing a mother say the words "General Sherman" with no less vitriol than had her grandmother; spending hours with elders who were in the riots and battles of the sixties, and hearing their wisdom of when to pick up the guns and when to put them down.

It is difficult to navigate between the double bind of myth and reality when passing down history. This is a particular problem for the historian or storyteller who wants to highlight the moments when actors and events appeared to shake and break with the common order of the day. We often hear elders talk about the savagery of the past while simultaneously alluding to the idea that "times were simpler" back then. In our work we have tried to reject the myth of a simple and peaceful past in order to see an image of the past in all its dangerous contours, and this practice has been informed by our own intimate relationship to this complicated history.

The remnants of these memories do not have to be mummified by nostalgia or fetishized as artifact. They are partial scabs constantly threatening to be torn open, and when they do, it us up to us as to how we handle the blood. These memories become alive when brought into a historical context. They are made richer through their contexts—through stories that challenge us to a deeper understanding of the world we live in and where we come from. We read them not simply so that we can know our conditions, but so that we can find strength when we need it most.

On this note, in our research it became clear that, if we wanted, it would be more than easy to add to the countless volumes of scholarship around the suffering of southerners—there are thousands of photos and stories of wrongdoing begging to see the light of day. But that is decidedly not our project. Instead we hoped to produce a text that breaks through the narrative of victimization that has characterized the typical southern history book, a text that conjures strength rather than pity.

Structure and Terminology

Each chapter is connected to the next by an interlude that "zooms out" to briefly summarize broader dynamics of struggle and development in the region. It is our hope that this pairing of a microscopic view on the actors and events with a more macroscopic perspective of the interludes will enable readers to connect the major transitions in time, terrain, resistance, and recuperation. We've also chosen footnotes over endnotes, so that the anecdotes and broader observations therein can provide useful context simultaneously with a reading of the main text.

Claiming to cover three hundred years of history in one book sounds brazen at best, arrogant at worst. We know it seems like a lot of time, but we also find ourselves in situations that make it feel like not much has really changed in these three hundred years. When Black, Brown, and white youth and families come together to protest the death of a young Latino teenager at the hands of the police, it is, broadly speaking, the same forces that repress these riots as did in the sixties, on the roads around the plantations, and on "the dividing line" between colonial Virginia and North

Carolina. Rather than write a detached history of revolt in days gone by, we wanted to—however incompletely—demonstrate the direct connection between the struggles against slavery and plantation society of the eighteenth and nineteenth centuries with the street battles and prison riots of the twenty-first. Very popular books like Michelle Alexander's *The New Jim Crow* have thoroughly demonstrated this historical connection, but it is a connection typically drawn from the position of the victim rather than the deliberate insurrectionary. Within this framing—a centralization of the victim of history—readers are left without a deeper understanding of what could actually destroy the prison society we are ensnared in. There is no social-democratic light at the end of this tunnel. We have to dig *ourselves* out, and it will be messy, complicated, and violent.

We are undoubtedly writing against the grain of a traditional ethnographic history, while also learning how to navigate those archives and libraries where our history is locked up. Even so, the broader writing of this book was directly influenced by several strains of thought: Specifically, we've been influenced by the theoretical traditions of autonomous Marxism, postcolonial theory, communization theory, historical materialism, and insurrectionary anarchism. As we have borrowed terms and trends, we hope it is to better push an analysis that is neither overly optimistic about the redemptive power of the struggles of the past nor overly cynical about a totalitarian future. Some of our influences manifest subtly while, other times, we overtly use specific terminology, which we introduce below to help readers better situate those ideas before meeting them in the chapters.

On the Theory of Primitive Accumulation

In her seminal history *Caliban and the Witch*, Silvia Federici writes about the centuries of resistance to enclosures and empire and the witch-hunts that ensued across the Atlantic world. Her work is foundational for us in a few aspects, specifically in the way she reclaims the term *primitive accumulation* from the annals of orthodox Marxism.

> Primitive accumulation is the term that Marx uses in *Capital* Vol. 1, to characterize the historical process upon which the development of capitalist relations was premised. It is a useful term, for it provides a common denominator through which we can conceptualize the changes that the advent of capitalism produced in economic and social relations. But its importance

lies, above all, in the fact that "primitive accumulation" is treated by Marx as a foundational process, revealing the structural conditions for the existence of capitalist society. *This enables us to read the past as something which survives into the present.*[1]

Federici uses the theory of primitive accumulation to understand the vast array of processes that lead to the development of a capitalist society by highlighting the witch-hunts as a vital, often overlooked enclosure. Women were "disciplined" away from reproductive freedom and autonomy in their communities in order to force their transition to reproductive laborers for a burgeoning industrial society. Autonomous Marxists like Silvia Federici and Peter Linebaugh, alongside the tradition of Caribbean Marxists like Eric Williams and C.L.R. James, have insisted that slavery and colonialism across the Atlantic, from European colonizers and slave traders to planters in the Americas and industrial capitalists in Europe and the Northeast, all were part of enclosing and disciplining populations to accept and produce a new society based on a racialized and gendered division of labor.

This book also characterizes the forces of primitive accumulation in this way so as to contextualize a resistance to those forces that continues to the present. In viewing history as an ongoing process in conflict that survives into today, we attempt to weave together the ruptures that broke out in response to the changing political, economic, ecological, and social terrain. We believe, alongside the work of many autonomous Marxists who have written extensively on the subject, that there was not one discrete period of transition into a capitalist democracy, but that the entire maintenance of capital and empire relies on continually finding, exploiting, and destroying the commons. This is a process that continues today in the South—whether through resource extraction like coal and hydrofracking, the construction of penal colonies in resource deserts, or the continued enclosure of women's access to reproductive freedom.

On Biopolitics,
From the Spectacle of Lynching to Life Without Parole
Since the late-seventeenth century, when the first laws were passed in Virginia to differentiate the fugitive indentured Anglo from the fugitive

---

1   Silvia Federici, *Caliban and the Witch: Women, the Body, and Primitive Accumulation* (Brooklyn, NY: Autonomedia, 2004), 12 (our italics).

enslaved African, each subsequent generation has been constituted through this legacy, with the intention of maintaining whiteness as a nonracialized, privileged identity. This has been written on the nonwhite body in numerous languages—of law and punishment, labor and discipline, science and reason, culture and taboo.

With regard to this racialized subjectivity and regimes of punishment, our writing is also influenced by historian and theorist Michel Foucault, who theorized the historical shift in the state's tactics of control and punishment from the spectacle of public death to the later management of populations. He used the term "biopolitics" to distinguish between the regimes of death that characterized antiquity's power (the slaveholder) to the contemporary regime of self-management and surveillance (the law-abiding citizen), where the state works from within the body of its subjects (biopower) amplifying the conditions of state and capital control accumulated by previous means.

Too often the haunting images of spectacular violence associated with southern history have brought with them the assumption that modern forms of control either do not work or even exist in the South. Anyone in this region who has visited a state prison, gone through public education, exerted self-control in front of a surveillance camera, or visited a museum dedicated to the Civil Rights era, however, has interacted with these mechanisms. Lest there be any confusion on this point: regardless of technological infrastructure, southerners today are no less constituted by evolving techniques of surveillance and management than metropolitan New Yorkers.

State and extralegal violence continue to reinforce the foundations of a racialized division of subjectivity, and should not be underestimated in their power to choose whose lives are literally disposable. The southern states contain the largest prison populations in the country; meaning that we live in a region that incarcerates the most Black men per capita in the world today. This turn toward the carceral state as a solution for economically "surplus" populations has its obvious roots in the histories of slavery and the early development of capitalism and the state.

Today we often see white, Black, and Brown liberals decry the property violence and self-defense tactics used by multiracial, disaffected youth who stand up when their peers are murdered by police. Liberals instead demand better education and job opportunities to keep youth safe from police and prisons. Those decriers forget that education and work are both the ancestors of prison and its logical descendants. Those who complain of the "school-to-prison pipeline," for instance, forget that with regard to the invention of mass compulsory public education there has never been anything *but* a school-to-prison pipeline. In general, we hope that the history in these pages might make the totality of apparatuses that we face—school, nuclear family, prison, economy, state, race, gender—a little more apparent.

On Messianic Time and the Insurrectionary Rupture

Behind the curtain of much of the writing in this book is also the notion of "messianic time," as used particularly in the later writings of Walter Benjamin. Our interpretation here is influenced by Benjamin's political theology and philosophy of history. Writing much of this material during the Nazi takeover of Europe, and reflecting back bitterly on the failures of progressivism and Social Democracy to stem the tide of fascism, Benjamin's "historical materialism" broke with both rational Marxism and Enlightenment history. The urgency of Benjamin's writing on history and time is infectious and opaque, with the messiah referred to in the term "messianic" not as some higher force but as a precarious power we all possess or can conjure. For Benjamin, the revolutionary did not have to go through any series of transitions as a worker or self-conscious individual to revolt, and there was no waiting for the congruence of material conditions; every moment held the potential for the time of this world to end and another to interfere and begin. We invoke his historical theory not as scholars of his work but as comrades with shared enemies.

Messianic time can be seen as a window. It could appear as the window of escape for the deserter or fugitive, or the shattering of a window by youth in the streets, or the break of time that happens when women in factories decide they're fed up and stop working. A "messianic cessation of happening" or "revolutionary chance" is any moment that bursts through to stop the time of work, social peace, and control.[2] Every act of desertion, refusal, and attack in these histories, whether by individuals or groups, can be read as a moment when a slave becomes free, a worker stops reproducing herself as a worker, or a prisoner ceases to be an object of discipline.

The moment of refusal is the historical subject's conscious coming to being. This is not to say that historical actors were not aware of their situations before rebelling, but that through the experience of breaking with

---

2   Walter Benjamin, "Theses on the Philosophy of History" in *Illuminations*, ed. Hannah Arendt (New York: Schocken Books, 1969): 263.

the current of productive time, they found a possibility or experienced a moment of freedom that was worth the sacrifices it would take to break with their conditions. Anyone who has found their bodies in the physical tumult of revolt can understand this sense of temporal rupture, this idea that "time stops." We use fluid concepts like the messianic moment or the revolutionary rupture to talk about the break of linear time that occurs during acts of refusal, sabotage, or transgression.

While it is safe to say that any term can become religious or ideological, it is our expressed desire to not overly reshape the already distorted figures of our past. This might be where we take our greatest liberties, in the spirit of historical materialism rather than ideology. We believe the subjects in this book made tiger leaps through history, not simply to secure a better future for themselves or their families, but for their ancestors whose memories were in danger. We, too, write for our ancestors—to redeem their past as our own, to hold a séance to invite them into our present terrain and help guide us to make our own ruptures. In particular this concept of messianic time appeals to us in opposition to the progressivism that suffocates so much of southern history, through distorting acts of resistance and delegitimizing conflictual narratives in order to align them within a vision of the future as a path of conciliatory and gradual reform.

This idea of a messianic break with time also points directly to the insurrectionary rupture sought by much of contemporary anarchist practice, and in particular to those individuals who refuse to wait for the correct "objective conditions" before acting. Just as a riot, land seizure, or occupation might be an opening move in an insurrectionary situation, an insurrection can in turn become an opening move in a larger revolutionary moment. Whether or not this happens, we see these opening moves, not as "necessary phases" that subjects must pass through but as breaks or ruptures with the existent world, as fundamentally changing experiences that seek to render impossible the return to normality.

On the Illusion of Peace and Other Enemies

Counterposed with this insurrectionary rupture is *social peace*, a vague term that we sometimes use in this book to describe the assemblage of conditions and dynamics that exist to maintain the illusion of a functioning, democratic, or egalitarian society. In a southern context this has roots in the mythology of the peaceful plantation, commune-like, where slaves and masters worked together to create wealth for the nascent nation. In the riots of the 1960s, it was the perversion of an imagined peaceful transition of Civil Rights integration, social welfare, and equality that was the real threat that rioters posed for both the newly constituted Left and national security. The idea that a discrete granting of rights was not enough to satiate the demands of urban youth or women in prison was infuriating to those organizations and institutions that sought to route others' rage into their own gain. These are the defenders of what we call the social peace.

Related to our use of this term is our use of "the Left," an admittedly overbroad and fluid term referring to the set of actors, institutions, and political interests that seek to preserve and guide the structures of capital and state toward their own ends, usually through the reform of a system in order to incorporate their own political base. In this sense the Left is characterized as the loyal opposition, those organizations and leaders that aim to "politicize" or "institutionalize" revolt into manageable and controllable forms, so that such revolt can be digested and spit back out as various reforms or cosmetic changes. This nexus of institutions has played a particular role in the South, ideologically pairing technological and industrial modernization with democratization and civil rights.

We understand that we're using this term in a way that may be unfamiliar to many readers.[3] We also acknowledge that "the Left" is by no means monolithic or homogenous. It has changed throughout history as its strategies and structure have shifted from the parties and organizations of Reconstruction and Radical Republicanism to the trade union management of the mid-twentieth century to the nonprofits and horizontal networks of the twenty-first. Likewise, this set of institutions and interests has, at any given point in time, reflected a wide degree of ideological difference and internal conflict, presenting itself as revolutionary and reformist, nationalist and internationalist in scope. Nevertheless, certain identifiable patterns exist throughout, from an emphasis on modernity, rights, progress, and industry on the one hand to a reliance on bureaucracies, political parties, civil society, legalized protest, and the federal government on the other. In all its forms the Left—whether that of Quaker activists, Democratic politicians, Communist Party members, trade union militants, or

---

3   We recognize that until recently most antiauthoritarians made some approximation of the distinctions we are making simply through the use of adjectives—the authoritarian Left, the liberal Left, the bureaucratic Left—while still considering themselves to be a part of some larger Left. Along with many others from different post-Left and insurrectionary circles, we are choosing to abandon this language as a whole because, to us, it reaffirms a position within the binary of state politics in which our modes of struggle remain legible to and representative of the state we're trying to destroy.

twenty-first-century community organizers—continues to play a crucial role in containing and managing revolt. Even the most "revolutionary" of these forces have always sought to position themselves as mediators and representatives of the dispossessed, turning angry mobs into controllable constituencies and numbing our capacities for self-organization and social conflict. As such we draw attention to this Left as an obstacle and an enemy, something entirely distinct from the kinds of rebellion and struggle we wish to see. Not surprisingly, the Left has also tended to present the history of this region in certain ways, which we hope to identify and depart from in this book.

Toward a History of the Present

To our knowledge, none of the protagonists in this book called themselves anarchists; few in fact subscribed explicitly to any known political label. Most of them, particularly from the seventeenth to the nineteenth centuries, left behind no words of their own, leaving the record of their deeds written only in the language of their enemies. As authors, this has sometimes left us in a bind, as we seek to present the actions in as honest a light as possible but find it difficult or impossible to present the rebels in their own words. We think it is just as profane and anachronistic to assume these protagonists were fighting for anarchy as for an industrial democracy, and we have no desire to "claim the dead" for our own. This is not a history of anarchists, but rather a history of revolt written by anarchists, who see in the complicated and contradictory dynamics of struggle multiple threads of antiauthoritarian possibility.

If we write history, we write it with confidence in the autonomy of those who rebelled, with the assertion that these people acted on their own behalf, with means they knew and innovated through need, and with their own ways of finding joy and fighting for freedom in an unlivable world. There is no single narrative that can encapsulate rebellion against oppression, no single revolutionary subject that can seize the reins of history to deliver us from our misery, no politician that can save us from this hell. There are many other stories of revolt yet to be liberated from archives or recirculated from a grandmother's mouth, but we can only find them if we stop needing them to be legitimized by anyone other than ourselves.

In that spirit, this project started a long time ago as a single 'zine, cautiously testing the waters of research and historical writing. Since then it has grown and evolved as a collaborative project with more ideas and curiosity than resources and time, but it has been a joy all the while. With every new experience gained in the streets and meetings and occupied spaces of the last few years, we've been forced to reflect anew on the material herein. As such, *Dixie Be Damned* aspires to be a history of the present. We hope that this book will resonate with others both of and beyond this region, perhaps inspire similar efforts by comrades in other parts of the world, and above all contribute in some small way to struggles here in our homeland. We are part of a long arc of revolt and defiance in this land that we love—let's fight as fiercely as if our ancestors were watching over us, guiding our hands and our hearts forward. They are.

A Home in Your Heart
Is a Weapon in Your Hand.

s. & n.

The "discovery" of the New World breathed new life into a European social system that was facing crisis and rebellion at home. Peasant uprisings across Europe in the fifteenth century took advantage of labor shortages, heretical religious ideas, and communal structures to eventually achieve a level of autonomy and self-sufficiency unknown to urban laborers centuries later. The existence of the commons—whether the fen, the field, or the forest—in which peasants and artisans could survive in hard times, proved a fundamental obstacle to the expansion of capitalism in Europe. The consequent destruction of these commons through the enclosures and expropriation of the fifteenth and sixteenth centuries opened the door to capitalist expansion and colonization, and forced entire classes of European laborers into intense poverty and despair. It was this class of newly proletarianized peoples that built and maintained the infrastructure of early capitalism's cities, ports, and colonies. These processes also resulted in new waves of radicalism among these dispossessed peoples, from the antinomian and the Anabaptist to the Levellers and the Diggers, who self-organized to destroy the hedges and fences that enclosed formerly communal lands.

The ripples of these developments were felt beyond Europe to the whole of the Atlantic world, from West Africa to the Caribbean and the Americas. This world was globalized on the terms of slave-traders, merchants, and politicians, but the heavy lifting was done by diverse crews of West African, Indian, and European laborers, prostitutes, domestic workers, field hands, and sailors—"hewers of wood and drawers of water"—who sought every possible opportunity to rebel. Whether one refers to the impressment of sailors, the capture of Indians, indentured servitude, or the later development of chattel slavery, labor under seventeenth and eighteenth century capitalism was predominantly some form of slavery.

This slavery was not initially organized on strictly racial lines: for example, an Irishwoman captured and forced into servitude by English forces might work on the docks alongside a West African Akan man, who himself had once sailed with unpaid men of a half dozen different nationalities. This contributed a global and multi-ethnic character to revolt, whether it was that of the pirates of Bartholomew Roberts who attacked the slave trade of the early 1700s, the diverse characters behind the New York Conspiracy of 1741, or the autonomous fugitive settlement of North Carolina's Albemarle Sound. The motley character of these rebellions was particularly terrifying to those in power, and in this fea-

one can find the origins of the racial hierarchies we encounter today. Everything from legislation to new divisions of labor—in particular the role of poor Europeans as police or overseers—sought to divide, break apart, and isolate the threatening cross-cultural alliances that formed in the daily lives of the dispossessed. This process kicked into full gear in the late-seventeenth and early-eighteenth centuries, sparked by events like Virginia's Bacon's Rebellion of 1676, which began as a ruling-class-led coup but grew out of control into an all-out war by English and African bond-laborers on the plantation elite. The word "white" did not even appear in legal records until 1691, but by the early-nineteenth century an entire code of racial categories, divisions of labor, scientific doctrine, and social conduct had evolved, which sought to shut out any possibility of meaningful, cross-ethnic solidarity.

This is not to diminish the importance of the mostly uniracial rebellions against southern chattel slavery, but to draw attention to the moments in which these racial codes were either not yet fully concretized or were simply thrown aside. The combative maroons of the Great Dismal Swamp, and the fugitive settlement that preceded them, present an illustrative example of the interaction between changing divisions of labor, the origins of whiteness, the development of a rebellious pan-African identity, and the solidarity of the criminal and the propertyless.[1]

"Maroon" is a generic word used to refer to a fugitive from slavery, typically one who joined with other fugitives to live in some kind of autonomous settlement. Those who escaped North to Canada as individuals are rarely called maroons, for example, while the large settlements of escaped slaves who banded together in the Great Dismal, Caribbean, and Central and South America usually are. Most historians in the United States have only used this term to refer to African laborers, but in other parts of the world it can refer

"For freedom we want and will have, for we have served this cruel land long enuff, and we are full able to conquer by any means."

—Correspondence between slaves in Greene County, Georgia, and Martin County, North Carolina, eighteenth century

"Like one of the Patriarchs, I have my Flocks and my Herds, my Bond-men and Bond-women, and every Soart of Trade amongst my own Servants, so that I live in a kind of Independence on everyone but Providence. However this Soart of Life is attended with a great deal of trouble. I must take care to keep all my people to their Duty, to set all the Springs in motion and make every one draw his equal Share to carry the Machine forward. But then 'tis an amusement in this silent Country and a continual exercise of our Patience and Economy."

—William Byrd II, wealthy seventeenth century planter, writer, and explorer

"Do not take me by my looks, I could kill a white man as free as eat."

—Jacob, a slave involved in Gabriel's Uprising

A SUBTLE YET RESTLESS FIRE:

Attacking Slavery from the Dark Fens of the Great Dismal

FROM 1790 TO 1810, THE TIDEWATER REGION OF SOUTHEASTERN VIRGINIA and northeastern North Carolina experienced perhaps the most turbulent, constant, and ambitious series of conspiracies and insurrections ever faced by the institution of American chattel slavery. The product of over 150 years of autonomous activity by slaves, servants, fugitives, and Natives in the area, this period of rebellion forever changed the scope of insurrectionary activity under slavery.

The majority of day-to-day slave resistance and planning was unreported and remains unknown, but even a very brief survey of this time period presents an incredible outgrowth of rebellious activity:

May 1792　　A conspiracy of nine hundred armed slaves, coordinated across multiple cities with plans to attack Norfolk, Virginia, is uncovered in a letter intercepted by slave-owners.

Summer 1792　Rumors of rebellion by slaves in Newbern, North Carolina, are reported in newspapers.

November 1792 An armed band of outlawed fugitives assassinates a plantation overseer in Charles City County, Virginia.

Summer 1793 Another conspiracy, allegedly involving as many as six thousand slaves, is discovered by slave-owners in a letter between fugitives in Richmond and Norfolk.

1795 A plantation overseer is murdered by fugitives or slaves in Wilmington, North Carolina.

1797 A group of fugitive slaves resist search by a white patrol in Prince William County, Virginia, killing four whites.

1799 Two whites are killed in Southampton County, Virginia when a group of slaves forcefully resist their transfer to Georgia.

August 1800 The famous Gabriel's Conspiracy erupts, in which one thousand armed slaves from across the state attempt to march upon and attack Richmond.

1800–1801 A conspiracy started by slaves in Petersburg, Virginia, which plans an attack on Norfolk, spreads to the interior.

1801–1802 Reported slave conspiracies increase in counties across northeastern North Carolina.

June 1802 Fugitives and outlaws stage an armed attack on the Elizabeth County Jail in order to free slaves arrested for conspiracy.

1805, 1808, Insurrectionary activity is reported in Isle of Wight, Nor-
and 1810 folk, and Chowan counties, on both sides of the North Carolina–Virginia border. Arson attacks and cattle raids become increasingly common throughout this period, and newspapers warn white people not to spread news about the attacks for fear of their contagion.[1]

Whenever and wherever there has been slavery, there has been resistance. This period, however, is unique in comparison to earlier times due

---

1   Herbert Aptheker, *American Negro Slave Revolts* (New York: International Publishers, 1943), 209–243; Hugo Prosper Leaming, *Hidden Americans: Maroons of Virginia and the Carolinas* (New York: Garland Publishing, Inc., 1995), 252–253.

to the increase of *coordinated* and *large-scale* conspiracies attempting, not just to alter immediate conditions, but to fundamentally overthrow bondage. The individual endeavor of escape took on more conspiratorial and collective forms as revolt changed in both frequency and content.

Historians have attempted to explain the exponential increase in rebellious activity in a number of ways: a contributing factor was the concurrent spread of revolt in the Caribbean and across South America, including the massive revolution that began in the French colony of Saint Domingue (Haiti) in 1791. Others have pointed to the growth of bourgeois revolutionary ideas and natural-rights philosophy at the time, and their possible introduction into slave circles.[2] Though this last theory remains untenable for a number of reasons, it does make sense that internal tension among the ruling class was an opportunity that was exploited by insurrectionaries at the time. Certainly it is true that word of rebellions in the Caribbean had spread to North American slave communities, and it's reasonable to assume that these revolts, in turn, may have influenced the timing of several conspiracies.

The questions remain, however: what could explain the geographic conglomeration of this period of revolt around the counties adjacent to the eastern North Carolina–Virginia border, and how were these attempted revolts coordinated on a larger scale than their predecessors?

Between the cracks of contemporary historical studies on slave revolt— and in the personal letters, General Assembly notes, and newspaper clippings of the time—a tentative answer starts to emerge: this period and territory of revolt can be seen as the direct product of the Great Dismal Swamp maroons, who were part of a series of permanent, overlapping communities made up, at any given time, of around two thousand plantation fugitives. Nearly all of the aforementioned rebellions or conspiracies took place in areas that bordered or encompassed parts of the swamp, a massive piece of land that originally included an estimated 1,500–2,000 square miles, and stretched from Norfolk, Virginia to Edenton, North Carolina.

---

2   It is true that some slaves may have interacted with these ideas secondhand, but when slaves and maroons took up arms during the Revolutionary War, they often fought *against* the "revolutionary" forefathers, sometimes even the very same elite who contributed to Enlightenment thought. This pokes a fairly giant hole in the idea that the revolutionary ideologies of Jefferson, Paine, and the like had much to do with slave insurrections. More to the point, it is patronizing and absurd to imply that slaves needed the white bourgeoisie to tell them that freedom was worth fighting for, or what that freedom should look like. The effort to characterize slave organizing as an outgrowth of bourgeois philosophical sentiment seems to have less to do with fact and more to do with absolving the slave-owning founding fathers of some level of guilt.

Charles Bridge Collection [portrait]

An early colonial governor of Virginia, Alexander Spotswood helped to consolidate the English Empire's control over the mid-Atlantic by breaking up the original Albemarle Settlement and destroying the Tuscarora Confederacy.

These maroons, who were of Native, European, and West African descent, built and held long-term communities in various parts of the swamp roughly from the end of the Tuscarora Wars in 1714 to the end of the Civil War in 1865. For 150 years these multi-ethnic rebels mixed and shared the diverse cultural and religious forms of the Tuscarora, Irish, English, and West Africans.[3] Forced to flee above-ground life as debt fugitives, runaway slaves, or refugees from the brutal wars waged on Indians, the maroons established a permanent life in the swamp while waging a long-term, unceasing guerilla war against plantation society in the form of arson, cattle rustling, crop theft, encouraging slave escapes, and coordinating insurrections throughout the area. At times, the maroons and related slaves allied themselves with larger political forces—affiliating themselves, for example, with the British to attack American slave-owners during the Revolutionary War, and forming autonomous forces to fight the Confederacy ninety years later.

---

3   "West Africans" of course includes a huge number of differing tribes and societies; there is little information on the specific origins of many of those who ended up as swamp maroons, though we do go into more detail later as to from where these men and women likely came.

The swamp was a key site of social organization behind multiple waves of rebellion, demonstrating that individual escape could, in the right circumstances, transform into a practice of collective attack. Always intersecting with this dynamic interplay was a diverse and, at times, bizarre mixture of cultural and religious practices, blending everything from Tuscarora rites of passage, heretical Christian thought, and self-described witchcraft to the serpent-centered spiritual and political councils of West African conjure men and women.

The Sink of America, the Refuge of Our Renegades

No history of the Great Dismal Swamp maroons would be complete without a brief mention of their predecessors: the fugitives, who were escaped bond-laborers of both European and African descent, pirates, landless paupers, and religious and political radicals who formed the semi-autonomous Roanoke Settlement of North Carolina's Albemarle Sound.[4]

Beginning in the 1640s, individuals and bands of escapees and rebels fled the plantation life of South Carolina and Virginia to what is now northeastern North Carolina, for the protection of the militarily powerful Tuscarora Confederacy.[5] Eventually this multi-ethnic population coalesced into its own settlement, which by all known accounts was a successful experiment in cooperation between neighbors of vastly different cultural backgrounds. The community of several thousand maintained itself by way of subsistence farming, hunting and gathering, mutual aid, and small trade with the larger Tuscarora communities. No orthodox church was allowed to establish itself, with the settlers militantly preferring an anticlerical version of Quakerism that emphasized "inner light" and "liberty of conscience," as well as adopting the practices of the Tuscaroras themselves.[6]

---

4 We use "indentured servant" and "bond-laborer" interchangeably; such a worker, who was unpaid and could be sold between owners like credit, was purchased with the owner paying the worker's travel cost or debts. Bond-laborers could be worked for a period of years or a lifetime, were often worked to death, and might be of West African, Irish, or English decsent.

5 A surviving expression hints at this early history, poking fun at South Carolina and Virginia by describing North Carolina as "a valley of humility between two hills of conceit."

6 Their version of "Quakerism" was nontraditional. Settlers did not build an official church, few adopted pacifism, and their practice as a whole may not have necessarily even been Christian. At least some Roanoke settlers were also adopted as members of the Tuscarora tribe, being given different names and instructed in local religious rituals and cultural practices. (Marcus Rediker and Peter Linebaugh, *The Many Headed Hydra: Sailors, Slaves, Commoners, and the Hidden History of the Revolutionary Atlantic*

As early as 1675 the settlers called for the abolition of slavery, and one of the few declarations or laws they passed established a kind of jubilee for fugitives fleeing bondage elsewhere:

Noe person transporting themselves into this County after the date hereof shall be lyable to be sued during the terme and space of five yeares after their arrival for any debt contracted or cause of action given without the County and that noe person liveing in this County shall on any pretence whatsoever receive any letter of Atturney Bill or account to recover any debt within the time above mentioned of a Debtor liveing here with out the said Debtor freely consent to it.[7]

To no one's surprise, the managers of profit and discipline in Virginia and South Carolina recognized the threat of such an appealing alternative that was ever present at their own borders. Virginia was physically separated from the Albemarle Sound by the dense and difficult Great Dismal Swamp, but since the very beginning of the colony, laborers had chosen to risk escape over the possible death and certain misery of enslavement on a plantation. Spelling out perfectly the early capitalist position on these settlers, the governor of Virginia wrote, "As regards our neighbours, North Carolina is and always was the sink of America, the refuge of our renegades: and till in better order it is a danger to us."[8]

Efforts to put the Roanoke Settlement and its Tuscarora neighbors in "better order" were soon to come. Trouble first erupted in 1677, when the Lords Proprietors—aristocrats appointed by the crown to exact fees and manage the territory—attempted to impose new restrictions on the inhabitants. Thirty or forty armed settlers seized the customs records and imprisoned the acting governor, along with several other officials. A group of West African and European fugitives from servitude in Virginia also managed to escape and join the rebellion at the same time. The Lords Proprietors backed down and replaced the governor. The conflict came to be called Culpeper's Rebellion, after the radical inhabitant John Culpeper,

---

[Boston: Beacon Press, 2000], 138–139.)

7   "Acts of the Assembly of Albemarle Ratified and Confirmed by the Proprietors the 20th Jan 1669 (–70)," Colonial and State Records of North Carolina (CRNC), vol. 1: 183–184.

8   "Lord Culpeper to Lords of Trade and Plantations" (December 12, 1681), in *Calendar State Papers, Colonial Series, vol. II, America and West Indies, 1681–1685* (HM Public Record Office, 1898), 155.

who had been involved in seditious activities from Charleston to Virginia and New England while "endeavoring to sett the poore people to plunder the rich."[9]

A new, larger conflict involving similar tensions rose to the surface in 1704. This time, the governor began requiring a swearing of allegiance to the crown for all offices, a practice harshly opposed by the dissident settlers, who physically removed him from office. A tense calm held, but by 1711 the "Quaker War" had broken out, pitting those who desired to maintain their non-plantation way of life against wealthier newcomers, who sought to turn North Carolina into a profitable, well-governed monocultural agrarian economy. The stakes were clear: either the Albemarle Sound would remain a free territory—multi-ethnic and with a cooperative basis for interactions between settlers and Indians—or slavery would reign supreme.

The stakes of the conflict extended well beyond the single settlement and had broader consequences for English imperial and economic aims: the vast majority of settlers brought to Virginia in the late-seventeenth century were bond-laborers of one kind or another, and from the moment of setting foot in the wilderness of this new world, many of these commoners sought an immediate escape from—if not the destruction of—the world from which they came. Governor Alexander Spotswood of Virginia understood this threat well. A clever statesman, Spotswood was more in tune with long-term, imperial, and capitalist strategy than many of his contemporaries. He had long manipulated and intimidated various Indian tribes into paying tribute to Virginia, and it was these tribes that in part helped to prevent the creation of permanent maroon settlements on the colony's western front in the Blue Ridge Mountains.[10]

Despite the overwhelming force of the English empire, the Roanoke inhabitants fought well. Aided in particular by the renowned skill of West African sailors in navigating the area's difficult waterways, the men and women built an impressive fort and won their first battle. After three years of large battles and small guerilla skirmishes, however, the combined forces of Spotswood's Virginia militia and the English

---

9   Leaming, *Hidden Americans*, 151–152.

10 Most famously, in 1712, Spotswood took the children of native tribes from these mountains as hostages, forcing them to speak English and adopt Christianity while interned at the College of William and Mary. The children were to be killed if their tribes refused to assist in the colony's war against fugitives; Anthony S. Parent, Jr., *Foul Means: The Formation of a Slave Society in Virginia, 1660–1740* (Chapel Hill: University of North Carolina Press, 1996), 163.

Royal Marines forced the settlers to either surrender or retreat into the nearby swamps.

After the defeat of the Roanoke Settlement, there was one final obstacle in the path of English imperial and economic strategy in North Carolina: only a few months after the Quaker War ended, forces from England, South Carolina, and Virginia waged a brutal campaign of extermination against the northern Tuscarora Confederacy. The Tuscaroras were more numerous and powerful than the Roanoke settlers, though, and were assisted by individual fugitive-fighters of African and European descent who were fleeing their own recent defeat in the Albemarle Sound. Thanks in part to the help of a brilliant fort-builder, engineer, and escaped "militant against slavery" known to us only as Harry, the Tuscaroras held off enormous European forces until 1713.[11] That spring, South Carolinian militia finally defeated the Tuscaroras' Fort Hancock, massacring nine hundred men, women, and children, and enslaving the rest.

Many of the surviving members of the Tuscarora Confederacy left the territory, fleeing as far north as Pennsylvania and New York. Some guerilla bands continued the fight as late as 1718, while others sought to create a life in the wilderness alongside the European and West African fugitive-rebels who had fought in the Quaker War. Many of these latter groups of Tuscaroras formed the nucleus of the first Great Dismal Swamp maroons, as not just isolated warriors but politically and socially unified communities. They were joined by more maroons from Virginia, in particular from the Powhatan Confederacy and Chowan Nation, and within a generation would form large communities capable of attacking and destabilizing one of the most profitable regional economies in the world.

The period of this mass escape represents a confluence of historically relevant developments. The decade in which power was consolidated by North Carolina's emerging planter class saw the end of the Roanoke Settlement and Tuscarora Confederacy and the beginning of the swamp maroons, and was pivotal in the larger history of Atlantic capitalism and English empire. For England and the colonies under English power, this period finalized

> the establishment of the limited monarchy, England's entry into continental European politics, the development of a bureaucracy, the rise of executive government, the emergence of high finance and public credit, the birth of tariff protection, the

---

11   Leaming, *Hidden Americans*, 197–199.

union with Scotland, the end of religious struggles, convulsions in the landowning sector of the economy, and rapid acceleration in the advance of the business and professional interest.[12]

All these changes were a distinct transition, a modernization of political and economic forces that coincided precisely with the end of a certain phase of primitive accumulation in the colonies.[13] For fugitive debtors, servants, and slaves, the living dream of an egalitarian and libertarian way of life, which had briefly taken root in Albemarle, was wiped out and replaced by the forced exodus, enslavement, and extermination of Indians; the forced labor of the poor; and the establishment of a violently maintained racial hierarchy. Though their struggle would seriously challenge the plantation system and inspire countless thousands to rebellion, the later swamp maroons emerged less as a lived alternative to this reality than as a fierce attack upon it.

A Bald Cypress emerges from the edge of Lake Drummond in the center of the Great Dismal.

Fleeing to the Swamp

The impassibility of the Great Dismal Swamp and the mythology that surrounded it provided protection to these early maroons, making their recapture cost-prohibitive and dangerous. Augustine Herrman, an early mapmaker, described the area in 1670 as "Low Suncken Swampy Land not well passable but with great difficulty. And herein harbours Tiggers Bears and other Devouring Creatures." In 1728, William Byrd II—slave-owner,

---

12 Ibid., 197–201.
13 "Primitive accumulation" is a term commonly used to describe the initial processes of development and forceful dispossession that laid the groundwork for capitalist economies around the world. As Marx wrote, "This primitive accumulation plays in Political Economy about the same part as original sin in theology." We would caution the reader to understand this accumulation not as a singular event that occurs at the dawn of capitalism, but rather as an element consistently present in every era: Just as the wars on peasant heretics and witches in Europe, and their maroon counterparts in America were a part of primitive accumulation in their time, so too were the later wars of imperial ambition of the twentieth century, along with the neoliberal reforms, structural adjustment programs, and prison industries of the twenty-first; Karl Marx, "Volume One: Capital," in *The Marx-Engels Reader*, ed. Robert C. Tucker (New York: W.W. Norton and Company, 1978), 431.

aristocrat, and credited founder of Richmond—was tasked with surveying the boundary line between North Carolina and Virginia, in part to help with jurisdictional conflict that had erupted between the states over the recapture of slaves.[14] After his difficult trek through the swamp, Byrd wrote, "The ground of this swamp is a mere quagmire, trembling under the feet of those that walk upon it."[15]

Poets who had never set foot in the area wrote of the territory as a metaphor for the darkness and hidden nature of the soul. Henry Wadsworth Longfellow mythologized the swamp in his poem "The Slave in the Dismal Swamp":

Dark fens of Dismal Swamp...
Where will-o-wisps and glow worms shine,
In bulrush and brake:
Where waving mosses shroud the pine,
And cedar grows and the poisonous vine,
Is spotted like the snake.

A generation later, Harriet Beecher Stowe explicitly acknowledged the Great Dismal as a harbor for escaped slaves in *Dred: A Tale of the Great Dismal Swamp*. Though she would have little grasp of the extent of cultural and political development held within its bogs and fens, Stowe presented the land as a symbol of the moral stagnation of white southern civilization. Her portrayal of the environment also perfectly suited the "dark" racial stereotypes she used in her writing.[16]

Many of these descriptions were designed to sell papers or books, or in Byrd's case, to garner a large paycheck from the English crown. The swamp was hardly the desert that early explorers described; though pits and peat bogs were dangerous to careless strangers, it was and remains a beautiful, biodiverse wilderness filled to the brim with otters, bobcats,

---

14 For a healthy reminder of the political and personal ethics of our country's early founders, we strongly encourage our readers to check out Byrd's diaries. His own accounts of perpetrating sexual assaults on domestic workers and slaves are written with bone-chilling nonchalance.

15 Jack Olsen, "The Cursed Swamp," *Sports Illustrated* 17, no. 22 (November 26, 1962): 68.

16 In *Dred*, Stowe describes the radical slave protagonist: "The large eyes had that peculiar and solemn effect of unfathomable Blackness and darkness which is often a striking characteristic of the African eye. But there burned in them, like tongues of flame in a Black pool of naphtha, a subtle and restless fire, that betokened habitual excitement to the verge of insanity" (Harriet Beecher Stowe, *Dred: A Tale of the Great Dismal Swamp* [New York: Penguin, 1995], 241).

deer, over two hundred species of birds, as well as a large lake, and juniper, gum, cypress, and southern white cedar trees. Islands between the fens and peat bogs made it possible to grow crops and raise livestock, and game was plentiful.[17]

Observers projected their own anxieties or affinities onto the mythology and ecology of the swamp depending on their position in plantation society. For example, the area around Lake Drummond at the center of the wilderness was long held to be of spiritual importance to swamp dwellers, who reported the existence of lights hovering over the water. While maroons and slaves viewed the phenomenon as "soft lights ... used by the Gods to guide us lost slaves," well-to-do white people outside the swamp referred to the lights as "the terrible people of the mist."[18]

Even the natural foods of the area bore a contested political significance, depending on one's position in the plantation order. Blue lupine, a plant that grows there wild, was considered devilish by proper society, but was consumed enthusiastically as a cereal grain by maroons, who credited its introduction to Grace Sherwood, a famous African herb doctor and witch of Currituck County.[19]

The emergence of white supremacy, new divisions of labor, new forms of misogyny, and a paranoid fear of magic and witchcraft all intersected with a fear of the wild.

This mythology about the natural world, paired with the very real dangers of the swamp, created a place the "better" sort of people tried to avoid—in other words, a perfect environment for the formation of hidden, yet permanent large-scale maroon communities, otherwise more common to the Caribbean than North America.

Some of the earliest known activities of these maroons included attacks on Virginia's cattle industry. Planters would guide their herds to the healthy grasslands west and north of the swampland, where, unbeknownst to them, they were vulnerable to cattle rustling by maroons.[20] Even before larger-scale settlement in the swamp, slaves could use the territory as a sort of backup plan: in 1709, for example, a slave insurrection planned jointly by Indians and Africans took place in Isle of Wight County, on the edge of the swamp, and when it was stamped out by the Royal Governor

---

17   Olsen, "The Cursed Swamp," 68.
18   Leaming, *Hidden Americans*, 340.
19   Ibid., 344–346.
20   These cattle were brought back to the swamps and bred as livestock to sustain the maroon communities, while others were allowed to re-wild in the swampland, eventually evolving into a mixed breed that observers have called Swamp Buffalos.

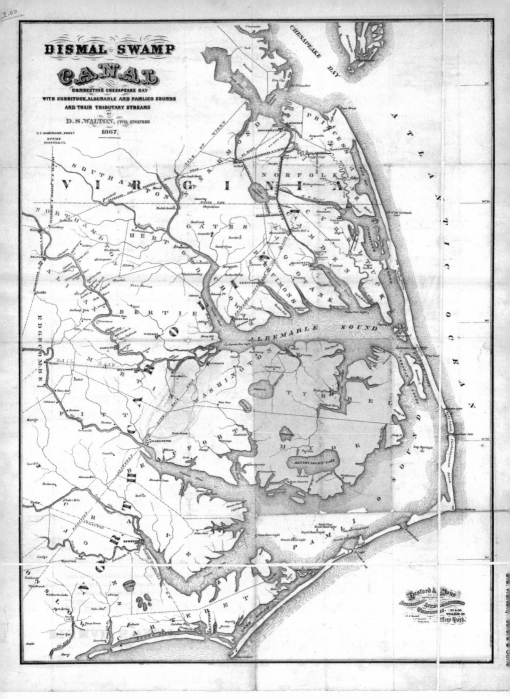

An 1867 map of the Great Dismal Canal portrays the Albemarle Sound and the counties surrounding the swamp on both sides of the Virginia–North Carolina dividing line.

of Virginia, one of the leaders, an African named Captain Peter, eluded capture by fleeing to the relative safety of the swamp.[21]

As word of these efforts spread through the slave and servants' quarters of the Tidewater region, and conflicts over the future of North Carolina ended, the population of the swamp grew rapidly, and the establishment of real settlements was possible. This process started with larger, unified groups of Tuscarora Indians, who provided a cultural and organizational foundation, and who were soon joined by the formerly European (and some formerly African) settlers of Roanoke. Some of the earliest fugitives to enter the area, likely from the Virginia side, were Irish, as evidenced by early Celtic trail names like the Shallalah and Ballaback roads, and by the continued use of words like "shanty" (from the Irish *shan tigh*, meaning old house) among African Americans into the early-nineteenth century.[22]

Many of the inhabitants of the Great Dismal were known to temporarily leave the swamp to do small jobs, either for trade or petty cash. In particular the maroons were known as excellent shingle-makers; nearby settlers would often turn a blind eye to their illegal status in return for help harvesting wood for roofs. One runaway slave who spent some time in the swamp, and was interviewed after he escaped to Canada, had this to say about the inhabitants' hospitality:

> I boarded wit a man what giv me two dollars a month for de first un. Arter dat I made shingles for myself. Dar are heaps ob folks in dar to work: Most on 'em are fugitives, or else hirin' dar time. Dreadful 'commodatin' in dare to one anudder. De each like de 'vantage ob de odder one's 'tection. Ye see dey's united togedder in'ividually wit same interest at stake. Never hearn one speak disinspectively to anutter one: all 'gree as if 'dey had only one head and one heart, with hunder Legs and hunder hands. Dey's more 'commadatin' dan any folks I's ever seed afore or since. Da Lend me dar saws, so I might he 'pared to spit shingles; and den day turn right 'bout and 'commodate demsels.[23]

The earliest known settlement, named Scratch Hall, was founded in the 1730s as the Tuscarora's numerical and cultural dominance subsided.

---

21 Leaming, *Hidden Americans*, 225.
22 Ibid., 224.
23 James Redpath, *Roving Editor: Or Talks with Slaves in the Southern States*, 243.

The wild cousins of the poor whites of the southern countryside, the Scratch Hall folk were tawny or tan-skinned descendants of the Roanoke Old Settlers, and probably had a good deal of Tuscarora ancestry as well.[24] They lived in the mixed swampland and pine barrens of the southern edge of the swamp. Guerilla raids on plantations that began in the area with the Tuscarora were continued by the Scratch Hall people, who harassed plantations by capturing horses, rustling cattle, and "committing other enormities." They were helped in these endeavors by reportedly ferocious dogs called the Scratch Hall breed, which they bred and trained with the specific purpose of hunting and herding animals like cattle and horses.[25]

Above: An early print of the blacksmith Gabriel Prosser that appeared in white newspapers.
Below: Images like this one appeared in white newspapers and journals after conspiracies like Gabriel's Insurrection, galvanizing white fear and hatred.

Colonial and, later, American newspapers often did not recognize these tawny maroons as properly white. Groups of white vigilantes attacking similarly multi-ethnic maroon settlements in South Carolina reported frustration at not being able to tell "who was a negro."[26] Laws against intermarrying between races, unheard of in the non-plantation-based Roanoke Settlement, can be understood to have emerged in this period not as the product of "prejudice" but rather as an attempt to biologically police boundaries that governed the social divisions of labor, wealth, and power in society. In this context the definition of race was clearly political, with whiteness seen as a social—rather than biological—inheritance of privilege and power, rooted in the plantation order and concretized by the loyalty one did or did not express to the economic system. In his surveying

24   We shift here to using more conventional "racial" rather than national designations (e.g., white instead of European) for these protagonists, in part because their own society was doing so at the time. "White" and "Black"—as terms that are used for categories of labor, power, rights, privilege, and conduct—emerge and concretize in this period, though the maroons themselves may have had very different ways of thinking about their own ethnic and cultural loyalties. "Black" as a category and identity can partly be understood as the product of chattel slavery and its legal and moral justifications, but is equally a product of the pan-African cultures of resistance that developed in places like the Great Dismal.
25   Leaming, *Hidden Americans*, 229.
26   John Tidwell, "Maroons: North America's Hidden History," August 26, 2002, 3. http://www.freewebs.com/midnightsea/maroons.pdf.

the border between North Carolina and Virginia, Byrd hinted at this distinction: "Most of the North Carolina whites were poor, but did not belong to the 'poor white' class, which was held in contempt even by many of the slaves. The term 'poor white' connoted more than poverty."[27] It is further telling that, over 130 years after the establishment of Scratch Hall, the maroons of European descent were considered "colored" by the Union Army and fought in tawny companies in Black regiments during the Civil War.[28]

The attacks on plantations and aid to escaped slaves that characterized early maroon resistance continued throughout the eighteenth century, despite efforts by both North Carolina and Virginia governments to stop them. During this period, the African presence in the swamp grew remarkably, reflecting changing demographics in the labor force and an increased colonial dependence on chattel slavery.

The West African men and women who were brought to North America in the seventeenth and eighteenth centuries, and who would have contributed their numbers to the swamp maroons, came from a variety of territories along the western coast of the continent, kidnapped from tribal populations in what is today the Ivory Coast, Ghana, Nigeria, Morocco, Senegal, and Gambia, among others. In particular, notable tribes like the Coromantee from the Gold Coast, who had lived communally in Africa, were fierce warriors, and often played central roles in slave revolts in the New World.[29] Many of these slaves passed through the Caribbean first, and their experiences opposing bondage there made them especially dangerous to the ruling class of the North American colonies. Recognizing

---

27 Political prisoner and ex–Black Panther Russell "Maroon" Shoatz has written about this distinction as well, arguing specifically that the origins of the term "white trash" lies in a derogatory reference to the class of "poor whites" who committed the ultimate act of race treason by marooning themselves with other servants, slaves, and Indians to attack the plantation order ("The Real Resistance to Slavery in North America," in *Maroon the Implacable: The Collected Writings of Russell Maroon Shoatz*, eds. Fred Ho and Quincy Saul [Oakland: PM Press, 2013], 131–156). A similar history could be ascribed to the word "redneck," which, though it was embraced proudly by the men it was given to, was initially a derogatory term invented by the media for the armed miners who fought to unionize in the Battle of Blair Mountain in 1921. "White" functions not just as a designation of racial loyalty and privilege but as a pledge of allegiance to capital itself (William Byrd, *William Byrd's Histories of the Dividing Line Betwixt Virginia and North Carolina* [Raleigh: North Carolina Historical Commission, 1929]).

28 Leaming, *Hidden Americans*, 225.

29 In 1733, for example, a group of about 150 mostly Coromantee slaves, armed only with knives, took over a Danish fort on the island of St. John and held their ground for *over seven months* (Rediker and Linebaugh, *The Many Headed Hydra*, 201–202).

this danger, the New York Assembly went as far as to impose a special tax on Africans imported indirectly via the Caribbean in order to discourage the practice.[30]

In the Great Dismal, a kind of division of labor evolved: Maroon settlements in the middle and northern areas of the swamp—which were constituted mainly by those of African descent, attacked plantations on the Virginia side—while tawny settlements attacked those on the North Carolina side. These guerilla struggles only intensified during the Revolutionary War.

In 1775, Lord Dunmore, the last Royal Governor of Virginia, cynically switched Virginia's traditional position on slavery and issued an emancipation proclamation that promised freedom to any slaves or indentured servants who would fight for the king. It was an early experiment with a policy that Britain later universalized across the continent when the Revolutionary War grew in scope. Maroon fighters answered the call, joining a band of six hundred ex–field hands and poor whites to successfully attack an American militia in Princess Anne County in 1775, and expropriating seventy-seven pieces of field artillery from American-held villages that autumn. Black crowds started gathering in Norfolk, which bordered the swamp, where they held meetings and created "disturbances." Throughout Dunmore's campaign in the Tidewater region, Black guerillas and white "Ragamuffins" (as they were termed by the American press) wreaked havoc on the plantation economy, expropriating livestock and crops, freeing slaves, and killing planters.

Spelling out quite clearly the extent to which their new natural-rights theory and revolutionary rhetoric extended to slaves and other laborers, the American State Legislature in North Carolina responded to these developments by forbidding the manumission of slaves by their owners in a law titled "An Act to Prevent Domestic Insurrection." Repressive legislation of this nature did not cease after the war. Though they changed their target from Loyalist slave-owners to Quakers and others considered subversive, the slave-owning American patriots remained extremely anxious about rebellion by this motley crew of maroons, slaves, and poor whites. The motivations of the American property-owning class remained consistent from before the War for Independence to long after the departure of the last British ship.

It is worth noting that on other parts of the continent, groups similar to the early swamp maroons played a key role in instigating action *against*

---

30   Ibid.

British authorities rather than on their behalf. One particular example is that of Black and white sailors in New England, who engaged frequently in strikes and sabotage in response to the British policy of pressing sailors into service against their will. For twenty-five years before the Revolutionary War, seamen in Boston led constant, militant riots against impressment by British officials, beginning in 1741 when a mob attacked a sheriff. Events ramped up over the course of that year and three hundred sailors—armed with "axes, clubs, and cutlasses"—attacked the commanding officer of a ship. Later that same year, a multiracial conspiracy by domestic workers and sailors, organized in taverns along the waterfront, threatened to destroy a British naval fort and burn down all of New York City.[31]

Nevertheless, efforts to "reclaim" the Revolutionary War, by pointing to its supposedly proletarian roots, or to the influence of Enlightenment philosophy on slave insurrections, are sharply contradicted by the guerilla bands of maroons, slaves, and servants attacking their "revolutionary" masters farther south. We mention this period not to take sides in a war between governments in which both sides deserve utter contempt, but to highlight the *social war* that was constantly taking place beneath the surface. That this other war manifested itself sometimes in favor of the British, and at other times the Americans, matters less than the deeper patterns of cross-ethnic alliance, revolt, and experimentation by the dispossessed at this time. The struggles of both the sailors and their maroon counterparts represent a liberatory self-activity, autonomously driven, that continued long after the American War for Independence was over.

Little changed after the war, then, for the classes of people driven to maroon themselves in the Great Dismal Swamp. The communities of the swamp continued to grow and develop their own ways of life, including their own unique cultural and religious practices. In the final decades of the nineteenth century, the swamp was home to around two thousand people—mostly of African descent but with sizable tawny and Indian populations—grouped in numerous, overlapping settlements throughout the roughly 1,500 square miles of swampland.[32] Though a canal was constructed by developers, which connected the Intercoastal Waterway to a lake in the center

---

31 Marcus Rediker and Peter Linebaugh, "The Many-Headed Hydra: Sailors, Slaves, and the Atlantic Working Class in the Eighteenth Century," in *Gone to Croatan*, eds. Ron Sakolsky and Richard Koehnline (Brooklyn: Autonomedia, 1993), 135; Rediker and Linebaugh, *The Many Headed Hydra*,174–193.

32 In comparison, the neighboring port city of Norfolk had roughly seven thousand residents in 1800.

of the swamp, efforts by the likes of George Washington and Patrick Henry to turn the wilderness into fertile farmland failed utterly.[33] Attacks on plantation society continued uninterrupted up to the turn of the century, when the rebels began to coordinate themselves across larger and larger geographic areas, seeking not just the immediate relief of individual escape from slavery, but the destruction of the entire economic order.

To No Longer Bear What They Had Borne

Rustling cattle, burning plantation property, liberating slaves, and stealing crops were frequent features of maroon life throughout the eighteenth century. As slaves were also engaging in similar activities, and because some slaves would escape for only short periods of time before being returned to the plantation, it is difficult to distinguish in the historical record between acts committed by true maroons and those by those still held in bondage.[34]

Regardless, new patterns of rebellion—distinct from the smaller and less "ambitious" raids of earlier decades—began to emerge around 1790. Coinciding with a huge period of unrest and maroon-driven revolution across the Caribbean, insurrectionary activity in the Tidewater region of Virginia and North Carolina began to take on a new character, as rebels sought to expand and coordinate attacks over larger and larger geographic territories, and as they directly targeted not just plantation production but also white-controlled cities and political centers.

---

33 In spite of the failed drainage efforts led by these founding fathers, massive logging and development made possible by the canal and later railroad construction have unfortunately reduced the swamp to roughly one-tenth of its original size. This reduction of habitat for would-be insurrectionaries and fugitives offers further insight into how private development and industrial attacks on the land have themselves functioned as part of a state strategy to discipline rebellious populations. The remaining portion of the swamp was turned into a wildlife refuge in 1974.

34 In Louisiana this clever tactic of temporary escape was explicitly acknowledged with a name: *petit marronage*. It described the common tactic by which slaves, in lieu of the possibility of permanent escape, would leave their work en masse for a week or two at a time until certain demands were granted by the owner (John Tidwell, "Maroons: North America's Hidden History." August 26, 2002, 5). The similarity with the later tactic of the labor strike is remarkable, and likewise brings to mind the early labor movement's characterization of work under capitalism as "wage slavery." Without diminishing the unique brutality and indignity of chattel slavery, this evolution of tactics offers one further reminder that slavery and wage work are not divided by some fundamental ethical/political boundary, but occupy one long, continuous development of bonded and exploited labor.

Between 1790 and 1810, attacks on the plantation economy occurred in nearly every season of every year, and any number of conspiracies and revolts could serve to demonstrate the changing focus of target. The three highlighted below were specifically chosen because they demonstrate the coordinating and encouraging role of the Great Dismal Swamp and its inhabitants.

Early Insurrection Attempts: 1792–1800

The first of these insurrectionary attempts began in May 1792, and involved over nine hundred slaves and maroons on the eastern shore of Virginia. As reported in the *Boston Gazette*, "about two weeks ago, the Negroes in that part of the State, to the amount of about 900, assembled in different parts, armed with muskets, spears, clubs, and committed several outrages upon the inhabitants."[35] Under the command of a leader known as Celeb, the slaves communicated with slave communities on the Dismal Swamp and Norfolk side of the bay, and secretly made weapons with the help of a blacksmith. Their intent was to cross the bay, join others on the mainland at the border of the swamp, and attack the arsenal at Norfolk, but their plans were discovered and the planters requested extra military supplies from the mainland.[36]

Conspiracies and underground organizing in the area continued however, as evidenced by one intercepted letter found in Yorktown, Virginia in August 1793:

> Dear Friend—The great secret that has been so long in being with our own color has come nearly to a head that some in our Town has told of it but in such a slight manner it is not believed, we have got about five hundred guns aplenty of lead but not much powder.... I am full satisfied we shall be in full possession of the [w]hole country in a few weeks, since I wrote you last I got a letter from our friend in Charleston he tells me he has listed near six thousand men....
>
> Secret Keeper Richmond to Secret Keeper Norfolk.[37]

---

35 *Boston Gazette and the Country Journal*, June 18, 1792. In Leaming, *Hidden Americans*, 367.

36 Leaming, *Hidden Americans*, 366.

37 William F. Cheek, *Black Resistance Before the Civil War* (Beverly Hills: Glencoe Press, 1970), 101–102.

Another letter was found addressed from Portsmouth, also in the Dismal Swamp region. The conspiracies failed to come to fruition, partly due to the intercepted communications and the shipment of arms from the mainland, but were notable for their size and ambition, and for their early attempts to communicate across vast areas. Their letters would have necessitated travel through territory either covered by the Great Dismal Swamp or bordering it.

In comparison, earlier known efforts at spectacular, collective resistance, like South Carolina's Stono Rebellion, appeared more as an effort at joint escape and involved hardly more than a hundred participants. Not surprisingly then, word of this significantly larger attempted rebellion sent shockwaves through both slave and planter circles. Despite the insurrection's failure, fear spread through white communities in the Tidewater region and beyond, and other slaves were encouraged to act. A letter sent one month after the failed conspiracy from Newbern, North Carolina confirms whites' fears:

> The negroes in this town and neighbourhood have stirred a rumour of their having contemplation to rise against their masters and to procure themselves their liberty; the inhabitants have been alarmed and keep a strict watch to prevent their procuring arms.[38]

The conspiratorial wave seemed to have a rippling effect: several months later, a group of armed maroons murdered an overseer on a plantation in Charles City County, also bordering the swamp.

Gabriel's Uprising: 1800–1801

The second major insurrectionary attempt of this period was Gabriel's Uprising. One of the most famous slave rebellions in North American history, the uprising involved an attempted attack on Richmond in 1800, and was coordinated over a huge territory. The conspiracy was led by siblings Gabriel, Nanny, Solomon, and Martin Prosser, among others, and participants were recruited from all over Virginia, including Gloucester, Cumberland, Henrico, Luisa, Chesterfield, Hanover, and Caroline counties. Martin Prosser was the rebellion's sword maker, and bitterly opposed any delay of the rebellion; according to a fellow

---

38 Aptheker, *American Negro Slave Revolts*, 213.

US Fish and Wildlife Service

Even the mist that rose off the surface of the swamp's Lake Drummond invited conflict, with whites fearing demonic spirits while slaves and fugitives found spiritual guidance and power.

conspirator, "before he would any longer bear what he had borne, he would turn out and fight with his stick." The intention was to march on Richmond, and as one group set fire to the warehouse district as diversion, others would capture arms, the capitol building, and the governor. Frenchmen, Methodists, Quakers, and other whites sympathetic to the cause were to be spared.[39]

The insurrection involved thousands. Secrecy was maintained for a time, but due to planning delays, word of it eventually reached Virginia's Governor Monroe, who, on April 22, wrote to Thomas Jefferson of the threat.

No immediate action was taken by the government, however, and the slaves continued to produce bayonets, swords, and ammunition through the spring and summer. Secrecy was mostly kept, though by August 9 word of a planned revolt appears in a letter between two whites of Petersburg and Richmond. The letter was intercepted and passed on, and military authorities were informed. Further word of the rebellion was provided to the governor by a slave-owner named Moseby Shepard, who "had just received advice from two slaves that the negroes in the neighborhood of Thomas H. Prosser intended to rise that night, kill their masters, and proceed to Richmond where they would be joined by the negroes of the

39   Ibid., 220, 224.

city."[40] Monroe finally acted, posting cannons outside of Richmond, informing militia commanders around Virginia, and calling into service 650 local soldiers.

At this exact moment, on the evening of August 30 an enormous rain began to fall, referred to later by whites as a "providential" downpour. The territory between the conspirators' rendezvous point and Richmond was separated by a torn bridge, and the flash flooding made crossing the waterway impossible. Despite the rain, one thousand slaves met at the agreed location, six miles outside the city, armed with hundreds of homemade weapons. Unfortunately, the attack was made impossible, and they were forced to disband. The following day the entire military apparatus of Virginia was aroused, and scores of conspirators and insurrectionaries across the State were arrested. Gabriel Prosser managed to escape on a ship in Norfolk at the swamp's border, but was recognized and betrayed by two slaves on board. He was taken to Richmond, and after refusing to give any significant information about the conspiracy, hanged on October 7.

At least thirty-four other conspirators were hanged as well, while one committed suicide and four managed to escape from jail and were never recaptured. Two of these escapes were the result of a mob action by Black maroons besieging the Hanover County courthouse, wherein they released the prisoners, charged the guard, "knocked him down" and "stamped on him," and ran away. According to one slave-owner, the break was planned throughout the previous week when slaves visited the prisoners, "under the pretence of a preaching."[41] A wave of repression and white paranoia erupted after Gabriel's Uprising, especially in Virginia but extending well beyond its borders. Arrests and hangings continued throughout the winter of 1800–1801.

Insurrections of 1800–1810

Almost as soon as Gabriel Prosser's body was in the ground, a third wave of conspiracy and insurrection occurred. Beginning in late 1800 in Petersburg, Virginia, by December unrest had spread to Norfolk on the northeastern border of the Great Dismal. The goal was again a coordinated attack on Norfolk, and word spread from the coast to the

40   One of these informant slaves was named "Pharaoh" (Cheek, *Black Resistance Before the Civil War*, 108).

41   Gerald W. Mullin, *Flight and Rebellion: Slave Resistance in Eighteenth-Century Virginia* (New York: Oxford University Press, 1972), 154.

interior of the region. Plans were shared throughout the following year, as is demonstrated by a letter dated January 1802, which was intercepted on its way to Powhatan. It stated, "Our friend has got ten thousand in readiness to the night." Small attacks and gatherings increased; on April 3, "four unknown men made an attack with bricks upon the sentinel at the Capitol, and were fired upon." Repression spread as well. Hangings and arrests occurred in Halifax, Hanover, and Princess Anne counties as well as in Norfolk. A letter from Richmond mentions that, "convicted slaves confined in the Penitentiary house [had] become so numerous as to render their maintenance burthensome [*sic*] and their safe keeping inconvenient."[42]

News of the planned uprisings traveled south to eastern North Carolina, where conspiracies were reported in May. Newspapers attributed these to the influence of a spiritual leader named Tom Copper, a maroon who, according to the Raleigh *Register*, had "a camp in one of the swamps" near Elizabeth City. Newspapers grew reluctant to report on the conspiracies, and silence took the place of their usual paranoia in an effort to prevent the spread of rebellion. At this time, large numbers of slaves or fugitives were executed or punished in counties adjacent to the swamp territory where Copper was headquartered and thought to be organizing (Camden, Bertie, Currituck, Martin, Halifax, and Pasquotank counties). In retaliation for this repression, in early June 1802, six maroons on horseback fought a battle with Pasquotank militia in a failed effort to liberate comrades being held in the Elizabeth City jail.

Historian Herbert Aptheker writes of the significant multiracial element in this period of revolt:

A striking feature of the Virginia conspiracies of 1802 is that evidence of white participation is fairly good. Thus, a Mr. John B. Scott, while informing the Governor on April 23 of the trial and execution of slaves in Halifax, stated, "I have just received information that three white persons are concerned in the plot; and they have arms and ammunition concealed under their houses, and were to give aid when the negroes should begin." One slave witness, Lewis, twice declared that whites, "that is, the common run of poor white people" were involved.[43]

---

42   Aptheker, *American Negro Slave Revolts*, 229.
43   Ibid., 233.

The presence and participation of the Great Dismal Swamp maroons becomes most clear in this third insurrectionary period of 1800–1802, when unrest spread across the state's border and involvement by whites as well as Blacks became explicit. Counties surrounding the swamp, three in Virginia and six in North Carolina, all saw increased guerilla raids in this time. War bands on the North Carolina side, led by Tom Copper, were multiracial and originated just east of the Scratch Hall maroon settlement.

Insurrectionary activity continued to occur over the next decade, with specific reports coming from counties that bordered the swamp in 1805, 1808, and 1810. Throughout the period, planters reported "distressing apprehensions of fire and other casualties." In 1808, the planter citizens of Edenton in Chowan County, North Carolina, established a Black Code to protect "our wives and children [who are] surrounded by desperadoes, white and Black." By no coincidence, Chowan County was the area most adjacent to Scratch Hall.[44]

The Influence of the Maroons on Slave Insurrection

The period between 1790 and 1810, and in particular the three insurrectionary eras discussed here, represent a tremendously inspiring yet difficult time in African American and labor history, with slaves facing as much repression and consolidation of white power as they did opportunities for rebellion. Compared with strategies of individual escape, these attempts at revolt often presented great risk and little immediate benefit for those participating. But on a systemic level, the increasing frequency, violence, and regional coordination of revolt at this time seriously destabilized the plantation economy. This social turbulence cost a tremendous amount of money in lost production and significant levels of anxiety and paranoia for white populations who, if we are to believe their newspapers, were in near-constant fear for their lives.

This fear spread like a virus. The increasing ungovernability of the plantation system in the Tidewater region did not go unobserved by the rest of the country. The specter of massive Black or even multiracial rebellion entered the consciousness of affluent white families, newspapers, and state assemblies up and down the East Coast, and can be directly tied to a number of important changes: First, by 1804 all states north of the Mason-Dixon line had either abolished slavery or passed laws planning for its gradual abolition. Second, in 1808, US and British law banned the

---

44 Leaming, *Hidden Americans*, 250–253.

international slave trade. Both of these things made the institution of slavery and the plantation system more vulnerable to attack.

The timing of both of these developments directly points to the increased unrest by slaves and their co-conspirators in the mid-Atlantic and the Caribbean regions. The slave trade and the plantation system it thrived upon were immensely profitable; these new legal constraints should not be understood as casual, insignificant, or inevitable. While certainly a variety of factors contributed to the political context in which these two developments occurred, we would argue that fear, rather than humanitarianism, was their driving force. Beyond catalyzing these policy shifts, we would point to the sense of pride and dignity that slaves across the United States could take in these rebellions. In lifting the sense of what was possible, this period forever changed the scope of insurrection from the local to the regional and national, from the individual relief of escape to a collective revolt directed at the destruction of the existing economic order.

Three factors help to explain the increasing size and ambition of the insurrectionary activity of this period. Already mentioned was the influential role of massive slave rebellions in the French Caribbean, specifically the revolution beginning in Saint Domingue in 1791.[45] Geography as well as timing would have played a role here, as Norfolk and Portsmouth were two important ports from which news of the Haitian revolution would have spread. These cities both lie near the edge of the Great Dismal; news of the slave takeovers in the Caribbean, carried north by the servants and domestic slaves of Frenchmen fleeing the islands, could have easily traveled by maroon from the port cities to any number of counties on both the North Carolina and Virginia sides of the swamp.

Government officials were well aware of the potential disaster if revolt spread from Haiti to the mid-Atlantic coast. It was documented by officials that a Black steward of the trade ship *Minerva* introduced insurrectionary literature from the Caribbean in 1809 in Charleston, which was read aloud to fellow slaves by Denmark Vesey. Shortly before the 1820

---

45   Maroons played a leading role in the Haitian rebellion as well, initiating revolutionary activity in the early period and continuing to carry it forward after Toussaint L'Ouverture and his army had agreed to play the role of French puppet. As Russell Shoatz writes in "The Dragon and the Hydra," "Consequently, we witness the decentralized hydra elements [the maroon bands] launching the revolution, being displaced by Toussaint's army—the dragon—only to resume their leadership roles during a crisis that saw the dragon capitulate to the French, thus showing [the maroons] as the most indispensable weapon the revolutionaries developed" (Shoatz, "The Dragon and the Hydra," in *Maroon the Implacable*, 121).

uprising that carries Vesey's name, South Carolina banned the import of such literature.[46] Though Charleston is far south of the Great Dismal, one can infer that similar processes played out in port cities like Norfolk on the swamp's border.

The second factor can be found in the demographics of the states in question. From 1790–1800, the Black population of North Carolina increased by 32 percent, while the white population increased by only 17 percent. In Virginia, a similar shift took place when one factors in the free Black population, and in particular when one focuses on the Tidewater region. Increasing ratios of Blacks to whites would have made autonomous travel, communication, education, and planning easier.[47]

Thirdly, and most significantly, lies the role of the maroon communities of the Great Dismal Swamp in encouraging and coordinating rebellion across the Tidewater region. Newspaper reports, letters between family members, and the counties in which revolt so consistently occurred, all point to the importance of the maroons in this period. The existence of a liberated frontier like the swamp would have been a tremendous encouragement for slaves considering escape or revolt in this period. In addition to providing refuge for would-be insurrectionaries, the maroons were mobile, offered rare military experience, and played a key role in coordinating revolt by way of spiritual leaders.

An important figure in this last element was General Peter II, a maroon leader who sought to more formally establish bonds with slave insurrectionists on the surrounding plantations.[48] In referring to this coordination, one supporter of Peter II was overheard saying, "there would be an earthquake here [as well as in North Carolina] in the same night."[49]

Though Black spiritual leaders traveled from plantation to plantation in the Tidewater area, their headquarters were in the swamp, and many of them reported to a central spiritual council. As Leaming writes on the subject,

---

46 Peter Linebaugh, "Jubilating, or How the Atlantic Working Class Used the Biblical Jubilee Against Capitalism, to Some Success," *The New Enclosures: Midnight Notes* 10 (1990): 94.

47 Aptheker, *American Negro Slave Revolts*, 209–210.

48 This Peter bore the same name as the insurrectionary maroon leader of exactly one hundred years before, and was headquartered in the same county. Leaming hints at a possibly spiritual explanation for the name, in the common West African belief in the supernatural possession of a living figure by a beloved, deceased hero (Leaming, *Hidden Americans*, 255).

49 Aptheker, *American Negro Slave Revolts*, 246.

These "slave preachers," chosen by their fellows in bondage, unrecognized by any white church, often unknown and generally disapproved of by the slaveholders, preached a faith and worship very different from those of Anglo-Saxon Christianity. Also in the society of the enslaved there were conjure men and women, sorcerers or folk psychotherapists who helped the sick to uncross or cast off their spells of depression, hysteria, or obsession.[50]

The spiritual messengers were an opaque force, unregistered and unmarked by plantation society, but highly respected by slaves and maroons alike. Their religious orientation varied greatly, ranging from Christian Methodism to a variety of traditional West African folk spiritual practices and magic. These practices had evolved for over a hundred years in the Great Dismal Swamp, resulting in the blending of the strange mixture of Quaker ideas and Indian religion that had come earlier, with the spiritism and mysticism of more recent Black maroons. At his trial, for example, one of the leaders of Gabriel's Uprising remarked that he was sent south to recruit with the "outlandish people" who were "supposed to deal with witches and wizards," and therefore would be useful to the efforts of their army.[51]

Though religious figures' involvement in slave coordination started much earlier, the recognized central council of conjure men and women, known as "the Head," emerged sometime around the end of the eighteenth century, during or after Gabriel's Uprising. What we know about this institution comes largely from the writings of an early Black nationalist named Martin Delany, who wrote a novel fictionalizing the travels of an escaped slave throughout the southern United States, Cuba, and Central America, documenting Delany's vision for Black liberation and his role in revolutionary Black politics. Delany wrote specifically about the conjure councils of the Great Dismal Swamp and, as his observations greatly reflect known West African practices of the time, is understood to be credible.

According to Delany, the Head was made up of seven leading conjure men and women, drawn from the plantation, town, and maroon communities, and known as the "seven-finger high-glisters."[52] The glisters held a

---

50   Leaming, *Hidden Americans*, 253.
51   Mullin, *Flight and Rebellion*, 154.
52   "Glister" is an older word for "glitter." Delany uses it to refer to the highest level of conjure-men and women of the swamp; how he came to use this word is unknown.

permanent location in a cave in the swamp, where they housed supplies, performed rituals, and kept their most sacred symbol, a large living serpent, considered a holy object in many West African practices and often used to represent the religions of African spiritism.

In addition to performing collective rituals, the Head's primary function was the ordaining and coordination of the many underground spiritual figures across the region. In order to be ordained as conjure men or women, non-maroons were forced to (at least temporarily) escape their bondage and find the council. As spiritual leaders returned to their fields and towns from the swamp, a link was established between the swamp maroons and aboveground plantation society, connecting slave communities to an underground council that had contacts all over the Tidewater region and beyond. As Leaming writes:

> The social impact must have been tremendous. Knowledge that such a council existed and was perpetually engaged in such ceremonies could only have been of inestimable value in the preservation of hope and the encouragement of struggle for those African Americans in bondage who believed. Above all else ... the Head, like the conjure person of the plantations, considered themselves to be the chaplains corps of the war on slavery. The Head deeply revered the memory of Nat Turner, and claimed to have been associated with his effort. As young conjure men they had fought alongside General Gabriel and took pride in that action forty years later.[53]

Baptist and Methodist ministers were involved in spreading word of slave insurrection and maintaining morale as well, though their level of coordination with the Head is less known. Many of the Black spiritual leaders of this time would have fallen somewhere in between the gospel Christianity of the Methodist preacher and the spirits-worshipping mysticism of the seven-finger high-glisters, mixing the two variably to suit the occasion. What resulted from the maroon experience and its influence on slave organization was not a religious or political orthodoxy, but a vast spectrum of spiritual, communal, and insurrectionary practices, the inheritance of over a hundred years of life among diverse co-conspirators in the wilderness.

The impact of these practices, whether in the swamps or in the fields, was no less than the development of an oppositional, pan-African identity.

---

53   Leaming, *Hidden Americans*, 258–259.

Slaves just arriving from the Caribbean or West Africa got off the boat speaking different languages and possessing markedly different cultural backgrounds; in short, they arrived as Akan, Coromantee, Asante, Malagasay, Igbo, or Papa.[54] It was the law, science, labor, and economy of the plantation, and the pan-cultural resistance to these things, that made these men and women "Black."

The maroon role in spreading the insurrectionary fires of the Tidewater region continued after the concentrated period of uprisings to which we draw attention here. Both isolated and coordinated expropriations of cattle and other plantation property remained common, and the settlers of the swamp remained active in coordinating this revolt. Though rebellious activity erupted throughout the southeast in the nineteenth century, it continued to disproportionately appear in areas bordering this swampland, and newspapers often reported the surprising presence of lighter-skinned people in the groups responsible.

At the outbreak of the Civil War, the maroons and the many slaves they helped to liberate autonomously attacked Confederate forces and plantation property and generally destabilized the economic production that was so desperately necessary for the South to remain in the war. For example, the Richmond *Daily Examiner* reported on January 14, 1864, that a group of 500–600 Black "banditti" was ravaging the countryside in Camden and Currituck counties, both of which closely bordered the Great Dismal Swamp on the North Carolina side. The paper argued, "This present theater of guerilla warfare has, at this time, a most important interest for our authorities. It is described as a rich country ... and one of the most important sources of meat supplies that is now accessible to our army."[55]

Alongside their tawny comrades, some of these autonomous maroon forces eventually joined Black regiments in the Union Army, while others continued guerilla activity and the liberation of the enslaved. Most of the maroon settlements voluntarily returned to life outside the swamps after Union victory, hopeful for the effects of emancipation, but the Great Dismal Swamp continued to be a major spiritual and political center for Black life long after. Though either forgotten or ignored by many twentieth century historians, the legacy of this territory and the resistance it enabled lives on in the memory of the communities to whom it provided refuge.

---

54 Rediker and Linebaugh, *The Many Headed Hydra*, 184–185.
55 Herbert Aptheker, "Maroons Within the Present Limits of the United States," in *Maroon Societies: Rebel Slave Communities in the Americas*, ed. Richard Price (Garden City, NJ: Anchor Books, 1973), 165.

The Promise of Escape and the Practice of Attack

The history of maroon settlements and guerilla struggle in the Tidewater region covers a long stretch of time and cultural development. From the early 1600s to the end of the Civil War, an ongoing, nearly uninterrupted war on early capitalism and its processes of primitive accumulation was waged by successive groups of maroons, fugitives, slaves, and Indians (who are included in the former groups as well). These were not conflicts that could be easily ignored by the dominant colonial and planter forces; maroon and fugitive existence consistently undermined English imperial strategy and later destabilized the consolidation of labor power needed for the development of early American agrarian capitalism, so much so that slave revolt ultimately helped to catalyze a civil war and force agrarian capitalism's transition from chattel slavery to wage labor. As subsequent chapters will demonstrate, the adoption of wages represents not a victory over or departure from the forces behind slavery, but a continuation of that method in new forms.

The early development of capitalist wealth and power was thus not a "natural" or tranquil process but one enacted through constant violence against populations of the dispossessed. These communities and individuals resisted such processes with their lives. Every period of primitive accumulation—from the European theft of the commons to the earliest theft of Native lands—required bloody wars and ever-larger state apparatuses for enforcement. Always bubbling beneath the surface of such wars was the forced rewriting of daily social life on the bodies of the oppressed, the whole remaking of spiritual, communal, ethnic, and gender norms. The very existence of whiteness as a political and social category finds its origins in this period. Laborers of European descent *became* white as they were subjected to the various forces of democracy, divisions of labor, nationalism, and war.

In providing a commons beyond the boundaries of capitalist life, the role of wilderness was fundamental to the resistance of the swamp maroons. By the early 1800s, however, this wilderness was an island surrounded on all sides by a well-consolidated state and economic system. What had begun in part as an open, highly experimental mixture of radical cultural elements and ideas—European, Native, West African—evolved into a network of hidden, strictly oppositional, mostly Black settlements.

In all the phases of this evolution, radical and unpredictable religious forms played a key role—providing everything from a coordinating military role to a defense of women's reproductive autonomy and their

Sometimes considered 'the grandfather of black nationalism,' Martin Delany was active against slavery, advocated for resettling former slaves outside the United States, and wrote the first novel published by a Black man in the United States, which highlighted the spiritual systems of maroons in the Great Dismal.

leadership in social and political life.[56] A cross-Atlantic similarity can be noted here, as revolts by laborers in Europe were also marked by the magical, the irrational, the heretical, and the supernatural. By no coincidence, it was the same rationalist institutional forces that sought to govern Roanoke, enslave the Tuscarora, and drain the Great Dismal Swamp, and that sought to murder ungovernable women and stamp out uncontrollable spiritual practices in Europe.[57] It is worth remembering that the quasi-atheist Deism of Thomas Jefferson, the man who ran Monticello like a well-oiled machine, was that of a slaveholder and politician.

Another theme emerges from the story of the Great Dismal, at what we might call the beginning of an anarchist history of the American South: that true affinity between differently racialized communities can only be found in a context of revolutionary violence. Even the process of forming the earliest Roanoke settlement must be understood in this way: the escape of fugitive servants and debtors was by legal definition an act of theft, and the constitution of the multi-ethnic settlement itself was made possible only by successive armed engagements with the English crown and an alliance with Tuscarora fighters. For the maroons of the Great Dismal, only through constant conflict with the plantation system was it possible to carve out settlements in which the racial order of the surrounding world could begin to erode. It was through acts of war with plantation society that various maroons could begin to approach each other as equals; only through the destruction of plantation society could that project have been completed.

Departing from the feel-good clichés and whitewashing of subjects like the Underground Railroad and Harriet Tubman that one finds in high school textbooks, this history broadly affirms that the promise of escape is only fulfilled by the practice of attack. It reminds us why Tubman carried a handgun on her at all times, why many escaped slaves did not flee to the North but instead remained South, stealing from the economy that stole them, liberating their former coworkers, and attacking their former bosses.

Ultimately, these efforts forced American elites to reconsider slavery as the most stable and profitable system of agricultural production. The Civil War that resulted brought together competing visions for agrarian and industrial capitalism alongside new practices of exploitation and control, but it also opened new doors for resistance by the South's angriest and

---

56 Leaming, *Hidden Americans*.
57 Federici, *Caliban and the Witch*.

most dispossessed. An equally violent social war continued underneath the formal national and racial divisions of the Civil War itself, with the poorest and most oppressed finding their own victories and defeats as one system of exploitation was replaced by another.

Near the end of the Civil War, in January 1865, Union General William Tecumseh Sherman arrived in Savannah, Georgia with his army of capital, "dripping from head to foot, from every pore, with blood and dirt."[1] The destruction caused by his army was general and total throughout Georgia, South Carolina, and parts of North Carolina. "One could track the line of Sherman's march ... by the fires on the horizon. He burned the ginhouses, cotton presses, railroad depots, bridges, freighthouses, and unoccupied dwellings."[2] The violence spared no one, neither plantation playboys nor poor laborers, owners nor fieldhands, free nor enslaved.

Thousands of formerly enslaved men, women, and children trailed the victors, many among them ambivalent to the Union, careless of the Confederacy, but with a burning hatred of the planter class and with a desire to take advantage of the opportunity opened up by the Union's invasion. Sherman's destruction not only served military interests, but industrialists as well, paving the way for reinvestment in the South by northern capitalists—what history will call the period of Reconstruction. For a very limited time at the end of the Civil War, attacks on the plantation economy by slaves and laborers partly coincided with the scorched earth policy of an army serving northern business interests.

The Civil War brought to a head conflicts over race and competing visions of economic production that had been simmering for decades, but it did so on the terms of the ruling class, answering these problems in ways that perpetuated capitalist and colonialist conditions while realizing modern forms of exploitation for a new era. Nevertheless, the power vacuum opened up in this tumultuous period offered an opportunity to former slaves and fugitives who had built up networks of resistance and established maroon communities before the war. Insurgents continued

1   "If money … comes into the world with a congenital blood-stain on one cheek, capital comes dripping from head to foot, from every pore, with blood and dirt." (Karl Marx, *Capital: A Critique of Political Economy* [New York: The Modern Library, 1906], 834.)

2   "John H. Kennaway, 1865," in *Standing upon the Mouth of a Volcano: New South Georgia, A Documentary History*, ed. Mills Lane (Savannah: Beehive Press, 1993), 3.

to attack the plantation system long after the military conflict had ended, taking advantage of the state's loss of regional control when possible, but also beginning to simultaneously respond to and reject northern models of democracy and wage work. Tactics shifted accordingly; sabotage against the plantations persisted, but was accompanied by strikes, the self-organizing of farm laborers, the rejection of labor contracts, the occupation of land, and armed community defense from white vigilantes.

In Savannah, where the ocean temporarily cooled the flames of Sherman's brutal march, Union troops arrived as a scattered mass. In one group stood the Union Army, who believed they were determining the fate of the South for years to come. In the other group were the fugitives and deserters, who were welcomed into the city, marshes, swamps, and islands by the thousands of men and women who would actually deliver the final blow to one of "the most close knit, aristocratic, and affluent group of planters [of] the antebellum South."[3]

3 Eric Foner, *Nothing but Freedom: Emancipation and Its Legacy* (Baton Rouge: Louisiana State University Press, 2007), 78.

"You ask us to forgive the landowners of our island.... I cannot well forgive. Does it look as if he has forgiven me, seeing how he tries to keep me in a condition of helplessness?"

—Anonymous former slave from Edisto Island, South Carolina, October 1865

"As to work, I do not imagine they will do much of it."

—Charles Heyward, a Combahee River, South Carolina planter, 1867

OGEECHEE TILL DEATH:

Expropriation and Communization in Low-Country Georgia

ON THE EVE OF 1868, WHILE PROMINENT SAVANNAH CITIZENS DELIGHTED in Christmas and New Year's festivities, another party was brewing in the swamps and rice fields of the Ogeechee Neck just twelve miles south of the city. Hundreds of rice workers and forest squatters were driving the plantation overseers off their lands, and concretizing their plans to occupy the land and create new lives for themselves, independent of the newly imposed rent and wage system.

The Ogeechee Insurrection would last only a few weeks, but its legacy lives on as the most coordinated series of occupations of the coastal southeast rice plantations. While rice workers all over South Carolina and Georgia were striking intermittently, the Ogeechee rebels went beyond work stoppages and transformed their lives by claiming the land that their ancestors had been forced to turn into rice fields. With arms and manifestos, the insurgents fought in the footsteps of the maroons before them and attempted to destroy the plantation system forever.

Land Contestation after the War

At the end of the war, many Black workers chose not to leave the plantations, homesteads, and cities where they were enslaved. The story usually goes that this was because they were isolated from survival networks away from their homes; however, many slaves had already freed themselves at home and did not need to leave to find sanctuary. The Emancipation Proclamation, which officially freed the slaves, was a militarily strategic move that legalized the incorporation of fugitive and contraband slaves into the ranks of the Union Army, while crippling the South's productive capacity during the war.[1] In effect, the Proclamation was symbolic; slaves had already been freeing themselves by the thousands, not to officially join a war they were already fighting on their own terms, but because "they wanted to stop the economy of the plantation system, and to do that they left the plantations."[2]

For many slaves who had been trying to rid the South of the planter class for decades, the presence of an invading army complicated their efforts at freedom. To begin to catalog the attacks on plantation society in the South from 1861 to 1865 would be impossible because they were occurring everywhere and all the time. Refusal continued as it had for generations: in the various forms of sabotage, strikes, insubordination, individual acts of violence, conspiracy, and revolt.[3] By 1861, to counter this rebellion, the entire South became one huge mobilized military camp, the effects of which perfected the systems of policing already created for slave labor.[4]

In the pre–Civil War era, slavery resisters made constant and diverse attacks against cash crop production to interrupt the flow of profit and to gain autonomy. With the war winding down, the introduction of federal troops, and the planters' attempt to return to the land, there was a distinct

---

1   We are reminded of Lincoln's infamous reply to abolitionist Horace Greeley's "Prayer of Twenty Millions": "My paramount object in this struggle *is* to save the Union, and is *not* either to save or to destroy slavery. If I could save the Union without freeing *any* slave I would do it, and if I could save it by freeing *all* the slaves I would do it; and if I could save it by freeing some and leaving others alone I would also do that. What I do about slavery, and the colored race, I do because I believe it helps to save the Union." Source: http://www.nytimes.com/1862/08/24/news/letter-president-lincoln-reply-horace-greeley-slavery-union-restoration-union.html.

2   This is not to hide the fact that there were countless ecstatic celebrations and riots at the announcement of the Thirteenth Amendment. To diminish this would be to ignore the importance of this event to the four million enslaved people and all of those who suffered under the planter oligarchy. Nevertheless, it is worthwhile to question what freedoms the amendment was intended to secure, especially considering its later use in re-enslaving many former slaves via new systems of incarceration, punishment, and forced labor; W.E.B. Du Bois, *Black Reconstruction in America 1860–1880* (New York: Simon and Schuster, 1935), 49.

3   Even in the heart of the Confederacy, the president was not safe. Jefferson Davis's home was burned down in Richmond in 1864, allegedly by slaves (Aptheker, *American Negro Slave Revolt*, 147).

4   Ibid., 360.

turn toward generalized expropriation and destruction by former rice and cotton workers in order to force the end of the system of plantation labor, prevent planters from recovering the wealth stored in their properties, and resist assimilation into wage slavery. These actions speak to the desires of the saboteurs, those who refused to forgive and forget their exploitation and who did not wait for Union bureaucrats to settle matters between the planters and themselves.

> More than in any other part of the South, the accumulated resentments of slavery burst forth in violence. In Georgetown, plantation homes and meat houses were pillaged by the freedmen. Chicora Wood,[5] the home plantation of Robert W. Allston before his death in 1864, was ransacked by his slaves—every article of furniture was removed and his meticulous plantation records destroyed.... On another Georgetown plantation, Blacks "divided out the land and ... pulled down fences and would obey no driver." Farther to the south, the magnificent plantation home at Middleton Place near Charleston was burned to the ground and the vaults in the family graveyard were broken open and the bones scattered by the slaves, including some who had escaped to enlist in the Union Army and who now returned with General Sherman to wreak vengeance.[6]

Surrounded by bands of refugees, fugitives, and guerilla soldiers, and with more showing up each day, Sherman couldn't leave Savannah until he made an attempt to address this impending crisis. Chiefly concerned with the fact that they were all unemployed, the Secretary of War General Edwin Stanton came in from Washington immediately to investigate the matter and work with Sherman toward a solution. After a few days of "examining the condition of the liberated Negroes," Stanton chose twenty men whom he determined were fit to be leaders, whose backgrounds ranged from barbers and ministers to former overseers, and sat them down with Sherman to discuss a plan of action.[7]

---

5   This plantation was named after the Chicora, a small Native American tribe in northeastern South Carolina. By the Civil War, all but a small remnant of the original tribe had been enslaved, murdered, or displaced by the planter class. One cannot help but be reminded of the many affluent gated communities in the modern-day South proudly named after former slave plantations, with street names indicating the flora or fauna that once thrived there.

6   Foner, *Nothing but Freedom*, 79–80.

7   Foner, *A Short History of Reconstruction*, 70.

In November of 1864, Sherman's troops took Atlanta and destroyed the entire railroad infrastructure in the city. They would return again, under different names, after the war to rebuild the railroads and the city but with northern, industrial investment and profit replacing the southern planter oligarchy.

From there, General Sherman issued the infamous "Sea Island Circular" of January 18, 1865, also known as the "Special Field Orders, No. 15," which ordered the redistribution of all abandoned and confiscated lands from Charleston, South Carolina, to St. John's River, Florida, including the Sea Islands and coastal waterways thirty miles inland. In effect, the majority of the South's coastal rice and cotton plantations were to be divided into lots to be leased or sold to their former workers. Having no presidential or congressional authorization for this wartime act, Sherman appointed General Rufus Saxton, who became an abolitionist before the war, to deal with the details. Saxton would go on to direct the divisions of the Freedmen's Bureau in South Carolina, Georgia, and Florida when they were established in March 1865.[8]

Charged with managing this process of redistribution and political transition, many contemporary historians consider the leaders of the Freedmen's Bureau to have been well-intentioned victims of their own bureaucracy. Regardless of individual Union officials' sentiments toward racial harmony, however, it is clear that the larger function of the Freedmen's Bureau and its policies was the smooth transition from one kind of class society to another, normalizing modern notions of landownership, contractual labor, and alienation. Another prominent leader of the Freedmen's Bureau, General Oliver Howard, for example, is described by historian Eric Foner as representing the dominant view of the Union officials that, "most freedmen must return to plantation labor, but under conditions that allowed them the opportunity to work their way out of the wage-earning class."[9]

As an institution, the Freedmen's Bureau was a direct descendent of the "experiments in freedom" that occurred throughout the Sea Islands in Georgia and South Carolina, the sugar country outside of New Orleans, and the Mississippi Valley. Since the congressional Confiscation Act of 1862, the Union Army was permitted to seize and claim any land that had been abandoned by its Confederate owners or any land where its owners ceased to pay taxes. It is no surprise then that the concentration of lands that the Union chose to appropriate were where the region's wealthiest cash crops were produced. In manipulating fugitives

---

8   It was General Saxton who devised the forty-acre allotment system. Accruing more and more land since the 1862 Confiscation Act, in 1865 the North controlled over 850,000 acres of land that the government considered abandoned. Of those, 549,000 acres were under Saxton's control in South Carolina, Georgia, and Florida (Du Bois, *Black Reconstruction in America,* 60).

9   Foner, *A Short History of Reconstruction,* 71.

and refugees of these areas, the Union set up a pseudo-military slave camp to entice workers to continue to produce crops for the benefit of the northern war effort.[10]

In the case of the Sea Islands, the cotton plantations were organized by Union textile and railroad capitalists who were sent down to teach Blacks that "the abandonment of slavery did not imply the abandonment of cotton, and that Blacks would work more efficiently and profitably as free laborers than as slaves," and to instill the free labor ideology that "no man … appreciates property who does not work for it."[11] The experiment on the Sea Islands was a total failure. The free workers preferred growing subsistence crops and refused to produce the profits that had been achieved in years before the war. The Yankees left in 1865, unable to secure a long-term investment in Sea Island cotton. Northern investors did not learn from this failed attempt at disciplining the Black worker through the wage-labor system, and they would continue to impose their definition of freedom as workers moved from subtle tactics of work slowdowns and workplace occupations to destroying the foundational infrastructure of the cash crop system.[12]

In the summer of 1865, the Freedmen's Bureau was still redistributing land that was covered under Sherman's field order while importing northern philanthropic missionaries to staff compulsory schools for children and to teach investment economics to the new landowners.[13] At this point, President Johnson received regular hate mail and threats from the previously wealthiest men in America, and would read reports from the

---

10　Du Bois, "Black Reconstruction," 68–72. Du Bois writes more extensively on the varying degrees and conditions of these experiments, particularly in Louisiana and the Mississippi Valley, indicating that those with forced plantation labor failed miserably while others that allowed for Black control over work and civic life in the camps were met with more success. These were all, though, still "experiments" controlled by generals who would go on to direct the Freedmen's Bureau, and as such ultimately produced a state of dependence on the Union for resources. In effect this reinforced white control over southern land and Black labor, just with the policies of the Union instead of the planter.

11　Foner, *A Short History of Reconstruction*, 25.

12　Ibid.

13　New research reveals that white northerners made up the smallest percentage of teachers (about one-sixth) and that while northern educational models were overwhelmingly employed in the new schools, Black southerners' struggle for literacy and autonomy was an initial driving force in the construction of many of these schools. For more on the complicated history of Black education in this era, read Ronald Butchart, *Schooling the Freed People: Teaching, Learning, and the Struggle for Black Freedom, 1861–1876* (Chapel Hill: University of North Carolina Press, 2013).

Agricultural Department stating that "labor [in South Carolina and Georgia] was in a disorganized and chaotic state, production had ceased and … the power to compel laborers to go into the rice swamp utterly broken."[14] Johnson reversed all orders by the Bureau and sought to immediately repossess the planters of their property.[15]

It was at this time that the Freedmen's Bureau revealed itself as the enforcer of the old economy in new terms:

> The "two evils" against which the Bureau had to contend, an army officer observed in July 1865, were "cruelty on the part of the employer and shirking on the part of the negroes." Yet the Bureau, like the army, seemed to consider the Black reluctance to labor the greater threat to its economic mission. In some

This engraving depicts the burning of a railroad depot, potentially in Atlanta, by Sherman's troops in the fall of 1864. Below the flames, fugitives and refugees—symbolized by their carried belongings—are seen in the wake of Sherman's army, representing the thousands that followed behind the advance of Sherman's troops to Savannah.

areas agents continued the military's urban pass systems and vagrancy patrols, as well as the practice of rounding up unemployed laborers for shipment to plantations. Bureau courts in Memphis dispatched impoverished Blacks convicted of crimes to labor for whites who would pay their fines.[16]

From late 1865 until its dissolution in 1868, the Bureau's chief occupation was to attempt, by any means necessary, to convince free Blacks to sign contracts to work for their former masters on plantations or smaller farms. When General Oliver Howard—an architect and proponent of the "Black yeomanry" model of freedom—had to go to Edisto Island, South Carolina, to tell people they were to quit the lands they had been squatting on and return to work on the plantations, the people who had been living free of labor contracts responded as follows:

> General we want Homesteads, we were promised Homesteads by the government. If it does not carry out the promises its agents made to us, if the government having concluded to befriend its late enemies and to neglect to observe the principles of common faith between its self and us its allies in the war you said was over, now takes away from them all right to the soil they stand upon save such as they can get by again working for *your* late and their *all time* enemies … we are left in a more unpleasant condition than our former…. You will see this is not the condition of really freemen. You ask us to forgive the land owners of our island…. I cannot well forgive. Does it look as if he has forgiven me, seeing how he tries to keep me in a condition of helplessness?[17]

Refusing to learn from the so-called experiments in freedom of the previous years, and still ignoring the clear words from the Sea Island people, in February 1866, Bureau officials attempted to bring former landowners back to the islands. The inhabitants armed themselves, drove off the bureaucrats and the planters, and barricaded themselves on the land, telling the capitalists, "You have better go back to Charleston, and go to work there, and if you can do nothing else, you can pick oysters and earn your living as the loyal people have done—by the sweat of their brows."[18]

16 Foner, *A Short History of Reconstruction*, 157.
17 Ibid., 73.
18 Ibid., 74.

Accounts like this one are innumerable from the islands of Georgia and South Carolina in 1865 and 1866. These islands were geographically strategic to squat and defend, as many of the planters had abandoned them at the beginning of the war. The former workers, who knew the ecological and economic flows of the waterways between the islands and mainland, had no intention of leaving.

Snap, Crackle, Pop! Tensions Build in the Rice Fields

Across from the Sea Islands where squatters were defending their land, woven together by intercoastal waterways and tidal marshes, were the mainland rice fields surrounding the port towns of Charleston and Savannah. Second only to the Georgetown County rice kingdom in South Carolina, the Ogeechee Neck in Chatham County, Georgia, was the seat of the most profitable rice bounties in the country before the war. As on the islands, by the summer of 1865, planters were already returning to the Ogeechee River network with the help of Union officials and devising ways to reinvest in the rice crop. When planters returned to find their former lands claimed by multiple new owners, the Bureau worked with them to help them reoccupy their plantations. Planter John Cheves, who owned the 2,014 acres he called Grove Point Plantation, refused to recognize the thirty families who had gained possessory titles to 245 acres of his land in his absence. The Bureau followed his lead. In the true spirit of the capitalist debt economy, the Bureau helped him borrow $11,300 to pay back his debts and reinvest in his plantation. The planters who did not borrow money from the bank simply redivided their land and tried the scheme of the northern capitalists: selling their own plots to the people who already leased the land from the Bureau. Some planters, like the bosses of Wild Horn and Oriza, were so eager to get production up and running again that they simply leased the land to skilled workers in exchange for a portion of the crops.[19]

The workers who leased, bargained, and contracted with the Bureau and former masters for employment and housing were in the minority of the 4,200 Black people living in the Ogeechee district. Hundreds, if not thousands more were squatting in the pine woods around the swamps and surviving between subsistence hunting, fishing, and farming, and the informal economies that existed throughout slavery with other poor Blacks

19 Karen Bell, "'The Ogeechee Troubles': Federal Land Restoration and the 'Lived Realities' of Temporary Proprietors, 1865–1868," *The Georgia Historical Quarterly* 85 (2001): 380.

and whites. Frances Butler Leigh, a Sea Island cotton planter's widow and mistress of three plantations after the war, attests to this lifestyle:

> Our neighbors on Saint Simon's are discouraged with the difficulties they encounter, having to lose two or three months every year while the Negroes are making up their minds whether they will work or not. There are about a dozen on Butler's Island who do no work. They all raise a little corn and sweet potatoes and with their facilities for catching fish and oysters and shooting wild game they have as much to eat as they want.[20]

Most historians who recognize the phenomenon of these Black autonomous communities at the end of the Civil War describe them as solely the result of rice production conditions and the social relations specific to that labor, ignoring the fact that it was the active refusal of those conditions—through attacking and abandoning the plantation society—that secured the possibility of that freedom. It is necessary, however, to examine the history of southern rice cultivation in order to learn the full history of these maroons.

The plantation economy relied on the skilled knowledge of slave laborers, who brought with them a long history of highly developed rice cultivation practices from West Africa. Planters considered the tidal marshes and swamps of coastal South Carolina and Georgia to be perfect for rice production because cultivating these areas forced people to uproot the massive bald cypress and tupelo trees in the swamps, thus extending and controlling the tidal marshes while partly taming the swamps. Preparation began in January and lasted through February, during which time men would dig trenches and repair the irrigation systems. In March, women would create the rice seed balls and plant them. From April through July, the fields were flooded multiple times for sprouting and early growth, then weeded and protected against other flora and fauna. During the height of the late summer malaria season, the fields remained mostly flooded while men stood on constant watch protecting the crop from "rice birds" and other marshland creatures. Flatboats would arrive in the early fall to carry the harvest to the mills for processing and then off to the Charleston or Savannah markets.

---

20 "Frances Leigh, St. Simon's Island, 1866–68," in *Standing upon the Mouth of a Volcano.*

While some of the division of labor was gendered, the field work was organized as a task system. This meant that there were very few overseers to the operation and workers self-organized based on their knowledge of the tasks that had to be completed and who could best get those done. What emerged was an intensely cooperative production process, aided by the fact that the planters and managers could not stand to be in the swamps during the summer malaria months. Slaves were disciplined to the extent that they were rewarded for high yields by being allowed to stay with their families, but they also constantly manipulated the labor time so that they had free time to do other things. Rice required slave labor to profit; no one who had other options for survival would do this work. Increasingly throughout the nineteenth century those who refused this brutal labor came to include the rebels called *maroons*. By placing hundreds of laborers in a single area with little white oversight, the cooperative labor structure of low-country rice production more closely resembled the sugarcane fields of the Caribbean than most other plantations in the southern United States.

The low country in which this rice production occurred is a flat coastal plain that lies in Georgia and South Carolina. After the Civil War, the low country was made up of the lands that extended fifty miles inland from the Atlantic, about one-third of which consisted of immense swamps that interlocked with each other to form a long chain, stretching several hundred miles along the coast. The plantations often faced the larger rivers, backing up into stagnant swamp areas where slave quarters were erected. These so-called back swamps were stagnant water (unlike the tidal marshes where the rice grew) and were dominated by large cypress trees. As one historian of the maroons of the area states, they were liminal "places that planters owned, but slaves mastered," where "white control was defined as loose at best."[21] Much as in the Great Dismal Swamp, the ecology of an undomesticated wilderness perfectly fit the needs of the bonded yet rebellious labor force.

Unlike the fugitive slaves who fled north and west, when maroons left their plantations they chose to make their homes in the nearby swamps. The survivalist skills and offensive tactics learned from over a hundred years of maroonage in the low country formed a collective knowledge base that people drew on during the Ogeechee Insurrection and throughout that larger period of revolt. Maroonage was not merely

---

21   Timothy James Lockley, *Maroon Communities in South Carolina: A Documentary Record* (Columbia: University of South Carolina Press, 2009), 32.

---

a lifestyle option for deserting enforced labor, but a specifically evolved method of attack on slave society. From the survival skills of hunting, fishing, tracking, and hiding to the conspiratorial skills of maneuvering within the swamps and plantation borders, navigating rivers, and setting up trusted networks for trading information and goods, the tactics of the maroons were just as essential to the attacks on the postwar plantations as in the antebellum period.

After the Civil War—with the power vacuum created between the planter class and the northern industrial class, backed by their respective political parties, and with the total destruction of the slave-based economy—these revolts took on new forms. A high-intensity class warfare emerged out of two hundred years of lower-intensity activities. The desires and demands of Black workers became total and generalized. When rebels organized the attacks and seized territory along the Ogeechee River plantations in 1868 they were continuing this maroon history, but with the new awareness that they didn't have to live at the margins of the rice empire: they could destroy it.

The Insurrection of 1868–1869

We had a small excitement in November, 1868, owing to a report which went the round of the plantations that there was to be a general Negro insurrection on the first of the year. The Negroes this year and the following seemed to reach the climax of lawless independence, and I never slept without a loaded pistol by my bed."

—Ella Thomas, daughter of a prosperous farmer in Augusta, Georgia[22]

By 1867, the rice plantation owners in the Ogeechee Neck had become more organized and effective in revamping the cash crop system of their former society through the labor contract system introduced by northern interests. The close-knit nature of the planter class allowed them to reorganize ownership and management of their lands without compromising their economic power. Three of the prominent plantations in the Ogeechee Neck hired Confederate officers Major Middleton and Captain

22   "Ella Thomas, Augusta, 1868," in *Standing upon the Mouth of a Volcano*, 73–79.

Tucker to run operations, and one of the first acts of these new managers was to evict everyone who refused to sign labor contracts. Those evicted and other sympathetic workers immediately began organizing around this hostility through the local Union League.[23]

Unrelated to the Union Army, the Union Leagues were a massively attended, decentralized, cross-racial political organizing body of southerners active during the Reconstruction era. Varying wildly in composition, style, strategy, and tactics, the local context of the League took precedent over any national doctrine that Radical Republicans might have been pushing at the time. Whether or not the Union League in the Ogeechee District began with the intention of becoming an insurrectionary force, leaders from the League moved beyond the marches, parades, strikes, and voter organizing that dominated other region's Leagues.[24] It can be gathered that in Ogeechee, those in the Union League were primarily concerned with getting land, and advocated for the direct action of setting up homesteads for themselves in the face of the government's inaction toward that end.

One historian of the Ogeechee rebellion, Karen Bell, asserts that—as tensions rose with laborers' refusal to sign contracts—it was the leaders of the Union League who initially rallied the Union Home Guard, a protective militia of and for formerly enslaved Blacks, which was created in 1866 to support those who refused to work. It is also entirely possible that affiliation with the Union League was merely a strategic choice, enabling those in Ogeechee to organize aboveground meetings. In February 1868, however, Major Middleton made it illegal for the League to meet on any of the plantations he controlled, which effectively sent the organizing body underground. From there, the conspiring that would lead to the rebellion the following winter began.[25]

Accounts vary as to how hostilities specifically manifested in the last week of December 1868, but it seems that for at least a year, hundreds of workers and refugees of the Ogeechee Neck (and probably throughout Chatham, Bryan, and Liberty counties) conspired about the actions that followed. These included setting up communication networks, accumulating weapons and materials, and expropriating crops to fund the actions. To get a sense of what took place during the roughly two weeks of action that became known as the Ogeechee Insurrection, we must use daily newspaper reports from Savannah, as well as the limited available academic

23 Bell, "The Ogeechee Troubles," 384.
24 Foner, *A Short History of Reconstruction*, 125–128.
25 Bell, "The Ogeechee Troubles," 385.

research, which aggregates the various paper trails left by property owners, court clerks, and military and state officials. While there is an abundance of testimonies from whites who fled the area and Black workers who were loyal to their employers, there are few firsthand accounts by those who participated in the revolt, save for one small manifesto by leader (and former Union League president) Solomon Farley.

It is worth noting that most of the daily events of the Ogeechee Insurrection were relayed through the *Savannah Morning News*, the prominent media outlet of the city. Throughout the nineteenth century, the media in the South operated as a legitimized amplification of the gossip and paranoia of white property owners; such reporting was encouraged by all sectors of society who were terrified of the upheaval of the conditions under which they were accustomed. This is not to say that conspiracies of slave insurrections and insurrections by free Blacks in the postwar south were not a constant threat to plantation society, but exaggeration was effective in efforts at controlling the majority of southern society who owned neither slaves nor land, i.e., poor whites and Blacks. The generalized fear of violent insurrection by Black men, a fear constantly reinforced by newspapers, was necessary to maintaining racial segregation between Blacks and poor whites. This obscured the reality: that the two often shared mutual interests and sometimes even a history of cooperation during rebellion.

Urban media outlets like the *Savannah Morning News* also functioned to maintain the myth that the African body was providentially ordained, and by implication psychologically inclined, to servility and thus bondage—a myth that was reinforced by the emerging "sciences" of phrenology and eugenics.[26] Though both were functional to maintaining the plantation system in their own way, the narrative of providential decree sat uneasily beside the constant paranoia drummed up by media outlets seeking to engineer poor white support. This inconsistency rendered the prospect of an organized insurrection by Black workers at once horrific and omnipresent, while simultaneously inconceivable.[27] The contradiction of these

26 Of course, Providence is a canvas that can carry many colors; as writes one historian of slavery and early capitalist development. "The planter looked upon slavery as eternal, ordained by God, and went to great length to justify it by scriptural quotations. There was no reason why the slave should think the same. He took the same scriptures and adapted them to his own purposes. To coercion and punishment he responded with indolence, sabotage, and revolt." (Eric Williams, *Capitalism and Slavery* [Chapel Hill: University of North Carolina Press, 2004], 202.)

27 Even so, media manipulation was not adequate in and of itself to guarantee poor white loyalty to the plantation system. A variety of structural incentives and penalties

A.R. Waud, *Harper's Weekly*, January 5, 1867

Entitled "Rice Cultivation on the Ogeechee River, near Savannah, Georgia," this illustration shows the multitude of tasks that were required to propagate the rice crops, as well as the presence of both men and women doing work side by side. This representation of rice cultivation, however, creates the illusion of a peaceful, well-functioning economy at a time when strikes, work refusals, and land occupations dominated the coastal landscape.

competing white supremacist narratives may also help to explain the differing accounts offered by certain white witnesses during the rebellion, as to whether the insurgents were an organized military outfit or more similar to a disorganized, riotous mob.[28]

Partly due to the unreliability of the media, precise statistics concerning participation in the insurrections are unavailable; so the number of people involved and actual dates of various actions are based partly on conjecture. What remains important is that between December 1868 and January 1869, hundreds of people were sick of negotiating with bosses, landlords, and Freedmen's Bureau agents, and consequently forced all planters and those loyal to them off the lands where they lived. Within

---

existed to coerce white participation in the policing of Black bodies, including the use of Irish and Scottish immigrants as overseers, the intentional settlement of immigrant communities in potential maroon territory, and the formal or informal punishments faced by whites who refused to participate in slave patrols. With no major interruptions in either personnel or procedure, these slave patrols evolved gradually into the police forces we know and love today.

28   This contradiction, between the spectacles of the highly organized professional agitators and the disorganized mob, continues to appear in the media today. Both are used to evoke fear in a passive middle class, and provoke divisions within social movements. Likewise, it is worth remembering how history has colored the mob as a subhuman and nonwhite phenomenon, regardless of who constitutes it.

a limited territory, the infrastructural and symbolic power of the planter class was destroyed, and insurgents set out to live a new life. The following accounts are an attempt to give a fuller picture of their tactics, desires, and lives as they converged that winter on the five rice plantations between the Ogeechee and Little Ogeechee rivers.

On December 23, the *Savannah Morning News* reported that there is "proof of organization and a complete league among the country Negroes."[29] The source of this information was a citizen who was stopped a few days before "by armed pickets at every cross-road" and was only allowed to proceed after tense discussion.

The next day, the same paper reported that,

> On all the Ogeechee plantations the Negroes appear to be banded together, thoroughly armed and organized. They will not work and, by threats of violence, prevent those who are willing to labor from serving their employers, their object being to prevent the rice crop from being secured by day that they may steal it at night.

Tucker and Middleton hired extra white men to watch the fields at night. Some night prior, a group of the rebels appeared in two fields owned by the planters and fired on the watchmen, wounding two and forcing the rest off the land. The band then stole sixteen sacks of rice, roughly 160 bushels. One source described the rebels:

> They drill regularly, are armed, equipped and organized in regularly military style. They live mainly off plundering the plantations of poultry and stock, stealing the horses and selling them and raiding the woods for game. One of the ringleaders goes about at all times with an armed bodyguard and puts on as much style as an army brigadier. In that section of the country there appears to be no longer any security for life or property.

Bell's history of the revolt further describes the attack on the watchmen above, stating that: "The Ogeechee insurrection had its origins on Southfield Plantation ... when between fifteen and twenty freedmen, armed

---

29 Unless otherwise noted, all *Savannah Morning News* documentation is taken from "The Ogeechee Insurrection, 1868–69," in *Standing upon the Mouth of a Volcano*, 79–90.

with muskets and bayonets, sought redress from Maj. J. Motte Middleton and Capt. J.F. Tucker for expelling them from plantation lands."[30] In the last week of December, watchmen, overseers, farm managers, planters, and others aligned with the management class of the rice plantations were driven off of the Neck by insurgents' hostility, and they consequently headed to Savannah.

Between December 30 and January 2, the county sheriff and his men got involved, and the antagonism between planters and ex-workers intensified. According to the *Savannah Morning News*, on December 30 warrants for larceny and assault with intent to murder were issued for seventeen Ogeechee Black men. Sheriff James Dooner was charged with executing the warrants and immediately called upon Major Perkins for military aid. Perkins jumped at the opportunity to help quell the rebellion, but was forced to rescind his offer hours later after higher-ups informed him that "under the existing state of public affairs no action could be taken by the military until every means and all energies of the civil authorities had been exhausted and they proved powerless to act in the matter."[31]

Without support from the military, Sheriff Dooner and two other officers left Savannah early in the morning to deliver the warrants. They arrived at Station Number 1 on the Atlantic and Gulf Railroad, mounted the horses that awaited them, and headed five and a half miles west to Heyward's plantation.[32] When they arrived at Vallambrosia, the sheriff was assisted by the local overseer in detaining five men, who were then taken to the train bound for Savannah. The officers then proceeded to the New Hope Plantation, owned by a "Miss Elliot," to find "the great rascal" Solomon Farley who, based on his political and criminal record, they believed was behind the plot.[33]

The officers broke into Solomon's home, read his warrant aloud, and after some arguing he agreed to go with them. Before leaving the house Solomon

---

30 According to Bell, the Ogeechee uprising followed two other minor revolts in the county in previous years, known as the "Yamacraw" and "Louisville" revolts.

31 Georgia was still under military occupation by the Union, who controlled the city, county, and state militias and placed very specific restrictions on former Confederate officers and rebel citizens showing any force ("The Ogeechee Insurrection," 80).

32 Planter Walter Heyward owned the plantation known as Vallambrosia. Wild Horn, run by planter William Burroughs, had been leased out to seventy-four Black workers after the war, and was said to be where "freed people exercised control over their work and their personal lives and never relinquished possession of the land they worked" (Bell, "Ogeechee Troubles," 383).

33 "The Ogeechee Insurrection," 81.

exclaimed that he was "not yet secure" and "drew something upon a slip of paper and handed it to his wife, who started off up the canal upon receiving

it." He then handed off more slips of paper to his friends and family, who followed his wife's example. As the officers began to realize what was going on, they ordered Solomon to stop writing and headed off toward the railroad station with him in custody. From here the *Savannah Morning News* reports that the crew of officers arrived with Solomon Farley at the train station around 2:30 p.m., and while eating lunch began to notice some disturbance up the road ahead. Black men and women from the Neck were amassing on the road leading to the train station, and as minutes passed their numbers increased. The *News* claims that it was a "great mob … armed with guns and other weapons. About 200, it was estimated, were present." When the

1863 map of the rivers and railroads between the Savannah and Ogeechee rivers.

Illustrated London News, January 1863

sheriff attempted to address the crowd, they replied that they "didn't care for the Sheriff or anybody else." The officers immediately deserted the train station and left Savannah by road, where the people followed "yelling like a pack of demons." The police didn't make it far before needing to leave the road and barricade themselves in a nearby house.[34]

In another account, the story goes that the crowd was not a disorderly mob, but rather that they attacked the police in "military formation."[35] Regardless of the competing accounts, the Ogeechee crew succeeded in de-arresting Solomon while disarming the sheriff and his officers, seizing their arms, warrants, money, and "whatever else of value they had about them." The officers were left at the house, embarrassed and alone, to catch the next train on the fly as the rebels secured Station No. 1 against transporting the officers back to Savannah.[36]

On December 31—the morning after the sheriff and his officers made it back home—Savannah was teeming with rumors and excitement. People gathered in the streets to read the news and discuss what should be done. The *Savannah Morning News* reported, in the classic gossip style

34   Ibid.
35   Bell, "Ogeechee Troubles," 388.
36   "The Ogeechee Insurrection," 81.

of the day, that it was "unanimous [in the streets] that things should be stopped and at once." Also arriving in town at the time were George Baxley and Mr. O'Donald, employees of Major Middleton who had both been forcibly removed from the plantations and consequently found fast friends with the *News* reporters and the sheriff.

George Baxley should have known that his days of micromanaging and punishing workers and their families in the Neck were numbered: not long before, he was trying to tear down an old house on the land when he was stopped by a rice worker named Hector Broughton who warned him, "Don't pull that house down, I'm coming back to get my forty acres and I want that house."[37] Baxley continued to manage the Southfield Plantation as usual until days later he was attacked and knocked unconscious by insurgents. Upon waking, he found a canoe at the river and fled to the city. As the *News* details:

> Deep in the Ogeechee woods, just before sunrise, two hundred members of the Ogeechee Home Guards divided into military companies and armed themselves with muskets and bayonets. The men had putatively secured weapons in Savannah months before the revolt. Plantation managers also provided muskets to "trustworthy" African Americans on the Ogeechee neck to drive off the ricebird. As the men marched toward the plantations, they met George Baxley, one of Middleton's overseers who had gone to investigate the commotion in the woods. The men lurched toward Baxley, surrounded him, confiscated his weapons, and struck him with the butt of a musket.[38]

Mr. O'Donald, a watchmen of Middleton's, experienced a similar expulsion. O'Donald stated that the armed former workers took him out of his house, beat him up, and then proceeded to march him up and down his front yard, stopping every few minutes to give him a beating. He was eventually told to leave and never come back. Removal of O'Donald and Baxley, and men like them, were clearly acts of revenge, but there was also the strategic importance of removing the management class from the territory. Overseers and watchmen safeguarded the agrarian capitalist class by physically and psychologically disciplining the workers. The way that O'Donald was made to march up and down in rows in his yard,

---

37   Bell, "Ogeechee Troubles," 375.
38   Ibid., 386.

receiving a beating at the end of each row, sounds strikingly similar to the movement of field workers, tending up and down rows of rice plants, while being tormented by overseers who were attempting to increase productivity. This ritual beating is also reminiscent of the paranoia and terror that was created years later when Black workers were stopped by watchmen along roads, their daily movements policed to re-create the conditions of slavery times when Black bodies were strictly relegated to their value as manual laborers.[39]

The same armed insurgents also forced the planter and owner of the Southfield rice plantation, Major Middleton, to abandon his lavish home. An account from the plantation manager stated that the "lawless vaga-bonds ... had completely cleaned it and the other houses of their contents ... all the houses had been plundered of everything they contained." The workers who showed for work had "no one to give them tasks" and simply loitered about.[40]

When the owners and managers had been run off, the rebels were said to have congregated at the Atlantic & Gulf Railroad Station Number 1, declaring that "no white man should live between the two Ogeechees."[41] This infamous declaration of the rebellion became a battle cry for Black laborers and struck fear into the hearts of whites who had abandoned the Ogeechee Neck, as well as those in Savannah who feared the spread of the insurrection. Black watchmen, who refused to join the rebellion, along with other Blacks who wanted to return to work or were friendly with the planter class, were pushed off of the land as well. Practically speaking, *whiteness* came to include not just a powerful racial caste but also those in collaboration with owners.

A brief aside on the racial demographics of the lowcountry is useful here. Before the war, one-third of low-country whites and nearly all free people of color lived in the urban areas of Savannah, Darien, Jefferson, and St. Mary's, while the vast majority of enslaved Black workers lived in the surrounding rural areas. In 1870, there were 4,201 Blacks and 411 whites in the Ogeechee district.[42] Regardless of these numbers, non-slave-holding white farmers did exist and intermingled within and

39   As in the border conflicts of our own century, the free movement of capital is made possible only by the physical obstruction of those whose labor creates it.

40   Getting rid of the managers helped to force a *total* work stoppage even when some workers didn't join the strike, because loyal workers had no one to receive orders from and no one to whom to report their tasks' completion ("The Ogeechee Insurrection," 82).

41   Bell, "Ogeechee Troubles," 386.

42   Ibid.

around the plantation borders; but the planters created a myth of gentility, which said there was no class disparity between whites. The repercussions of this myth were that poor whites were socially invisible in geographic areas dominated by the plantation economy. Widespread illiteracy and their being absent from state property and court records reinforced the legal and historical invisibility of poor whites in areas like Chatham County.

Timothy Lockley, in his book on race and class in the antebellum low-country, describes the myriad ways that poor whites and Black workers interacted and relied on one another. Particularly of interest are the informal economies they created through trade and crime. Even as many were ultimately recruited to police the territory, some poor whites would inevitably have been trading partners with rebel Ogeechee workers in the preparations for and during conflict.[43] Any efforts by poor whites who did aid in the rebellion's efforts were undocumented or concealed, while the spectacular accounts of those who fled the area were publicly used to incite and justify later military intervention.

New Year's Eve wore on in Savannah with Sheriff Dooner summoning a *posse comitatus* after he was refused military aid for the second time that week. Latin for "force of the county," *posse comitatus* was a common law that allowed for a county sheriff to summon the arms of any number of able-bodied men over the age of fifteen to help in the apprehension of criminals or convicts. This legalized form of vigilante justice was common in the rural South, especially when the conflicts between Union and Confederate allegiances in state governments created gaps in the smooth functioning of law and order. Savannah judge Philip M. Russell, Jr. issued 150 warrants against Ogeechee rebels, both men and women, seemingly with lists of workers' names from planters and managers who were driven out of the area. The warrants charged the individuals with "insurrection against the State of Georgia, robbery by force, robbery by intimidation, assault with intent to murder and larceny." The sheriff went out by train with his first posse, but returned immediately, frightened of being outnumbered, and proclaimed that "that no legal process should be served in

---

43   It is possible that it was poor whites in Chatham County that helped the Ogeechee rebels secure arms before the insurrection and facilitated communication lines between the city and the country. In the South Carolina and Georgia rice country, "there were also widespread complaints of low-country Blacks thieving from the planters, a practice ... encouraged by crossroads country stores and trading vessels that anchored offshore to purchase stolen rice and meat" (Foner, *Nothing but Freedom*, 87).

their neighborhood, that they had possession of the country and a government of their own, and no white man or office of the State should molest them with impunity."[44]

On January 1, 1869, the *Savannah Morning News* reported:

> The Negroes are receiving reinforcements from Bryan and Liberty Counties, and trustworthy persons from that section report that they are plundering all the plantations and threatening destruction to all who dare to meddle with them. They are said to have thrown up some sort of a fortification at Peach Hill and have all the roads and approaches strongly guarded.

Alongside the continued destruction of plantation homes, Middleton's house was rumored to have been torched after its contents looted. Up until that point, his plantation home had been used as a central strategic location for the rebellion.[45]

At this point, Major Middleton was becoming an organizing force in Savannah. He called a public meeting at the courthouse, where he seduced the crowds to his side with the impending threat of an armed and brutal mob surrounding Savannah. Middleton showed his true interests when he told the assembled crowd why they should hasten to intervene: "Capital which has fed these people, who are now deriving sustenance from plunder, would cease to be invested here."[46]

On the evening of January 1, when the train stopped at Station No. 1, there were no rebels in sight. A sheet of paper was flapping in the wind, nailed to a post. A manifesto of sorts was written on the page by Solomon Farley:

---

44 "The Ogeechee Insurrection," 82.
45 During the war, the Union Army used the grounds at Wild Horn Plantation, and constructed a signaling station at the rice mill at Grove Point, both of which were under Ogeechee rebels' control at this point. Whether or not any structures useful for the insurgency remained in existence at these locations is unknown. It is possible that Wild Horn and Vallambrosia had been under workers' control for some time, and Southfield, Prairie, and Grove Point plantations were targets to extend that control. Additionally, these three other plantations were where Tucker and Middleton instituted more restrictive labor policies and encroached on the autonomy of the rice workers.
46 The remaining accounts for the last days of the insurrection are taken exclusively from "The Ogeechee Insurrection, 1868–69" (in *Standing upon the Mouth of a Volcano*, 79–89) and Karen Bell's "The Ogeechee Troubles" (*The Georgia Historical Quarterly* 85, no.3 [Fall 2001]: 375–397).

To the publick at large. I has been accused in the midst of 17 or 18 men's as a Capt. which cants not be approved for Stealing Tucker & Middleton's Rice. the party Has Accused Me & Drawn me in for a Old Grudge. the Sheriff Arrested me and Brought me Some 4 or 5 Miles to Station No. 1. and their Came up a Party of the Loyal Leaguers. And Released Me in Regard that there is no Stay laws Which will Give the Republican Party no Particularity. If it was they would not Stopped my Going with the Sheriff to Savannah. If you should not See Me I will make my Appearance Just as Soon as the law Being Essued for the Right of all Classes & Color!!! Yours, Ogeechee Until Death.

The manifesto is one of the only documents written by the insurgents themselves. While it is difficult to understand the lexicon of the time, we interpret the manifesto as a rejection of the legitimacy of the planters, the sheriff, and the Republican Party to charge Solomon with any crime or to apprehend him. The last line stings with irony. Solomon never appeared again, at least not to those who record the history, and neither did Reconstruction's laws ever fulfill its promises of wealth redistribution and equal citizenship for former slaves in the South.

On January 2, rumors continued that the Ogeechee occupation of the rice plantations was beginning to spread to neighboring Bryan and Liberty counties, and that other poor people were hearing about the actions and migrating "across Augusta Road" to the Neck. It was also clear that a more definitive territory west of the railroad and between the two rivers was being secured: pickets emerged at the railroads to restrict the movement of trains through Station 1, and there was a twenty-four-hour watch on the roads. These strategic maneuvers were reportedly carried out by different insurrectionary bands of eight to twelve men and women. A country man who fled to Savannah on January 1 shared his story with the *Savannah Morning News*:

The Negroes, in strong force and thoroughly armed, were lying near the railroad, watching the movements of and prepared to resist the Sheriff's posse which went down on Wednesday. When the train moved off ... some six or seven hundred Negroes came out on the railroad and the leaders went about cursing and saying, "The white sons of bitches were afraid to come and attack and have gone back for more men!" He says that there is a very large force of the Negroes at No. 1 and that they are determined to resist any attempt to arrest them."

Two other men arrived in Savannah with similar stories, including one produce peddler from Liberty County, who claimed he was stopped by five different picket parties, who each told him to "tell the white men of Savannah to come on, that they were ready for them."

From about January 2 to January 4 more Chatham County citizens took refuge in the city, either because they were scared since they'd refused to join the rebellion or because of their complicity in counterinsurgency efforts. The *Savannah Morning News* admitted that rumors "of every kind" were flooding the city and it was difficult to know what the insurgents were doing. The Atlantic & Gulf Railroad's railroad master, Mr. Snyder, reported that the overseer on section No. 1, Mr. Hinton, was confronted on the tracks near the station by "an armed band, numbering from two to three hundred," and told that, "no white man should live between the two Ogeechees." This message was relayed frequently by white men driven out of the area, and seems a demand that forced key figures in the Neck (like the overseer of the only train station with access to the area) to choose between their loyalty to the planters—and by proxy, Savannah—or to those who had occupied the fields and plantations.

In a separate incident, David Corker, a country store owner on Ogeechee Road, left for Savannah with his family after his store was emptied by "a large band of armed Negroes … [who] proceeded to sack the place, carrying off the goods and fixtures and destroying what they did not steal." Corker mentioned that he overheard that they were collecting provisions to take back to their strongholds, the occupied plantations at Southfield and Prairie or their fortification at Peach Hill, where they must have expected imminent intervention by outside forces. It was also at this time that the overseer at Prairie Plantation told a plantation owner in Bryan County, where he had fled, that armed bands of rebels had made off in wagons and carts with all of the stored rice crop.

In the midst of the insurrection, a Black man from Ogeechee arrived in Savannah claiming he had been sent by the insurgents to relay a proposition that "ten or twelve colored men be sent out there by the citizens to treat with them and arrange the difficulty in a manner satisfactory to all parties." He was immediately taken into custody, however, as he was identified as one of the instigators of the rebellion. It is unclear how true it was that he represented the Ogeechee rebels, but at that point in the rebellion, Savannah Radical Republicans—including spiritual and labor organizers—were attending nighttime prayer meetings on the Ogeechee Neck with the insurgents, lending credence to the claim that the rebels were willing to meet with trusted Black outsiders from Savannah.

Karen Bell, perhaps the only historian to have done any digging into this history, claims that the prayer meetings intensified within the final days of the revolt as military intervention appeared imminent, and that the meetings were a way of bolstering faith in their desires. Most likely, the meetings would have been spent discussing their goals and strategies, followed by "ring-shouts," a song-and-dance ritual that continued to evolve in the low country and Sea Island communities of former slaves. Ring-shouts were influenced by West African drum song and dance, but because drums were previously banned in the slave territories in the United States, a complex clapping took their place. The songs of the ring-shout tradition were recited in a call and response style, with one or a few lead singers calling out the verses, while everyone else sang the response. Lyrically, these were jubilee songs that used scriptural verse and words of the Old Testament prophets (often Isaiah and Ezekiel) to code proclamations of emancipation and autonomy from oppressive forces.

Songs like "Moses, Don't Get Lost" warned rebels not to give up, reminding them that they were constantly pursued by forces that wanted to destroy them and warning them to stay one step ahead of their enemies. The songs were sung mostly in the present tense, with urgency. As Peter Linebaugh interprets, jubilee songs proclaim *"Now* is the time. It is not a question of time being ripe, or of objective circumstances being ready."[47] That jubilee songs were sung in revolts *after* Emancipation and the end of the Civil War reminds us that Lincoln was not seen as the Messiah, but that the Ogeechee rebels, like those before and after them, sensed that they were about to make the continuum of history explode.[48]

> Oh Day, Yonder Come Day (call)
>   Day done broke into my soul
>   Oh come on day (response)
>   I heard him say

---

47 Linebaugh "Jubilating," 84–98.

48 "The awareness that they are about to make the continuum of history explode is characteristic of the revolutionary classes at the moment of their action.... For every second of time was the strait gate through which the Messiah might enter" (Benjamin, "Theses on the Philosophy of History," 264).

It's a New Year's Day
Oh come on day[49]

As the rebellion in the Neck was growing more uncontrollable each day—and after his posse's retreat at the railroad station—Sheriff Dooner met with Savannah's mayor Edward Anderson to request military assistance. General Meade granted the request, Dooner surrendered his duties to military officials on January 5 and the civilians who volunteered to invade the Neck were let go. Meade deployed the Sixteenth Infantry Regiment, commanded by Major Thomas Sweeney. The Regiment was composed of two units from Augusta and two from Atlanta. The soldiers were instructed to restore peace to the territory and assist in the arrest of 150 insurgents whose warrants were issued earlier in the week by Judge Russell.

In 1898, a category three hurricane devastated coastal Georgia, crippling what was left of the rice plantations from south of the Sea Islands to further north of Savannah, as well as destroying over 60,000 barrels of rice due to the damage at warehouses and shipping docks such as the one depicted here in Brunswick." Even after limping on after the insurrection and the land contestations during early Reconstruction, the rice economy in coastal Georgia was not able to recover itself after this final, inevitable blow.

With news of the approaching military intervention, Solomon Farley, Captain Green, and other Union League members and Ogeechee men and women destroyed the bridge over the Big Ogeechee River in an attempt to make invasion more difficult, and perhaps also to revel in their final moments of freedom. The insurgents continued to use Heyward's plantation as their holdout, and the remaining plantation houses at Grove Hill, Grove Point, and Southfield were emptied and destroyed. With the added stress of military troops arriving in Savannah and preparing for invasion the following day, heated discussions about whether or not to surrender led to some factions forming. On January 5, fourteen men and one woman turned themselves in to authorities in Savannah, while hundreds remained on the Neck deciding their next move.[50]

49   This song was preserved by Bessie Jones, one of the Georgia Sea Island Singers, who inherited it from her grandfather who was born in Africa and enslaved in Georgia. Bessie saw the act of passing down slave songs as a spiritual gift and political work: "The Lord blessed me not to forget these things ... and keep them up among people who weren't studying it. White people know our backgrounds, but they're going to try to hold it back and keep us back as long as they possibly can" ("Bessie Jones," National Endowment for the Arts biography: http://arts.gov/honors/heritage/fellows/bessie-jones).

50   Bell, "Ogeechee Troubles," 390.

The military units and civil authorities, including Sheriff Dooner, eight deputies, and planters Major Middleton and Captain Tucker, left Savannah at dawn on January 6, prepared to stay in the Neck until the rebellion was put down. The expedition first examined Wild Horn Plantation, which was found to be quiet. Upon their arrival at Grove Place, the authorities found that:

> Everything movable about the premises was gone. The house had been ransacked from bottom to top, the mantelpieces broken and several of the sashes stove in. The door of the storeroom had been cut open, and its contents stolen. The house was filled with dirt and filth, and its whole appearance changed from a fine residence to a ruined and desolate building. One of the watch dogs lay dead under the steps.

Despite the ruins, the military companies set up camp to strategize further counterinsurgency actions. Colonel Sweeney and the planters then traveled on to Southfield Plantation, where insurgents had first attacked and gained control in late December. At Southfield they discovered that the entire lot of rice in the mill, around 4,000 bushels, was gone. Colonel Sweeney ordered no arrests be made until messengers could "summon the Negro leaders" and inform the insurgents that any resistance would result in punishment. From here it seems that some began to surrender at Grove Place, where the military had its headquarters, while others were arrested by soldiers. Some insurgents had been convinced by other "colored men" to go to the headquarters to discuss surrender, and when they arrived, they were immediately arrested. By mid-afternoon, sixty-some insurgents were amassed at the military headquarters, formed into a line, and placed under armed guard. The *Savannah News* informant reported that some refused to leave and told the officers that they could not take them, at which point muskets and bayonets were laid on them and they were marched to the station. On the evening of January 7, the sheriff and his deputies arrived back in Savannah with sixty-eight prisoners, but with none of the desired-for leaders in custody. The military stayed in the Neck for nine days, which resulted in 143 arrests and the clearance of the area.

It is not known whether Captain Green—a close comrade of Solomon's—was captured or if he voluntarily surrendered, but he was the first of the 143 insurgents to be seen during pre-trial hearings, which took place

January 15–29. With a packed courtroom, Green and his codefendants refused to confess, and nearly all of the men and women arrested denied involvement in the insurrection. As one would expect, the prosecution relied on testimony from the sheriffs and civilians who fled the area when the revolt erupted. The defense called upon Union League and Home Guard members who had not been arrested, and in an ironic strategic move, called on two plantation owners, William Burroughs and William Miller, who claimed that the rebellion was really just a labor dispute over contracts. By the end of pre-trial hearings, 116 insurgents were sent to trial, while twenty-six who could not be identified by State's witnesses, were released.

Talk of conspiracies was rampant throughout the trial process, with many whites believing that the insurrection was orchestrated by the "radical" Governor Bullock and labor organizer Aaron Bradley.[51] Again, whites who wanted to maintain the plantation's way of life in coastal Georgia could not believe that former slaves had carried out an autonomous and organized attack on their society without the seductive influence or aid of white agitators.

The trial began on May 12, and ultimately only six men were found guilty of insurrection, robbery by intimidation, and assault with intent to murder, with the remaining 110 defendants found not-guilty due to lack of corroborating testimony. The six men—Captain Green, Dandy McNeil, Ned Edwards, Jack Cuthbert, Thomas Benedict, and Nick Bailing—were sentenced to five years hard labor at the reconstructed state prison in Milledgeville, but were pardoned and given amnesty in July by Governor Bullock.[52] Bullock was famous for using the full extent of his pardoning powers to bolster Radical Republican activity in Georgia, which is consistent with Republican backing of the re-allocation of plantation land to former slaves. He was also pressured by some citizens to not waste money on unnecessary imprisonment, indicative of the cash and labor crises facing the former Confederate states at the end of the war.[53]

Solomon Farley, and many other rebels whose names and stories are left to our imagination, escaped capture to bordering counties. While we

---

51 Aaron Bradley was a radical labor organizer who visited the Ogeechee rebels during the revolt. He was famous for being arrested for "insurrectionary and seditious language" in 1865 when he organized former slaves in Chatham County to demand land under Sherman's Special Field Orders, No. 15.

52 For all the racial and social progress that has supposedly taken place since this period, one can only imagine the kinds of sentences and punishment that would await the captured participants ("terrorists") in a modern-day, armed, Black insurrection of this kind.

53 Bell, "Ogeechee Troubles," 393–393.

do not know their fates, it is entirely possible that they were able to find refuge in the neighboring Georgia Sea Islands, where former cotton and rice workers were able to create longer-lasting autonomous communities.

The Legacy of the Lawless Vagabonds

Karen Bell's history of the Ogeechee Insurrection ends by documenting the transition of the land around William Burroughs's Wild Horn Plantation into a self-managed subsistence and commercial farming settlement by free workers, who eventually accumulated enough savings to buy out most of the land in the area and start the town of Burroughs in 1897. Bell claims that through the failure of the Ogeechee Insurrection, those who returned to the land were forced to come up with other solutions for securing property and autonomy by engaging in the rice market as planters. This market was already in its end-game, however; unable to recover the level of profits made possible by slave labor, a series of hurricanes in the late 1890s delivered the final infrastructural blow that workers in the Ogeechee Neck had attempted twenty years before.

This is an all-too-familiar transition for historians to make: to leap from the revolutionary activities of those who desired the end of the rice plantation economy, to those who sought to slowly rebuild it as workers striving toward the goal of individual property ownership. Some workers—perhaps even some who participated in the Ogeechee rebellion—did end up conceding to labor contracts brokered by the Freedmen's Bureau, and even began to identify as a new class of planters, reborn in the image of free labor. But this does not account for the majority of landless Blacks in the region, and furthermore, in its Unionist logic, eclipses the magnitude of the struggle for autonomy that was being waged across the coastal areas of the Southeast during the 1860s and 1870s.

From the numerous armed standoffs in the Sea Islands along the coast of South Carolina and Georgia, to the series of organized strikes in the rice fields of the Combahee River region of South Carolina, to the destruction of the plantations in the Ogeechee Neck, whenever northern interests attempted to quell relations between former masters and slaves, they were met with resolute refusal. Whether in racial or economic terms, the planter and the industrialist both referred to a harmony between capital and labor as the secret behind the success of their system, blissfully ignoring the constant clash of interests and desires that defined these systems. The psychological logic of Reconstruction demanded forgiveness as a necessary step toward the reconciliation of capital and labor within the wage system. By refusing to forgive the planter and make amends with the society that had enslaved them, the Ogeechee rebels fought for freedom, not as a means for progress, but as the possibility of a full and unrestrained life.

Even W.E.B. Du Bois succumbs to the seduction of the industrialist's marriage of democracy and free labor; he does so as an orthodox Marxist, with the eventual goal of the demise of capitalism, yet his analysis is unsurprisingly statist. On the one hand, Du Bois's theory of the Black general strike as the true cause of northern victory in the Civil War was groundbreaking in its redefinition of the rebellious Black southern slave (rather than the white northern liberator) as the central protagonist during the war. Nevertheless, Du Bois uses a dialectical method that results in an orthodox, industrialist result:

> These men saved slavery and killed it. They saved it by leaving it to a false seductive dream of peace and the eternal subjugation of the laboring class. They destroyed it by presenting themselves before the eyes of the North and the world as living specimens of the real meaning of slavery. What was the system that could enslave a Frederick Douglass? They saved it too by joining the free Negroes of the North and with them organizing themselves into a great Black phalanx that worked and schemed and paid and finally fought for the freedom of Black men in America.[54]

He recognizes the "false seductive dream and the eternal subjugation of the laboring class," yet his protagonist is the Black worker who leaves the South, whether before the war as a fugitive or long after the war in the Great Migration. The assertion that before liberation can occur workers must first build up their "productive capacity" through industrialization traps Du Bois in a doomed narrative that is incapable of understanding revolts like the Ogeechee Insurrection. When explaining the failure of Union impressment of ex-slaves' labor, he assures the reader that this was "not because the Negroes did not want to work, but because they were striking against these particular conditions of work."[55] As former slaves, these men and women had not yet passed through the correct stage of

---

54   W.E.B. Du Bois, "John Brown," in *The Oxford W.E.B. Du Bois Reader*, ed. Eric J. Sundquist (London: Oxford University Press, 1996), 258–259.

55   Du Bois, *Black Reconstruction in America*, 72.

history, and so Black protest and work refusal could only be understood as a rejection of specific conditions of the plantation economy, rather than a rejection of wage work or capitalism as a whole. The refusal of waged labor and immediate communization of the land that occurred in places like Ogeechee was dialectically "impossible," and so it was simply written out of history. The historical figures of the maroons and their legacy in rebels like the Ogeechee men and women become the myopic southern dropouts, guilty of political immaturity in their refusal of contracts and tendency toward immediate revolt, and in need of rescue by the more disciplined political approach of their northern kin.

By the late 1870s, most of what was considered the period of Radical Reconstruction, including the first wave of Freedmen's Bureau land distribution policies, had finally been crushed by the Johnson administration. Andrew Johnson's policies were backed by the military occupation of the South, and the Union Army's protection of the former landowners of the coastal territories. Though the coastal rice and cotton industries were ultimately doomed, the former landowners successfully recolonized the area, and the Bureau began to focus on creating systems that would coerce former slaves into signing labor contracts. Such contracts promised certain wages and set rents, but ultimately recreated feudal conditions of commercial farming, a process that would come to be called sharecropping.

Labor contracts and sharecropping would trap many in the area, but not all. The inhabitants of the Sea Islands were able to establish a long-standing autonomy, due to a combination of their geographic isolation, the strength of autonomous cultural practices, the endurance of their resistance to recolonization by planters, and the fact that many former slaves who bought land early on were able to hold onto it and pass it down through the generations. Since slavery times, Gullah-Geechee people engaged in subsistence farming, relatively unfettered by mainland politics,

Historic American Buildings Survey / Library of Congress

A survey photograph of the abandoned Wild Heron Plantation in the Ogeechee Neck. Wild Heron, also known as Wild Horn, was one the occupied estates during the Ogeechee Insurrection. The delapidated state of this house in 1936 is reminiscent of the reports by authorities of the state of its ruin during the 1869 insurrection.

and provided some haven for those escaping the struggles further inland. Many academics and activists alike have fetishized the unique spiritual and cultural practices of Gullah-Geechee people in the Sea Islands, yet credit the high percentage of land and resources controlled by Blacks in the region to the legacy of Freedmen's Bureau policies rather than maroon resistance or community organization. This completely obscures the history of the islanders' initial armed defense against recolonization by planters and their ongoing struggle to resist ever-encroaching resort development.

Back in the low country, the failure of the rice industry to recover and the spread of the commons in the immediate postwar coastal areas necessitated a different plan for northern industrialists to profit off the area's resources and labor. Former rice workers and pine woods squatters were punished for and brought out of their tradition of not participating in waged work, in some cases through imprisonment, but also through the destruction of the longleaf pine ecosystem by the turpentine industry. Much like the eventual destruction of large segments of the Great Dismal Swamp, this eliminated a former commons that had provided refuge to those who refused slavery or wage labor. New forms of labor power and industry were gradually integrated into a newly built industrial transportation system created first by the Confederacy and then sustained by reinvestment from northern capitalists.

Trapped between the death gasps of the old conditions of the plantation system and the slow grind of an approaching industrial revolution, landless southerners found themselves exposed to a highly adaptive and hybrid disciplinary system. In Marx's elaboration of the theory of primitive accumulation, he exposes this disciplinary tension that had occurred centuries earlier in Western Europe:

> These men, suddenly dragged from their wanted mode of life, could not as suddenly adapt themselves to the discipline of their new condition. They were turned en masse into beggars, robbers, vagabonds, partly from inclination, in most cases from stress of circumstances.... Legislation treated them as "voluntary" criminals, and assumed that it depended on their own good will to go on working under the old conditions that no longer existed.... The history of this, their expropriation, is written in the annals of mankind in letters of blood and fire.[56]

---

56   Marx, *Capital*, 806.

The end of the Civil War represented a major crisis for capital in this country, one that could not be solved militarily. Reconstruction thus inaugurated a new era of government for the South, not just in the traditional understanding of courts and laws and police, but also in wage contracts, the elimination of ecological territories considered ungovernable, and the creation of new, more manageable divisions of labor. While largely catalyzed by Black struggles for freedom and autonomy, new practices of government affected everyone, including poor whites.

The Ogeechee Insurrection was definitively a Black rebellion, from the battle cry of "no whites between the Ogeechees" to the eviction of Blacks sympathetic with the planters. Whiteness was defined as a practice of dominating land and labor; thus resistance to that organization of life— and with it the understanding of Blackness—was defined oppositionally to both capitalist and racist social relations.

The new wage system that northern investors brought with them to transform and assimilate southern resources was not able to absorb the millions of propertyless southerners at an even rate. In order to maintain white supremacy as a political mode in the South, white southerners in power created elaborate written and unwritten social codes, backed by localized regimes of terror, to attempt to control this period of transition from bondage to wage labor. The increased segregation of daily life, armed resistance to white vigilantism, and the nationalist character of the later resistance culture that helped to defeat Jim Crow have all encouraged historians to apply a separatist lens to the struggles of the Reconstruction era. As a distinctly Black rebellion against white capitalist control, the Ogeechee insurrection can certainly be seen to reinforce this perspective. The insurrection is also part of a larger history, however, that includes the legacy of conspiratorial relationships that crossed racial boundaries in the swamps of the maroons and in other areas where the workforce differed racially from that of Georgia's rice fields. Ultimately, the racial character of different revolts was driven as much by local divisions of labor, along with the repression of cross-racial affinities, as by any explicitly articulated nationalist identity.

Ogeechee was a battle in a very different kind of civil war, one that continued in new forms as former slaves refused their reconstitution as workers and governable subjects by northern victors. The occupation of plantations, the expropriation of the rice crops, and the burning of bridges were unique eruptions on the Ogeechee rivers, but they had been planned in the same swamps in which maroons had dug hideouts many years before.

Like the resurrection ferns that cluster on coastal oaks in the low country, which shrivel inward to protect themselves from drought but with just a mist of water burst back to life, the ghosts of this rebellion would emerge again years later in the flames of arson attacks against the sharecropping system of the cotton empire.

During the Civil War, the necessity of building and supplying an army forced the Confederate states to begin to industrialize themselves, even as they supposedly fought to preserve an agrarian way of life. Forced labor at the Confederacy's new mines, railroads, and military forts in turn brought together massive numbers of laborers who had little interest in preserving plantation society. This labor degraded the autonomy and status of those on the edges of the region's racial boundaries, such as the many Indians, who had previously occupied a precarious position somewhere between Black and white. As the status of these remaining Indians declined, new alliances between the dispossessed sometimes became possible.

The war's end created power vacuums across the South, where for a period state control was minimal, economic norms were in flux, and populations of laborers were relatively free to experiment with new forms of resistance or shore up community infrastructure built underground during slavery. This process looked different in different places: Sometimes these efforts were solely the province of Black communities, while at other times anticapitalist activity offered the only meaningful venue for cross-racial alliances. In the lowcountry of Georgia, where the rice industry had long relied on and brought together large numbers of recently transported slaves, the Ogeechee Insurrection was entirely enacted by Black former slaves. In other areas with a different industrial and racial character, such as southeastern North Carolina, the process had a multiracial component and would involve individual acts of banditry, expropriation, vengeance, and work refusal.

Henry Berry Lowrie where are you?
    Sleeping in an unknown grave.
Does the grass grow above your breast,
    Or do dark waters flow
With secret sounds through your bones
    That will confuse mankind
Until the end of time.
    From ever lasting to everlasting
You are the hero of a people.
    Keep your secrets as you sleep—
That is part of your greatness.

                                —Adolph L. Dial

THE LOWRY WARS:

Attacking Reconstruction and Reaction in Robeson County, North Carolina

ON DECEMBER 21, 1864, A WEALTHY SLAVEHOLDER AND MINOR OFFICIAL of the Confederacy named James P. Barnes was ambushed on his way to the post office in Robeson County, North Carolina. After being initially cut down by a shotgun blast, Barnes was shot in the head at point blank range. While the assassins fled into a swamp, two nearby white residents arrived on the scene just in time to hear the dying slave-owner accuse two Lumbee Indians, William and Henry Berry Lowry, of the murder.

As a slave-owner and official in the Confederacy, Barnes was hardly an innocent man. Specific to this murder, he had recently accused several Lowrys of stealing his hogs, in an example of what many Lumbees still describe as "tied-mule" incidents.[1] It was common practice for white men to tie up their own livestock on an Indian's land, and return at a later time to accuse the family of stealing their animals. Knowing the family had little chance for justice in white courts, the white man would agree to not press charges if the Indians would cede over a portion of their land, or agree to work the white family's land for free. Such injustices were only one of the many strategies by which plantation society succeeded in gradually reducing the size and quality of Lumbee lands, undermining native autonomy, and pressing Lumbee men into forced labor, either on white plantations or

---

1   Adolph L. Dial and David K. Eliades, *The Only Land I Know: A History of the Lumbee Indians* (San Francisco: Indian Historian Press, 1975), 45.

at the Confederate forts on the coast.[2] James Barnes had recently used this exact strategy to force several Lowry sons into working at fever-infested labor camps to help build the Confederate Fort Fisher in Wilmington, thus unintentionally arranging his own death at the hands of Henry Berry Lowry, a man whom he had seriously underestimated, and whose legend would continue to grow over the next decade.[3]

This sort of revenge killing was not necessarily rare in the mid-1800s, when family feuds were common, and vigilantism and the law often went hand in hand. But due to a number of factors—including the fact that thousands of other Black and Indian laborers were being forced into new conditions of servitude on the supposed eve of "emancipation," the imminent arrival of a victorious Union Army, the escape of large numbers of Yankee soldiers from Confederate prison camps, and the relative cultural and economic autonomy of North Carolina's Lumbees—what could have been seen as an isolated act of vengeance came to be seen and experienced by many as a righteous act of political rebellion against forced labor and white supremacy.

Thus began the Lowry Wars, a period of roughly eight years of almost uninterrupted, multiracial attacks on plantation society in southeastern North Carolina. Dozens of sheriffs and white supremacist militia were murdered, plantations and white-owned stores expropriated, and five different successful prison breaks carried out, in what to this day represents a period of marked pride and dignity for North Carolina's Lumbees. It was a time of drastic economic and racial transition, as new avenues opened to different kinds of solidarity and political alliances between poor white families, newly "freed" Black laborers and Indians, but also to new forms of economic and social bondage. Above all, the Lowry Wars illustrate the kinds of racial hypocrisy, betrayal, and recuperation that could be expected from northern industrialists and their Radical Republican allies, and what their industrial vision would soon do for the race relations and economic servitude of poor people in the rural South.

On the Lumbees
Understanding the constellation of cultural practices and economic conditions that surround the Lowry War requires a brief background on the

---

2   Such methods bring to mind the same affect plea bargaining has today upon millions of Americans trapped in our judicial archipelago.

3   It should be pointed out that two hogs' ears with Barnes's mark were indeed found on the Lowry property, so it is possible the theft actually took place, for which we can only commend the Lowries more.

A Lumbee family outside their cabin in Robeson County, around the turn of the nineteenth century.

NC Museum of History

Lumbee Indians of southeastern North Carolina. Many historians and anthropologists disagree as to the exact origins of the tribe, how the Lumbees came to be in the area around the Lumber River, and who exactly their ancestors are. The lands now occupied by the Lumbee Indians were once controlled by members of Eastern Sioux bands like the Catawba, Cheraw, and Waccamaw, and it is assumed that some members of these bands mixed with the Lumbees.[4] Others have staked a claim on a Cherokee influence, which is supported primarily by the oral tradition of the Lumbees themselves, as well as by anecdotal evidence like the fact that one major Cherokee chief was named George Lowery. It is also documented that the more assimilated elements of Cherokee culture interacted sporadically with the Lumbees in the eighteenth century, prior to the forced removal of the Cherokee to western territories by white people in the nineteenth century.[5]

Language studies are of little help in determining Lumbee origins; two historians of the Lumbees, Adolph Dial and David Eliades, write that early recorded observations of Lumbees document their *already speaking English* upon initial European contact, specifically a style of English unique to the sixteenth century. There is no known native language of the

---

4   Dial and Eliades, *The Only Land I Know*, 16–17.

5   The process of Cherokee removal by white settlers and the federal government began long before the period known as the "Trail of Tears" in the 1830s. Andrew Jackson's intensification of "Indian removal" was largely fueled by the combined white planter and yeoman farmer classes' desire to expand cotton production across arable land in the Southeast (farther) into the remaining portions of land that were still occupied by southeastern Native peoples.

Lumbees, though due to their own cultural and economic autonomy, they continued to speak an older style of English long into the nineteenth and even twentieth centuries.

The predominant historical explanation for this bizarre language phenomenon, which has emerged alongside an array of other evidence, is that the Lumbees of North Carolina are the primary descendants of Lord Raleigh's famous "Lost Colony." These 117 men, women, and children, led by Governor John White, were sent from England to settle Roanoke Island in 1587. Governor White soon left the colony to return to England for supplies in August 1587, but was unable to return for three years due to a naval war with Spain. Upon his return, he found no one, only some abandoned supplies that would have been too large to carry, and a strange marking on a gatepost that simply read, "CROATOAN."

For many years it was simply assumed by historians, all evidence to the contrary, that the colonists had perished. The idea that colonists voluntarily "went native," to live in peaceful relations with their supposed inferiors, was absurd, despite the reality of positive relations with the nearby Hatteras Tribe (the birthplace of one member being, in fact, named "Croatoan"). Despite the initial white denial of this voluntary exodus, a legend and mythology of the Lost Colony grew anyway, and to this day functions as a kind of "origin myth" of radical escape from civilization, dreamed about and built upon by the contemporary anarchist imagination.[6]

Strange, then, that for many historians and Lumbee authors, the mystery of the Lost Colony is now no real mystery at all. With an understanding of patterns of native migration at the time, the most simple explanation for the Lumbees' use of English—as well as their strange lack of shared cultural practices with nearby natives, their many English agrarian and kinship customs, and the existence of phenotype characteristics like blonde hair and blue eyes—is that the Lumbees shared lineage and community with refugees of the Lost Colony. Oral history reinforces this conclusion. An excerpt from a speech given at the funeral of two Lumbee boys murdered by a member of the Confederate Home Guard serves as an example:

> We were a free people long before the white men came to our land. Our tribe lived in Roanoke in Virginia. When the English came to our land, we treated them kindly. We took the English

---

6   For a longer history of the Croatoan debate, and how this concept of escape and redemption plays out in the radical mind, check out *Gone to Croatan* (eds. Sakolosky and Koehnline).

to live with us. There is the white man's blood in these veins as well as that of the Indian.[7]

One final piece of evidence: of the ninety-five different surnames of the original Lost Colony, forty-one of these are shared with early Lumbees. Combined with a likely blood and cultural influence from other native tribes, this means that the Lumbees emerged as their own unique grouping fairly recently, as a kind of refugee tribe, built together from Anglo-Saxon escapists and those Indians who had left their native regions either by choice or because of tribal rivalries of some kind. While fully self-identifying as Indian, culturally they were a bridge between Anglo-Saxons and the Native cultures of the surrounding areas. Traditionally they practiced both small-scale subsistence agriculture and hunting, and had mutual-aid-based kinship networks.

Given the Anglo-Saxon cultural influence on the Lumbees, it is not surprising that for a time the tribe was able to live in relative peace with English settlers.[8] Lumbees often sided with settlers in conflicts with other Natives, and mainly kept to themselves. They also traditionally occupied the difficult lands in between acres and acres of swamp, leaving little immediate incentive for a large-scale white-orchestrated land theft, as long as greener pastures lay elsewhere.

This is not to say that the Lumbees had not defended themselves before: in 1754, for example, when the state of North Carolina sent troops to Virginia to help in its war against Indians, a surveyor was sent to Robeson County to inquire about men for military service. The governor's agent noted at the time,

> Drowning Creek [Lumbee River] on the head of Little Pee Dee, fifty families, a mixt crew, a lawless people, possessing the land without patent or paying any quit rents; shot a surveyor for coming to view vacant lands.[9]

The Lumbees must have been well aware of the precarious nature of their existence, surrounded as they were by a hostile state and an emerging economy that enslaved Indians, West Africans, and poor fugitive whites

---

7   Dial and Eliades, *The Only Land I Know*, 49.
8   Early European observers found much that was familiar in Lumbee culture, including the subsistence agriculture practiced, kinship patterns, and the kinds of gendered divisions of labor. Dial and Eliades, *The Only Land I Know*, 6.
9   Dial and Eliades, *The Only Land I Know*, 31.

Four members of the Lowry Gang: Clockwise from upper left: Thomas Lowry, George Applewhite, Henderson Oxendine, and Calvin Oxendine.

Harper's Weekly, 1872

THOMAS LOWRY.

GEORGE APPLEWHITE.

CALVIN OXENDINE.

HENDERSON OXENDINE.

with impunity. But it wasn't really until the great age of Jacksonian Democracy—a time of increasingly hostile racial caste systems and the uncertain future of the plantation economy—that the Lumbees were forced en masse into the social conflicts of the day. Surrounded on all sides by European political and economic forms, there was suddenly no retreat.

Several legal developments reflect this change, though the everyday practices of white power structures were really the catalyzing force. In 1835, North Carolina revised its constitution to officially disenfranchise all free nonwhites. In 1840, in a foreshadowing of the American use of gun control to disarm potentially insurgent populations, particularly people of color, the general assembly passed a law prohibiting free nonwhites from owning or carrying weapons without getting a license from the court.[10] This legislation emerged in response to a growing swell of antislavery sentiment and slave rebellions nationally. Locally, these legal changes occurred alongside cultural and economic practices by Robeson County whites that gradually but forcefully functioned to steal land from the Lumbee community, and thus turn them into a landless people. Lumbees increasingly found themselves forced to work on white plantations or industrial projects, like railroads, under threat of hunger, the point of a bayonet, or both.

Insurrections like those of Denmark Vesey, Nat Turner, and John Brown offered hope to many and succeeded, to a large degree, in destabilizing this early capitalist system, and heightened the racial anxieties of white elites in the process. The need for unpaid, forced labor to kick-start the Confederate war machine, however, worsened conditions even further. By the end of the Civil War, despite a "victory" for emancipation, the

---

10   Ibid., 43–45.

Lumbee community was facing the destruction of its traditional cultural practices, the decline of its legal status to that of Black ex-slaves, and a future of landlessness and forced wage labor on industrial projects owned in part by northern "liberators."

The War Begins

The Lowry Wars began with a vengeful assassination visited upon a Confederate sheriff who was responsible for forcing Indians (as well as still-enslaved Black men) into labor camps. Less than a month later, another Confederate figure was murdered by ambush. That man was James Brantly Harris, a known rapist, liquor dealer, and an officer in the Confederate Home Guard, a local policing body that hunted down deserters, escaped slaves, and union prisoners.[11] One Lumbee author described him as a "230-pound, swaggering, cursing, redfaced bully ... remembered in the folk stories of the Lumbees as a man 'mean as the devil, the meanest man in Robeson County.'"[12]

Harris was charged with "keeping the peace" in Scuffletown, the center of social activity for the Lumbees in Robeson County. To this day, it is unclear whether Scuffletown refers to a precise location or merely functioned as a name for any place where Lumbees gathered to share news or have a good time. Some believe it is in the general area of Pembroke, others at Moss Neck, and still others argue that it was a "floating or moving community." When interviewed, the Lumbee Reverend D.F. Lowry said that Scuffletown "was similar to the end of a rainbow.... You never could find the place." All that is known is that it referred to a gathering place of some kind, either a permanent or rotating and temporary zone, autonomous from surrounding white society, where news could be passed along, goods traded or shared, and festivities and decision making could take place.[13]

In any case, while attempting to police Lumbee gatherings, James Harris paid the ultimate price for his bullying. His murder was catalyzed by his own brutal bludgeoning to death of two boys of the large and respected

---

11 Several writers have pointed out that institutions like these Home Guards transitioned seamlessly after the Civil War into the modern police forces we've all come to know and hate. One can draw a wavering but unbroken line from the fugitive slave bounty hunters of chattel slavery, to the Confederate Home Guards of the civil war, to the KKK and local sheriffs of Reconstruction and Jim Crow periods, and then finally to the police departments of the modern era.

12 Ibid., 48.

13 William McKee Evans, *To Die Game: The Story of the Lowry Band, Indian Guerrillas of Reconstruction* (Baton Rouge: Louisiana State University Press, 1971), 29.

Lowry clan, who had stood up to him when he had made unwanted advances upon an Indian relative. Both whites and Indians sympathetic to the Lowrys attended the boys' funeral, and despite a warrant for Harris's arrest, he never made it to trial: while pleasure-riding in his buggy on Sunday, January 15, 1865, Harris was ambushed and killed by a barrage of gunfire. One account says that his body was taken from the buggy and thrown into a well; another says that Harris was so hated by the Indian people that he was "buried in an unmarked grave, lying north and south, 'crossways of the world,' rather than east and west as the Lumbees traditionally bury their dead.'"[14]

At this point, surely realizing that the assassination of both a civil and a military officer would not go unnoticed by the state, the informal band of multiracial rebels responsible for the assassinations got proactive. In response to the ban on Indians and Blacks owning weapons, they boldly raided arms and ammunition from the Robeson County courthouse in Lumberton, which also functioned as an armory for the local militia.[15] The expropriation was successful, and the Lowry Band, as they came to be called, began a series of ambitious raids on prosperous planters in the area, distributing the plunder in the ever-mysterious Scuffletown. They avoided the property of Buckskins, Blacks, and Indians, which helped them maintain a broad base of support, and is probably a reflection of the band's multiracial character.[16] The final notable raid in this period, which took place February 27, 1865, was an attack on the Argyle Plantation, which turned into an intense gun battle. After gaining entry to the house, one of the band's members, a Yankee regular named Owen Wright, was injured, but the Confederate officers and wealthy widow who owned the plantation soon gave up. While no one was killed, this incident prompted a retaliation by the Home Guard soon after.

Some notes should be given on the composition of this emerging band of insurgents: Most of the people who joined the group were Lumbee Indians, many of them related by marriage or blood to the extensive Lowry clan. This includes members like Henry Berry's brothers Stephen and Thomas Lowry, his first cousins Calvin and Henderson Oxendine, his brothers-in-law Andrew and Boss Strong, and many others. Some were

---

14   Dial and Eliades, *The Only Land I Know*, 49.
15   Wilmington *North Carolinian*, February 15, 1865.
16   Buckskins were typically poorer Scotch-Irish immigrants living in Robeson County. In the racial hierarchy of the time, they usually occupied a place somewhere between Indians and full whites, though there were also fully integrated, wealthy Scotch planters active in plantation society and Confederate circles.

simply friends who had an axe to grind with the white political and economic establishment, like John Dial, an Indian blacksmith apprentice whose father was harassed at bayonet point by the Home Guard. At least two Black former slaves joined as well: a skilled mason named George Applewhite and another man named "Shoemaker John." Another member was Zachariah McLaughlin, a young Buckskin Scot who had developed an affinity for the Lumbees after attending many of their festive, all-night corn-shuckings. Betraying his Calvinist background or any yearning for white respectability, McLaughlin joined the band in 1870 after being denounced by a member of the white community.

All of the gang tended to carry large amounts of weapons, typically two or three revolvers, a shotgun, a rifle, and a bowie knife apiece. Descriptions from contemporary journalists described the gang's leader, Henry Berry Lowry, in particularly spectacular terms. A pamphlet printed in 1872, which admittedly sought to sensationalize the outlaw band, reported that, "His forehead is good and his face and expression refined—remarkably so, considering his mixed race, want of education, and long career of lawlessness.... The very relatives of white men killed by Henry Berry Lowry admitted to me that, 'He is one of the handsomest mulattoes you ever saw.'" Multiple reporters praised Lowry's skill with banjo and fiddle, and many observed that, for a leader of men, Lowry was remarkably quiet: "His voice is sweet and pleasant, and in his manner there is nothing self-important or swaggering. He is not talkative, listens quietly, and searches out whoever is speaking to him."[17]

The band itself was overwhelmingly young; in the beginning the majority were teenagers, with both Henry Berry's right hand man Boss Strong, as well as John Dial, being only fourteen. They were unique for a guerilla operation in that their numbers and participants changed regularly, ranging from a small handful to dozens. Initially, members lived their lives out in the open in the community for many months at a time, only returning to hide in the swamps when the militia came around or when federal troops later occupied the area. The deep kinship networks of the Lumbee and the emerging communities of sympathetic free Blacks made this possible, and the constant interaction with non-outlaw society allowed them to avoid their own political isolation, as well as vigilante posses and police informants. It was not unusual for Henry Berry Lowry to show up at church one day, singing hymns alongside a Confederate officer, only to

17 George Alfred Townsend, *The Swamp Outlaws: or, The North Carolina Bandits; Being a Complete History of the Modern Rob Roys and Robin Hoods* (New York: Robert M. DeWitt, 1872), 12.

Quick with a bowie knife, accurate with a rifle, and tal-
ented with a fiddle, even a relative of someone killed by
him dubbed Henry Berry Lowry, "One of the handsomest
mulattoes you ever saw."

miraculously disappear to the swamps before a militia could be mustered
by the terrified soldier.

It is difficult to know how decisions were made internal to the band
of outlaws—Henry Berry Lowry certainly functioned as some kind of
leader, but it is hard to know to what extent his power extended beyond

community respect. Outside of oral history, much of what we know about the band relies on contemporary journalists, who were preprogrammed for a variety of reasons to portray such a movement as the product of a singular, charismatic individual rather than group reflection and process. One of the only known examples of internal conflict took place in regard to the proposed execution of a captured undercover police detective. Several band members opposed the execution, but were overruled by a majority vote. Generally, no formal organization was necessary beyond the community process already present in Scuffletown; larger decisions regarding communication networks and scouting were undoubtedly made on the ground by the family and community members who participated.

There were no known women members of what came to be called the Lowry Gang—if by "members" we refer to the rotating cast of armed individuals outlawed by the state, who lived clandestinely in the swamps of Robeson County. It is certainly possible that journalists would have refused to "see" women of the Lumbee community as possible robbers or bandits even when they were active in this regard, but other sources such as firsthand accounts and the oral history of the Lumbees themselves offer no solid evidence to the contrary. The modern reader is left speculating. Nonetheless, ample circumstantial evidence, along with a certain degree of logic, tells us that women in the Lumbee and Black communities played key roles in communication, scouting the movements of enemy militia, and storing arms. At least one woman, Rhoda Strong, played a direct role in two or three different jailbreaks.

The importance of these roles cannot be underestimated. The band of armed fighters hiding out in the swamps absolutely could not have functioned without other community and family members' active support. The direct targeting of Lumbee women by white militia in 1871 is in part a testament to the state's realization of this fact. Beyond the survival of the band, it was the broader community participation in the struggle that allowed it to transform from a small guerilla attempt at revenge into a burgeoning insurgency. Though when referring to the Lowry "gang" we primarily (and somewhat arbitrarily) mean the small, self-contained unit of armed outlaws, the "insurgency" as a whole should be understood as a more generalized affair. This involved the active and passive resistance of hundreds if not thousands of people—Black, Lumbee, and some white people, men and women—either through work refusals, scouting, the sharing of stolen goods, passing information along the railways, healing injured outlaws, hiding fugitives, and even, at times, volunteering en masse for militia duty in order to directly obstruct white search efforts. To privilege specific acts of banditry over this larger network of resistance would be to misunderstand the roots of a rebellion that had already begun well before the first assassinations of Confederate officers, and would result in an overemphasis on the "men's work" in an insurgency that actually involved an entire community.

The Home Guard Lashes Out

With the assassination of two officials and a series of expropriations against several prosperous plantations, the worst fears of Robeson County's white establishment were beginning to come true. While much of the ex-slave community was still hedging its bets on the imminent arrival of the Union Army, the Lumbees had seized the initiative.

The white supremacist response materialized in March 1865, when, frustrated by the outcome of the war and by the recent attacks against planters and police, eighty men of the Home Guard captured a half dozen Lowry family members and put on a rushed "trial" for theft. Two of the men, Allen and William Lowry, were hastily executed by firing squad. Then on April 1, upon visiting the home of Sinclair Lowry to search for weapons, a firing squad isolated Mary Lowry, an elderly matriarch of the Lumbees, tied her to a stake and blindfolded her, just as they had done only a few weeks before to her son and husband, Allen and William. A soldier interrogated her as to the location of stolen arms, but she refused to answer, and another soldier cried out, "Fire!" The shots were aimed above her head, intending to terrify her into talking. She still refused, and the men eventually untied and returned her to the cabin. The woman's courageous silence forced the Guard to leave without obtaining the locations of her guerilla sons and their hidden weapons.[18]

The summer and fall of 1865 continued on relatively quietly, with no particularly notable robberies or attacks taking place. It almost seemed as if the end of the Civil War would come to pass with a return to normality. But then on December 7, the situation exploded again. The teenaged Henry Berry Lowry was to marry Rhoda Strong, and the wedding was a massive event, celebrating the feats of the young Lowry and the incredible courage of his mother. Despite the Civil War years of poverty and hunger, that wedding feast remains legendary to this day, as it took up a seventy-five-foot-long table on the yard of the old Allen Lowry Homestead.

---

18   Evans, *To Die Game*, 51.

Unfortunately, the festivities were broken up by a troop of the Home Guard, led by Lieutenant A.J. McNair. The officers leveled their guns at Henry Berry Lowry and attempted to place him under arrest for the murder of Barnes. Lowry resisted, jumping behind one of the only two white men present, and yelling, "Men, are you going to see one man tie me here tonight?" After this appeal to the crowd, about half of the two hundred people gathered proceeded to march upon the Home Guard as they dragged Lowry away. Unarmed, they were beaten back by the butt ends of muskets, and ultimately forced to abandon their efforts.[19]

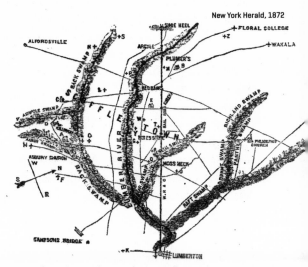

A map of Lumbee territory and surrounding areas, printed in 1872 by the New York Herald.

Because General Sherman had burned the county jail in Lumberton, Lowry was instead taken to the Columbus County jail in Whiteville, and charged with the killing of James Barnes. According to court records, Lowry treated the proceedings with "proud contempt," refusing to answer questions or counter-examine witnesses.[20]

It did not matter. As a local white reported, Lowry "filed his way through the iron bars of his cell and broke down the wall of the jail while the jailer and family occupied rooms beneath," and was thus able to "escape to the woods with handcuffs on, and make his way back to his wife in Scuffleton. This was the first escape ever effected by a criminal confined in jail at Whiteville. How he came in possession of a file, no one in the confidence of the whites can tell."[21] A Lumbee folk tradition says, however, that the file was brought to Lowry concealed in a cake by his new bride, Rhoda

---

19 Ibid., 70–71.
20 Ibid., 72.
21 Mary C. Norment, *The Lowrie History, As Acted in Part by Henry Berry Lowrie, the Great North Carolina Bandit. With Biographical Sketches of His Associates. Being a Complete History of the Modern Robber Band in the County of Robeson and State of North Carolina* (Wilmington: Daily Journal Printer, 1875), 13.

Strong. Along with fueling a cartoon cliché of outlawry that persists to this day, this was to be the first of five dramatic jailbreaks to occur throughout the Lowry conflict. Strong was to play a prominent role in several of these.

In the year and a half after this spectacular escape, the Lowry band spent more and more time in the swamps of Robeson County, hiding from an increasingly frustrated and angry white supremacist establishment. Plantation expropriations continued intermittently as well. New members joined the gang periodically, adding numbers to replace the rogue Union soldiers who had rejoined with General Sherman when he passed through in early 1865 or who had gone back to their own homes at the end of the war.

None of the bandits or their many Lumbee community accomplices were caught in this period, despite the Sheriff, Reuben King issuing thirty-five separate writs for Henry Berry alone. The Lowry band was self-disciplined in its targets and affinities: in almost nine years of attacking Planter society, it did not once target the property of Blacks, Indians, or the Buckskin poor.[22]

In the years between 1866 and 1868, President Johnson willingly turned a blind eye to both the return of ex-Confederate figures to power and to the racist KKK terror that accompanied this development. It comes as no surprise, then, that it was not to the courts or police that poor Robesonians turned to for justice, but to the Lowry gang. When one local Black woman was interviewed by a northern reporter, she showed him her mouth. When she was a slave, her master had knocked out all but two of her teeth with an oak stick. She was quoted, "Oh dis was a hard country, and Henry Berry Lowry's jess a paying 'em back. He's only payin' 'em back! It's better days for the Black people now."[23]

Republican Rule and the Lowrys

The Conservative Johnsonian state regimes were overturned in 1868, resulting in a power vacuum whereby, for a short time in some parts of the South, no specific state power existed with certainty. Some of the most exciting experiments in communization and self-determination that the United States has ever seen occurred in this short time period, whereby the idea of freedom would be radically reinterpreted by millions of poor people of color.

---

22 The gang once robbed the presumably wealthy Buckskin John McNair but, finding only fifteen dollars on his person, they returned the money and left quietly (Evans, *To Die Game*, 137).

23 Ibid., 77.

The brief rise of southern Republicanism, on the backs of masses of newly enfranchised Black voters, has often been interpreted by left historians as a brief period of hope and possibility for those who suffered from white supremacy in the Old South. While it is true that these regimes were initially greeted with enthusiasm by many, it is clear that the actual function of Republicanism—in both its moderate and Radical forms—was to subdue and constrain any possible expansion of the meaning or scope of emancipation. From the minor social programs of the Freedmen's Bureau to the use of landless workers in new industrial enterprises, from the "law and order" rhetoric aimed meekly at the Ku Klux Klan to the outright repression of popular uprisings like the Lowry War or Georgia's Ogeechee Insurrection, the Republican Party built the foundation of its new exploitation and oppression firmly upon the old.

In Robeson County, the Republican Party found itself in a peculiar bind. The party was nationally committed to a law-and-order platform, in an ultimately vain attempt at isolating and discrediting the waves of KKK vigilantism that were sweeping the South and keeping Black voters from the polls. Such terror had increased drastically when Republicans took over; as the Conservatives lost control of the legal means to inflict violence, they shifted easily into extralegal means. A law-and-order position meant that Republicans had positioned themselves to be equally opposed to any kinds of popular rebellion or direct action, or for that matter to Black or Brown self-defense. Locally, however, the party's base constituency was overwhelmingly supportive of the popular vengeance and collective theft represented by the Lowry gang, and so the party was conflicted.

A second issue confronted the local Republican Party as well: certain members of the old Home Guard were now active in the party organization, and any resurrection of concerns about the Lowry violence would bring this embarrassing fact to the fore.

In the end, the national and industrial concerns of the party inevitably took priority. In October 1868, a sheriff of New Hanover County asked Republican governor Holden whether he intended to honor an earlier bounty put on Henry Berry Lowry's head. Soon after, thirty men raided a company store in McLaurin's Hill, South Carolina, followed by three large plantations in Robeson County. On November 30, at the behest of a Conservative petition, Governor Holden issued a proclamation of outlawry against Henry Berry Lowry and many of his companions. Less than a year after taking power, the party of the Union had turned its back on the communities it had claimed to "liberate."

Several days later, aware of the precarious position into which the local party apparatus had placed itself, an agent for the newly formed Freedmen's Bureau and the newly elected sheriff paid a cordial visit to the cabin of Henry Berry Lowry and Rhoda Strong. After a large meal and entertainment from Henry Berry Lowry's deft fiddle-playing, they begged him to turn himself in, promising fair treatment and an impartial trial in the new Republican courts. Strangely, Lowry agreed, and allowed himself to be taken to a jail newly rebuilt by the Republican government in Lumberton.

Rumors of a possible lynch mob, however, reached Lowry's ears in jail, and after noticing that security was strangely lacking, he planned his escape. On December 12, when the jailor brought Lowry his evening meal, he was confronted with a pistol and bowie knife. Lowry complained about his treatment, reportedly saying, "I'm tired of this," and walked out of the building.[24]

Six weeks later, the gang reappeared. The wealthy landowner and former sheriff Reuben King, a man detested for his eighteen-year legacy of brutalizing Indians, catching escaped slaves, and evicting debtors, was shot in his own parlor by George Applewhite. The gang proceeded to ransack the plantation and escaped to the swamp.

The Lowrys, and by extension their vast community network of Lumbee and Black supporters, had unofficially declared war on Republican Robeson County. There was no going back.

Retaliation and Capture, Assassination and Escape

As one would expect, there was a shortage of Republican officers with military experience in the post–Civil War South, and so the new regime resorted to hiring aging ex-Confederate officers to do their bidding. The most competent man they found was Captain Owen Norment, who had made a name for himself hunting Indians in earlier years. Now, just three years after the Union's victory, he was being rehired to do the same for the Republican victors, this time in the name of property, law, and order.

Norment was more skilled than his predecessors in the Home Guard, and by September 1869 he managed to capture eight members of the Lowry gang. Two of these men, Shoemaker John and John Dial, initially gave corroborating testimony about the gang's involvement in the murders, but later repudiated their statements, saying they were made under torture. Foraging raids and expropriations against large landowners

---

24 Ibid., 106.

Harper's Weekly, 1872

The Lowry Gang camps out in the swamps.

continued, however, seeming to imply that as soon as some men were caught, others from the community could easily take their place.[25] Many of these raids even occurred in areas where the militia was most actively in pursuit.

Then, on March 19, 1870—just two weeks before the trials of the eight men were set to begin—the new regime suffered a major setback. Captain Norment was sitting at home with his wife when he heard a noise at the door. He walked out into the night and was quickly cut down by a shot in the dark. A doctor was called, but the mule pulling his buggy was shot on the way, and the doctor consequently arrived too late to save the Confederate-turned-Republican Indian hunter.[26]

On April 1, two of the captured men, George Applewhite and Stephen Lowry, were tried for the murder of ex-sheriff Reuben King. Despite the repudiation of John Dial's earlier statements, and the assassination of Captain Norment, the men were convicted and sentenced to hanging. While they sat in jail in Wilmington, three of the four other captured comrades managed a daring escape from their confinement in Lumberton. According to a local paper, a "low white woman," likely Rhoda Strong, managed to pass onto them an auger during visitation, with which they cut a hole in the wall and escaped.

Not to be outdone by their comrades, the remaining captured members of the gang set themselves to escaping from their own jail in Wilmington.

25 The racist and somewhat sensational Wilmington *Weekly Journal* suggested the gang had as many as three hundred active members, though in all likelihood the paper greatly exaggerated in order to justify state efforts at repression (*Weekly Journal*, September 24, 1869).

26 Besides a brawl with a servant during an ill-chosen and drunken raid on a distillery, this murdered mule was the only known "collateral damage" of the Lowry's war against plantation society. The authors would like to express our deepest sympathy for this courageous creature, and hope that his or her sacrifice, in hastening the death of Captain Norment, in turn saved the lives of many other innocent creatures.

On June 13, at 2am, the night guard made his regular rounds to the cells, only to find the one holding the Lowry gang members completely empty. The mystery was eventually unraveled: while guards and prisoners alike were distracted by a beautiful female accomplice earlier in the day, a second accomplice outside the building helped Stephen Lowry haul up a hatchet, chisel, and file through a jail window. The innovative prisoners then used the tools to fashion a makeshift key from a tin spoon, opened their cell door and escaped through a hole they had cut through the wall on a different floor. George Applewhite, Stephen Lowry, and Henderson Oxendine all managed to escape, while Calvin Oxendine decided to stay, insisting that he was innocent and had a solid alibi.[27]

Failing miserably in their strategy of militia-based Lowry hunting, the regime chose a new strategy: an undercover police informant. For many months a Boston detective named John Saunders lived in the area, cynically pretending to be a compassionate reformer aimed at teaching Indian children to read and write, while really under the direction of the state to find and capture the Lowry gang. The man had some initial success, ingratiating himself among the outlaws and viewing some of their swamp hideouts, but he was eventually caught talking to Conservatives about his work. After a heated debate, in which some of the men strongly opposed killing him, the outlaws decided that the only available course, given his knowledge, was execution. Following his death, the gang mailed Saunders's last letter and a photograph to his wife.

While the Republican authorities had enjoyed a certain initial success in stopping the Lowrys, the summer of 1870 proved how little they had actually achieved: nearly all of the band's captured members had escaped, the raids on plantations and the redistribution of planters' wealth had continued, and the county's most capable members of law enforcement had all been assassinated. The Republican party had lost all credibility with both the explicitly racist Conservatives and the poor communities that comprised the party's own local base.

Posses on the Prowl

In this context, the elections in the fall of 1870 were a disaster for the Republican Party. The party was seen as impotent by white elites and Conservatives, and was (accurately) viewed as having betrayed the hopes of

---

27 His decision worked out: when Oxendine later stood trial, an employer vouched for him and he was acquitted of all charges. Oxendine went on to live a normal life in the community (Evans, *To Die Game*, 120–123).

the poor people of its own base. Combined with a major railroad scandal, which engulfed certain members of Robeson County's own Freedmen's Bureau, and the active intimidation of voters by KKK terror, the results were predictable.

In an effort to avoid impeachment by a newly elected Conservative legislature, Republican governor Holden actually requested that federal forces be pulled from Klan-terrorized areas and relocated to Robeson County, where they would help hunt the insurgent Indians and former slaves of the Lowry gang. Though they were far more hesitant than the local militia to attack the Lowrys directly, the numbers of these federal forces made larger military operations possible.

The Lumbees' extensive knowledge of the swampland made surrounding and capturing the Lowry gang difficult, however, and the strategy failed a number of times. On more than one occasion, the gang slipped through their net with ease—sometimes even with members of the gang donning militia uniforms and joining in the hunt for themselves. At other times, entire troops of Lumbee men would volunteer for a militia unit, apparently with the sole intention of leading the search along a false trail.[28]

Nevertheless, the increase in militia numbers had some effect. On October 5, 1870, a militia unit, frustrated with the hunt, went to the houses of several Lowry relatives, apparently content to just murder them instead. Andrew Strong and Malcolm Sanderson were captured, and though Strong managed to escape by cutting his bonds and fleeing into the swamp, Sanderson was not so lucky. Revenge was swift, though. On January 14, 1871, KKK leader John Taylor, who had executed Sanderson three months before, was ambushed and shot in the head less than a hundred yards from the spot where Sanderson was murdered.

The white militia retaliated again in February. Targeted for being a Black radical, a Lowry supporter, or both, Benjamin Bethea was beaten and shot by a mob of angry whites. His family called on the Lowrys to come and help stop the beating, but they arrived too late. Shortly thereafter, two more white anti-Lowry people were shot down in revenge.

The Conservative legislature at this time began to offer massive rewards—up to $12,000 dead or alive—for members of the Lowry gang. Remarkably, the gang themselves then offered a similar reward (albeit smaller) to anyone who could deliver to them specific heads of state. Writes one historian,

---

28   Ibid., 142, 189.

George Alfred Townsend/The Swamp Outlaws, 1872

The story of the Lumbee rebellion in Robeson County was picked up by northern journalists, including one who printed this small, spectacular booklet in 1872.

If the legislators and county commissioners were demonstrating a marked liberality in offering rewards, the members of the Lowry band showed themselves to be of comparable mind. They offered one thousand dollars for the head of Angus Mc-Lean, a county commissioner, in 1870 and two hundred dollars each for a list of individuals they had declared "outlaws" in 1872, their more modest rewards resulting from the limitations of their resources rather than from a more miserly spirit.[29]

The rewards offered by the state certainly had an effect, as more and more posses of eager racists from around the region joined the hunt. On April 15, 1871, one such group ambushed George Applewhite while he was walking up the path to his cabin. He recognized the trap and ran, but not before being brought down by a bullet in the mouth, and then a second in the back. Fearing the rest of the gang was nearby, the posse left his body and returned the next day with the militia. The body had disappeared, and Mrs. Applewhite refused to answer questions. In frustration, the militia arrested her brother Forney Oxendine instead on trumped-up charges of theft.

It took the militia nine days to find George Applewhite's body, and it happened quite by accident. A small group led by the Conservative sheriff McMillan was in the vicinity of Henry Berry's cabin when they heard banjo music. They crept up slowly, surprised to find Lowry family members hanging out on the porch, as well as Applewhite, who was resting in the sun. After being shot twice, he had miraculously crawled into the swamp, "spit the bullet out" of his mouth, and found his way to the cabin of Henry Berry Lowry and Rhoda Strong. Some of the militia opened fire on the men, who fled into the house and began returning fire, while other soldiers left to get help. The skirmish lasted several hours, but at some point the militia realized the outlaws had ceased firing. After slowly approaching the cabin, they found it was empty. The soldiers discovered "a trap ... concealed in the floor, the hinges hidden or mortised beneath. This trap afforded admission to a sort of mine or covered way, which ran under the surface about sixty yards to the swamp."[30]

Not one to leave a family member behind bars, on May 10 a large band of armed men convened in Lumberton to stage a spectacular attack on the jail. With most of the force left surrounding the building to prevent

---

29   Ibid., 155.
30   Ibid., 170.

a counterattack by federal forces, Henry Berry Lowry, Steve Lowry, Boss Strong, and the now-recovered George Applewhite forced the doors open with tools on hand, held up the guards, and released Tom Lowry (who had been captured earlier) and Forney Oxendine from their cells. They returned to Scuffletown in triumph. Writing to the governor after this incident, local reverend James Sinclair pleaded, "At this moment the outlaws rule the county."[31]

War on Scuffletown

Around this time, the mood began to shift in Conservative circles toward the idea of targeting the entirety of the Lumbee community of Robeson County, rather than just the Lowry gang. It was becoming increasingly clear that the Lowrys had a massive support network and that there was a reason they always knew where the militia would be long before they got there. Wrote one officer in charge of the federal units, "The Lowrys have almost as many friends as enemies" who give them "information of any expedition against them and resist the civil law themselves. Taxes cannot be collected ... nor warrants served on any of the inhabitants of this settlement."[32] This kind of solidarity was not limited to the Lumbee community; members of the Black community also sought to help the insurgents. One journalist wrote in 1872 about how the Lowrys were forewarned of federal troop movements by rail, observing that:

> A movement among the negro train hands will be observed as the locomotive approaches the stations of Scuffletown.... When the troops pursued the scoundrels they could hear a peculiar bark like that of a cur precede them, and die away in the distance.... It was passed from shanty to shanty to put Lowery on qui vive.[33]

These acts of popular solidarity goaded the more aggressive elements of the white supremacist establishment into shifting to a strategy of general terror against the Lumbees. There was tension internal to the ruling class over this approach, with Republican moderates still attempting to isolate the band rather than punish the community as a whole. Nevertheless, July of 1871 saw this strategy implemented on the largest scale yet. Colonel

31 Ibid., 182–183.
32 Townsend, *The Swamp Outlaws*, 20.
33 Ibid.

Frank Wishart organized an anti-Lowry campaign with 117 men at arms. Rather than attempt to find the Lowry gang, the militia split into detachments to harass the community at large and capture Lumbee women at their homes. Four were arrested. One can speculate that at least one reason for this shift in strategy lies in the state's recognition of the strategic role played by these women and the large community network they managed.

Though the gang engaged the militia in several shootouts during these operations, the most notable incident occurred by accident. On July 10, in the midst of their campaign and with four women already in custody, a troop of eighteen men accidentally stumbled upon Henry Berry Lowry rowing by himself down the Lumber River. The militia immediately recognized the leader and opened fire. He was too fast, however, and—after diving into the water and tipping up his boat to use as cover—Lowry began returning fire. Rather than retreat, Lowry actually swam toward the men, picking them off one at a time from the cover of his upturned boat. Eventually the militia captain ordered a retreat, giving Lowry one more story by which to become legend.

A few days later, several members of the gang sent a letter to the sheriff of Robeson County, which read:

> We make a request, that our wives who were arrested a few days ago, and placed in jail, be released to come home to their families by Monday Morning, and if not, the Bloodiest times will be here that ever was before—the life of every man will be in Jeopardy.[34]

Three days later, civil authorities in the county held a meeting at which they decided to release the prisoners. The following day, the westbound train arrived at the Lumbee village of Red Bank carrying the four women. They had left as prisoners, but returned as heroes.

Henry Berry Lowry Disappears

Although the federal troops proved consistently unwilling or unable to apprehend the insurgents, their presence in the area made large-scale expropriations of plantations increasingly difficult. Outside of a generalized insurrection against the Conservative-turned-Republican-turned-Conservative regime, the gang simply could not survive in the same territory forever.

---

34 Dial and Eliades, *The Only Land I Know*, 74–75.

In late 1871, several peace treaties were attempted, separate from any influence of the gang's members. Various Republican and Conservative moderates proposed petitions that might pardon the outlaws and allow for a return to normalcy, but a strictly Conservative state legislature made these efforts hopeless. The state was positioned well enough to isolate and contain any large-scale rebellion, but it remained committed to a repressive course of action with the Lowrys that it was incapable of actually carrying out.[35] Asked by one of the political moderates why Lowry did not just leave North Carolina, he replied, "Robeson County is the only land I know. I can hardly read, and do not know where to go if I leave these woods and swamps, where I was raised. If I can get safe conduct and pardon I will go anywhere.... But these people will not let me live and I do not mean to enter any jail again."[36]

On the night of February 16, 1872, after giving up on a series of fruitless talks with politicians about a pardon, the insurgents drove a horse and buggy to the store of a prominent merchant in Lumberton and proceeded to steal a thousand dollars' worth of merchandise, as well as an iron safe from the sheriff's office that contained about $22,000. This was by far the most profitable expropriation the band had ever carried out. After the raid, Henry Berry Lowry and many of his co-conspirators disappeared.

The *Baltimore Weekly Sun*, 1871

Into a regular battle, which lasted some time. The sheriff's posse fought and followed the negroes into the recesses of the swamp, but it is not certainly known that any of the outlaws were killed. Lowry, the leader of the band, and Capt. F. M. Wishart had a regular duel on the railroad track, each loading and firing deliberately five or six times, but neither was wounded. The whole county of Robeson is aroused, and it is believed a campaign will now be inaugurated that will result in the extermination of the band. A committee of the citizens of Robeson county came to this city to-day to secure arms and ammunition. Every member of the Lowry band is a negro.

A news clipping discusses the kidnapping of Rhoda Strong and others, and the subsequent retaliation by the gang. The short article makes it a point to note that, 'Every member of the Lowry band is a negro.

The Mystery and Legend of Henry Berry Lowry

In the following two years, pursuit of the remaining known members of the gang by bounty hunters had some effect: Tom Lowry, Andrew Strong, and the young Zachariah McLaughlin were all ambushed and murdered

35 A brief anecdote from the Wilmington *Star* to highlight the utter incompetence of the government troops at this time: In September 1871, "an officer received a message from Lowry, stating that he had visited their camp the night before and inspected their arms to see if they were in proper condition. As proof of this assertion he stated that he had left his 'card,' which would be found attached to one of their guns. Upon examining their weapons the name Henry Berry Lowry was found inscribed upon the breach of one of them" (Wilmington *Star*, August 18, 1871).

36 Dial and Eliades, *The Only Land I Know*, 78.

by opportunistic bounty hunters driven by the most massive rewards North Carolina had ever offered for outlaws. The bounty hunters generally left the area in a hurry after collecting their pay. But the mystery of what happened to Henry Berry Lowry, or the money stolen on February 16, has never been solved.

Over 140 years later, historians and members of the Lumbee community still disagree about the leader's disappearance. A variety of folktales, legends, and hypotheses exist, some supported by more evidence than others, but all unproven: that Lowry escaped the county undercover as an injured soldier with the help of a sympathetic general; that he faked his own death and funeral with a straw-stuffed "corpse," later escaping from the county in a stolen military uniform; that he escaped by train in his own coffin; that he survived his endeavors and emerged under a different name as a leader of Native resistance in the Pacific Northwest a few years later; that he died on his brother Tom's land by accidental discharge of his rifle, secretly buried by his comrades to perpetuate his legendary status and the rebellious energy his life inspired. Local newspapers tended to prefer the accidental death story, but these papers had a political interest in undermining the legend of the man.[37] Neither the body nor the gravesite of Henry Berry Lowry have ever been found.

What remains clear is that, whether Lowry died young or old in his own homeland, or in another struggle far away, the insurgent gang that bore his name lives on in infamy to this day. Lowry historian William McKee Evans writes in his book *To Die Game*:

> The Lowrys clearly made an impact on the home territory of the Lumbee River Indians. They appeared on the scene at a particularly difficult period in the history of the Indians. At this time the armed resistance of the plains Indians was being smashed, their numbers decimated, while the Indians of the eastern seaboard had known little but defeat and increasing humiliation for a hundred years. With the triumph of a frankly racist party during Reconstruction, it appeared that nothing could stop the winners from putting the Lumbee River Indians into the same half-free place in which they generally succeeded in putting the Blacks. But this effort failed … to a great extent because of the bold deeds of the Lowrys, which filled

---

37 One is reminded of how both fascist and Communist mouthpieces manipulated news of the mysterious death of Spanish anarchist leader Buenaventura Durruti during the defense of Madrid; even in death our enemies cannot let us live.

the Lumbee River Indians with a new pride of race, and a new confidence that despite generations of defeat, revitalized their will to survive as a people.[38]

A brief story will illustrate just how strongly the legend of the Lowry gang remained to inspire the Lumbee people. In January 1958, while attempting to resurrect their presence in Robeson County, the KKK burned a cross near the home of an Indian family who had moved into an all-white neighborhood. A similar attack was carried out the same night in nearby Saint Pauls, in the driveway of a white woman allegedly having an affair with an Indian man. The Klan then announced an open-air rally to be held on January 18.

Unfortunately for the KKK, another clan attended the rally, too. The Chavises, Hunts, Locklears, Lowrys, Oxendines, Sampsons, and many other descendants of the Lowry insurgents arrived in force, resulting in what one reporter called "the shortest Ku Klux Klan rally in history."[39] A *Newsweek* journalist wrote,

> The Indians let the Klansmen set up their microphone and a single electric-light bulb; they let about 100 Klansmen assemble around the truck. Then they began to move forward, roaring: "We want Cole!" (The Rev. James W. Cole, self-styled grand wizard of the Klan) Cole stayed precisely where he was—behind the truck. The Lumbees began firing their guns in the air; a sharpshooter shot out the light bulb. There was pandemonium in the darkness; the guns spat flame into the air; the amplifying system was torn apart; auto windows were shattered by bullets. The Klansmen, themselves well armed, decided to run for it; there was the roar of automobile engines. Then the sheriff's deputies fired the tear-gas bombs. When the gas cleared, the Lumbee raid at Maxton was over. The Indians had won.[40]

Four Klansmen were injured in the exchange, and as the Klan left, the Lumbees burned their regalia in celebration. The incident became known as the Battle of Hayes Pond, and is still celebrated as a Lumbee holiday. The men and women who fought there were raised on stories of similar battles that occurred almost a hundred years earlier, stories that inspired

---

38 Evans, *To Die Game*, 259.
39 *Lumberton Robesonian*, January 20, 1958.
40 Evans, *To Die Game*, 256.

an identity and culture of rebellion and dignity. Needless to say, the Klan did not return to Robeson County.

This should not be understood simply as a "happy ending" for the Lumbees. The Lumbee community, constituting as much as 50 percent of Robeson County, continued to struggle with poverty and exploitation, white supremacy, and marginalization at every turn. The insurgency after the Civil War led to an unprecedented level of community coherence, political consciousness, and pride, which concretely contributed to a number of community institutions, especially Lumbee-centered schools, as well as the successful effort to resist the Klan. Nevertheless, the Lumbees faced the same reality as other communities of color after Reconstruction and did so long into the twentieth century. The relatively assimilated nature of Lumbee social life was no protection against poverty and unemployment. Many were eventually forced to leave Robeson County in search for work; one 1970s study of such Lumbee refugees in Baltimore found a tight-knit community in which one-third were on welfare, few owned their own homes, and nearly all children were stuck in the city's worst public school.[41] In forcefully displacing large numbers of the proud Lumbees from their land, the twentieth-century economy had finally succeeded where the seventeenth- and eighteenth-century militaries of colonialism had failed.

Reflections on Reconstruction and Resistance

Like many other Native tribes, the Lumbee community had been struggling to maintain its own economic and cultural autonomy for centuries. The chief avenue for this had historically been a degree of "looking and acting white," thanks in part to the tribe's English ancestry, as well as living in territories unsuitable for large-scale plantation development. But flareups of violent rebellion had happened before, and when the Jacksonian and Confederate regimes began to further erode the Lumbees' autonomy, the Lumbees had that history to turn to.

Much like the Ogeechee rebellion in Georgia, the power vacuums created at the end of the Civil War in Robeson County allowed for renewed efforts at direct resistance and new experiments in expropriation and mutual aid. The tensions internal to the ruling class, as well the complete incompetency of Yankee efforts to understand and manage southern social relations, made for an environment ripe for the community-wide passive resistance and guerilla tactics of the Lumbees.

---

41   Dial and Eliades, *The Only Land I Know*, 156.

Republicans were better at understanding how to incite industrial growth than how to appease racial strife. The party was incapable of pleasing both the white-supremacist planter class and exploited people of color, and clearly preferred the former to the latter. Though unable to ever secure the loyalty of the Lumbees, the party did play the vital role of political anchor to the otherwise rebellious tendencies in Robeson's Black communities. This anchor was made of hope, keeping a majority grounded in the idea that change and freedom could and would eventually be provided to them. While the Lowry conflict—which included some Black partisans as well as Lumbees—directly demonstrated the betrayal of the Republicans, *most* of the Black population remained content to wait and see what the Yankee liberators would do, preferring a passive support and sympathy for the rebels to active rebellion alongside them. While the Lowrys and their Lumbee comrades were more than capable of terrorizing the white supremacist establishment of Robeson County on their own, one can only dream of what would have happened had the much larger populations of former slaves set aside their lukewarm loyalty to the Republican Party and also joined in.

It cannot be emphasized enough that resistance like that of the Lumbees was *not* an extension of Radical Republicanism into deeper waters, but rather something entirely different. Thousands of Black and Brown (and some poor white) people across the South continued to organize and rebel long after Union victory. The nature of this resistance and the social forms it adopted—not to mention the fact that rebels like those of the Ogeechee Neck and Robeson County directly attacked Republican institutions—cause us to reject simplistic interpretations of their insurgency as an expression of "extreme liberalism" or a militant push for civil rights.

The realigning of southern political interests—with Republicans hiring ex-Confederate fugitive slave hunters, rebuilding old jails, and securing easily exploitable, cheap labor to industrialize the South—demonstrates beyond a doubt that, for the country's political elite, the Civil War was over. For them, it was time to put aside old rivalries and get back down to business. Whatever the benevolent intentions of individual Radical Republicans may have been, Yankee-engineered Reconstruction was chiefly a step in forcefully reintegrating newly available populations of desperate and destitute former slaves into industrial and agrarian production. The biopower of whipped slaves, landless Indians, and indentured servant whites eventually became the biopower of starving workers, all (some more, some less) free to sell their labor to large landowners or planters-turned-industrialists—in many cases the same men they had worked for previously. Post-Civil War regimes integrated old and new methods of disciplining these bodies, combining the traditional vigilante white militias of an earlier era with federal troops, courts, and a newly emerging network of state prisons.

These new forces of discipline represent an entire archipelago of state institutions from which Black and Brown bodies had been largely absent just a decade earlier. Courts, police, prisons, and jails—in much of the South these had been primarily reserved for white people, as slaves and laborers were generally disciplined privately. Now these public institutions faced a period of massive growth and expansion, after which they would eventually play the role of disciplining a much larger body of waged, un-waged, or indebted workers.[42] Thanks to emancipation, these oppressed were now semi-citizens, free to participate in civil society; to press griev-ances before the government; to invoke the almighty Law; to sign a labor contract; or to sit in a witness stand, a voting booth, or a prison cell.[43] Understood in this way—as a process of disciplining the newly emanci-pated—we can see this integration into civil society not as a small step forward but as a giant leap *sideways*, into a world where rebellion could be endlessly recycled through the legitimate channels of political spectacle. Bondage had not been abolished, it had been democratized.

The acts of those like the Lumbees in North Carolina—in presenting a challenge not just to old methods of discipline but also to the new state apparatus—represent a continuation of a different kind of war. This was

---

42 Though this process cannot be understood outside of its economic context, it also should not be understood in a vulgar way, as having *only* an affect upon "economic" life—the patterns of disciplining communities of workers in new ways after the Civil War affected the whole of social life in the South, from the policing of women's bodies and reproduction, to altering the gendered division of farm labor, to changes in racial codes of conduct.

43 As mentioned in the previous chapter, the Freedmen's Bureau itself supervised and enforced the creation of labor contracts between former slaves and planters, operating to normalize and stabilize relations between these two classes. Government and civil society evolved to not just discipline strictly in a "negative," repressive sense—with apparatuses like police and prisons—but also though the wide range of emerging "positive" institutions of social democracy. The end of Reconstruction signaled the end (and failure) of this experiment in positive social control, but the strategy would return with a vengeance a century later at the end of the Civil Rights period. It wasn't until this period, one hundred years later, that Black people would truly become "citizens" in the complete sense of the term, but the earlier emancipation did never-theless signal a fundamental legal shift in which the white discipline of Black bodies transitioned from the private to the public sphere.

not the Civil War that ended on April 9, 1865, at Appomattox Court House, but the social war that periodically reignited across the farmlands, swamps, and forests of the American South, that saw its hopes temporarily dashed on October 16, 1859, at Harpers Ferry. Their struggle cannot be properly understood as an attempt to spread the effects of democratization further for those who benefited from Union victory. From the moment of Henry Berry Lowry's first jailbreak—after voluntarily giving himself up to Republicans and then changing his mind, vowing to never "enter any jail again"—this struggle embodied a rejection rather than an acceptance of such democratic processes, preferring the direct expropriation of wealthy planters and the self-determination of an autonomous Lumbee community to a capitalist-driven and state-directed Reconstruction. The Lowrys are often portrayed as struggling for Indians' rights; these men and women may or may not have expressed themselves in such a way, given the chance. Regardless, we would point out that this rights discourse was a philosophical framework far more in line with the Republican Party of the time, a party whose sheriffs, officers, and wealthy elite the Lowrys were in the habit of shooting.

Assessing the political motivations of this diverse insurgency is complicated, made no less so by the historical distance one must travel to walk in the shoes of a community whose every daily activity was not managed by state and capital, like our own. Nevertheless, in rejecting the white supremacy of the Conservatives and the false peace of the Republicans at a pivotal point in the history of our region, the insurgency that took hold of Robeson County, North Carolina, is a struggle worth remembering. Traveling in southeastern North Carolina today, one can still occasionally find a large button with Henry Berry Lowry's handsome face for sale at small rural gas stations. Like many others, we imagine him with his comrades emerging from the swamps to raid the plantations and jails of nineteenth century Robeson County, or to assassinate a Klansman or sheriff, and we smile.

After the occupations, attacks, and be- trayals of the Reconstruction period, the South navigated its way toward a new normality. To varying degrees, depending on the state, northern-style industrial development was imported and built up on a foundation of southern agrarian cultural norms and white supremacy. Industrialists sought a replacement for the free slave labor of the antebellum period and, perhaps taking subconscious inspiration from the Thirteenth Amendment, looked to new regimes of punishment and social control to solve this problem. The convict lease emerged as a stopgap measure to help govern the rebellious Black communities of Reconstruction while simultaneously guaranteeing windfall profits, but in some places resistance to the lease brought about unpredictable new alliances in the war against capital.

In filthy rags, with vile odors and the clanking of shack-
les.... They were going to the mines.

—A visitor to Alabama, 1885

Some people say a man is made outta mud
A poor man's made outta muscle and blood
Muscle and blood and skin and bones
A mind that's a-weak and a back that's strong

You load sixteen tons, what do you get
Another day older and deeper in debt
Saint Peter don't you call me 'cause I can't go
I owe my soul to the company store.

—"Sixteen Tons," Merle Travis

Now therefore ye are cursed, and there shall none of you
be freed from being bondmen, and hewers of wood and
drawers of water for the house of my God.

—Joshua 9:23, *King James Bible*

THE STOCKADE STOOD BURNING:

Rebellion and the convict lease in Tennessee's Coalfields

ON THE NIGHT OF JULY 14, 1891, IN EASTERN TENNESSEE, A BAND OF about one hundred armed coal miners and local citizens marched on a newly built prison stockade owned by the Tennessee Coal Mining Company. The miners and their allies compelled the guards to release the forty inmates imprisoned there, put them on a train, and sent them to Knoxville. Without firing a shot, the miners disappeared back into the darkness.[1]

Over the next thirteen months, the workers would repeat this scene over and over, eventually torching company property, looting company stores, and aiding the prisoners' escapes. The miners were rebelling against the use of convict labor in Tennessee mines, which was being used to cut company costs and disastrously undermine the employment prospects and solidarity of free laborers. In the words of the president of the Tennessee Coal and Iron Company, "We were right in calculating that the free laborers would be loath to enter upon strikes when they saw that the company was amply provided with convict labor."[2] But, as David Oshinsky writes in his book about the development of early southern prison systems:

---

1   Karin A. Shapiro, *A New South Rebellion: The Battle Against Convict Labor in the Tennessee Coalfields, 1871–1896* (Chapel Hill: University of North Carolina Press, 1998), 79–81.

2   Ibid., 45.

Something happened in Tennessee, something almost unimaginable to the mine owners and politicians of that State. When the companies tried to intimidate their workers by bringing in convict labor to take over their jobs, the workers responded by storming the stockades, freeing the prisoners, and loading them onto freight trains bound for Nashville and Knoxville and places far away.

What began as an isolated protest in the company town of Coal Creek spread quickly across the Cumberlands to engulf most of eastern Tennessee. Thousands of miners took part in these uprisings, and thousands of armed State guardsmen were sent to face them down. The Tennessee convict war was one of the largest insurrections in American working-class history. And yet, unfolding at exactly the same time as the more publicized labor wars in Homestead, Pennsylvania, and Coeur d'Alene, Idaho, it was largely ignored.[3]

At a time when the post–Civil War South was trying to reinvent its economy, penal institutions, and racial caste system, the actions of the miners and their allies, combined with the resistance of convicts, created a perfect storm. Within a couple of years of the rebellion's beginning, it was clear that the brutal system of convict leasing, by which state and county prisoners were literally sold off to private railroad and coal companies, had become totally unsustainable. Again and again, all across eastern and mid-Tennessee, miners released prisoners and burned company property to the ground. The costs of militiamen needed to guard the prisoners, along with the sabotage, work slow-downs, and rebellions by the convicts, made the system cost-prohibitive both to the state and coal companies. By December 31, 1895, Tennessee became the first state in the South to abolish the tremendously lucrative convict lease.

The convict wars symbolized the continually violent transition of chattel to wage slavery in the South, in terms of both the southern states' attempts to industrialize as well as in the violent reactions of a newly industrialized proletariat to such efforts. Miners' participation in this insurrection also catalyzed a change in the thinking of many poor whites, who went from using forms of rhetoric traditional to a Jeffersonian Republic and commonwealth to those of class war. As shown by both the wildcats

---

3   David Oshinsky, *Worse Than Slavery: Parchman Farm and the Ordeal of Jim Crow Justice* (New York: Free Press, 1996), 81–82.

of the 1960s and '70s and the modern resistance to mountaintop removal mining, an uneasy combination of these different modes of thinking still remains in Appalachia to this day, creating the potential for movements that are at once quintessentially American yet simultaneously radical, violent, and autonomous in nature.

The convict lease sought to preserve the benefits of enslaved Black labor in the "New South." This insurrection can therefore be seen as an indirect assault by white and Black miners upon older notions of white identity and loyalty to the racial caste system. Though this form of race treason never became more than a secondary factor in the miners' economic self-defense, it would be wrong not to consider the meanings of such a self-interested racial solidarity, particularly at a time when the racist prison-industrial complex has now grown to such gargantuan proportions, and neoliberalism has eliminated so many of the industrial manufacturing jobs once occupied by white workers. For those of us interested in kindling future insurrections, there are many things worth considering in the convict wars.

The Rise of Convict Labor

By the end of the Civil War, the economic and social fabric of the Old South had been torn at the seams. Huge numbers of slaves had been "freed" with little or no resources at their disposal, only to be surrounded on all sides by a white supremacist society hostile to their presence. The South's small, battered jails started filling up with former slaves guilty of stealing items that were worth a few dollars or less. While the Tennessee board of prison directors used racist appeals to argue that these inmates should be put in a yet-to-be-built state prison, the Tennessee legislature thought otherwise. As Oshinsky writes:

> Railroad fever was sweeping the State, and unskilled labor was in short supply. After little debate and much bribery, the legislators turned over the entire prison system to a professional card gambler named Thomas O'Conner for $150,000 on a five-year lease. By 1871, State convicts were laying track and mining coal from Memphis to Knoxville. Each morning their urine was collected and sold to local tanneries by the barrel. When they died, their unclaimed bodies were purchased by the Medical School at Nashville for the students to practice on.[4]

---

4   Ibid, 57–58.

A drawing from Harper's Weekly portrays miners firing down upon state militia stationed at Fort Anderson.

The biopower of this newly created, expendable social class combined with northern investment to fuel the rapid development of southern industrial capitalism. Convict labor was significantly cheaper than waged labor, and relied on much of the same white paternalism common in chattel slavery. Convicts could appeal their cases to white benefactors such as well-known lawyers or industrialists, who would in many ways act as their "owners" through a process of appeals for pardon or clemency. If a convict presented himself in the correct light, telling white elites what they wanted to hear about their own system, they would often get their pardon. The convict lease system was an attempt, both economically and socially, to preserve the social character of chattel slavery in everything but name, throughout the drastic changes of industrialization.

This is further supported by the example of Arthur Colyar, the one-time president of the Tennessee Coal and Iron Company (TCI), newspaper editor, and passionate Democratic Party ideologue, who, after the

Civil War, put his own former slaves to work mining coal in Grundy County. It was he who, as part of the emerging Democratic faction devoted to industrialization known as the Farmers' Alliance, lobbied the state legislature to lease convicts to the state's industrial elite. Thus TCI, which later grew to become the Tennessee Coal, Iron, and Railroad Company (TCIR), eventually became the primary convict lessee.

Up until the coal miners' uprising and the Depression of 1893, the TCIR's profits grew tremendously. The company remained the main lessee throughout this time, but sublet convicts to a number of smaller eastern-Tennessee coal companies such as the Coal Creek Mining and Manufacturing Company and the Tennessee Coal Mining Company (TCMC). The legality of this subletting arrangement remained controversial throughout the 1890s, though attempts to abolish the lease through the courts were unsuccessful. Further controversy was generated by southern states' tendency to manipulate local vagrancy or larceny laws when increased laborers were needed. Oshinsky writes:

> Their numbers ebbed and flowed according to the labor needs of the coal companies and the revenue needs of the counties and the State. When times were tight, local police would sweep the streets for vagrants, drunks, and thieves. Hundreds of Blacks would be arrested, put on trial, found guilty, sentenced to sixty or ninety days plus court costs, and then delivered to a "hard labor agent," who leased them to the mines. In an average year, 97 percent of Alabama's county convicts had "colored" written next to their names.[5]

A brief look at the crimes for which Black men found themselves arrested paints a poignant picture of the criminalization of Black life. In one Alabama county, convicts were predominantly sentenced to mining coal for crimes such as "obscene language," "selling whiskey," violating a labor contract with a white employer, selling cotton to someone other than their landlord, "vagrancy," "illegal voting," carrying a concealed weapon, and miscegenation.[6]

Despite the occasional pardon for such crimes, the convict lease was incredibly brutal. In many states the inmate laborers died faster than they could be replaced. The G&A Railroad in South Carolina lost over

5   Ibid., 77.
6   Douglas A. Blackmon, *Slavery by Another Name: The Re-Enslavement of Black Americans from the Civil War to World War II* (New York: Anchor Books, 2008), 99.

50 percent of its laborers between 1877 and 1879. "A year or two on the Western North Carolina Railroad was akin to a death sentence; convicts regularly were blown to bits in tunnel explosions, buried in mountain landslides, and swept away in springtime floods," writes Oshinsky. When asked about the brutality of the convict lease, one railroad official explained, "Why? Because he is a convict, and if he dies it is a small loss, and we can make him work there, while we cannot get free men to do the same kind of labor for, say, six times as much as the convict costs." On railroads, convicts were forced to sleep in rolling iron cages, which could barely contain the men crammed inside them. "It was like a small piece of hell, an observer noted—the stench, the chains, the sickness, and the heat."[7]

The labor was regulated and managed by way of a task system, which required convicts to mine a certain amount of coal per day or else face punishment. Convicts were beaten repeatedly with a leather strap to encourage greater production; in Georgia the device was affectionately called the "negro regulator." Nevertheless, as one ex-prisoner testified, 40 percent of the workers were unable to fulfill their allotted quota. Companies attempted to further motivate convicts by augmenting the stick of the task system with the carrot of the piece-work system, offering cash bonuses to those who mined more than their required tonnage. The financial incentive was rarely achieved, as the company typically raised the quota once a prisoner could reach it; regardless, the cash payment provided managers a secondary technique of control alongside physical punishment.[8]

Middle-class reformers tried to speak out against the lease through newspapers and with political lobbying, but could not be heard above the roar of southern industrial progress. It was the rebellion of the convicts themselves, and later the efforts of free miners, that ultimately rendered the system unsustainable. As Karin Shapiro writes in her study of the convict wars,

> Convicts engaged in escapes, sabotaged the mine, and shirked work. Roughly one in twelve prisoners successfully fled incarceration in one of the mining stockades.... Sabotage took many innovative forms. Overcharging the holes with powder or engaging in "some pyrotechnic display ... directed towards the roof" seemed to be favorite methods of damaging a mine.

7   Oshinsky, *Worse Than Slavery*, 59.
8   Alex Lichtenstein, *Twice the Work of Free Labor: The Political Economy of Convict Labor in the New South* (New York: Verso, 1996), 134.

Inevitably officials would have to close the shaft while guards, miners, and some convicts cleared away the rubble.[9]

Prisoners also organized large-scale attacks on their confinement. In October 1890, inmates at the Nashville penitentiary set their workshops on fire, destroying many of the penitentiary buildings. In July 1894, seventy-five Tracy City inmates placed a dynamite bomb in a mining car and pushed it down a side entry. They managed to kill the deputy warden and two guards, and then refused to leave the mine. When a guard killed a convict thought to be a ringleader, the inmates posthumously labeled that man the leader so as to avoid punishment.[10]

Similar conditions sparked revolts among convict miners in Georgia. From 1886 to 1892 there were at least four major revolts or mutinies in the mines of or near Dade County, including a July 12, 1886 strike by 109 prisoners who refused to leave the mines and had to be starved out. In June 1891, a mutiny turned into a mass escape attempt—a new tactic for both free workers and prisoners alike.[11]

Less spectacular but equally participatory work slowdowns and intentionally poor mining probably made the biggest impact on the coal companies' bottom lines. Everyday resistance involved a number of tactics, from filling the bottom of coal cars with slate to better meet the required quota and knocking out timber supports to cause well-timed cave-ins, to feigning illness and actively aiding the sick or injured to fill the required tonnage.[12] As one prisoner's song said:

> The captain holler hurry
> I'm going to take my time
> Says he's making money
> And trying to make time
> Says he can lose his job
> But I can't lose mine.[13]

---

9   Shapiro, *A New South Rebellion*, 68.
10   Ibid.
11   Lichtenstein, *Twice the Work of Free Labor*, 126–127.
12   It is also worth noting that all of these strategies were equally used by free miners, who, despite the absence of corporal punishment, confronted the same task and piece-work systems—both systems created to help bosses to manage a workplace environment that did not easily allow for direct supervision (Lichtenstein, *Twice the Work of Free Labor*, 137).
13   Shapiro, *A New South Rebellion*, 69.

In this way, notoriously low-grade coal came out of convict-mined sites. The inevitable result was damage to the profit margins of most mines that relied on prison labor. For this reason, few coal companies chose to exclusively use convict labor; the vast majority were forced to mix free miners with inmate workers at their worksites. In this sense, the interaction between these two classes of laborers was the direct result of the resistance of the convicts themselves. In turn, it is easy to infer that this mixing of company in the mines was at least partly responsible for the solidarity and communication maintained between convicts and free laborers throughout the duration of the insurrection. While most of this story is necessarily told via the better-documented experiences of free miners, it is important to remember that the entire labor system was already consistently destabilized by the day-to-day disobedience and sabotage of prisoners.

Life as a Free Miner in Tennessee

The rebellion of Tennessee's coal miners took place primarily in eastern Tennessee, though it eventually spread to the small mid-Tennessee towns of Tracy City and Inman, and involved militiamen brought in from all over the state. Significant cultural differences existed between eastern and middle regions of the state: the most marked difference at the time was East Tennessee's unionist and Republican background. The small coal towns in eastern Tennessee, such as Coal Creek, Briceville, and Oliver Springs, consistently voted overwhelmingly Republican in elections, despite racist poll taxes and other laws meant to exclude Black and Republican voters from the electorate. Many eastern Tennessee miners had fought on the Union side during the Civil War.

While the Republican Party ultimately distanced itself from coal miners' actions, the relatively integrated social life and prominence of several Black union leaders, and the Unionist background of many whites, were important factors in the miners' ability to conduct large-scale, well-organized revolt. To some who had been fighting to abolish slavery, the new convict-lease system must have seemed a disturbingly familiar regression. At the same time, this support for the Union may also have played a part in the miners' initial refusal to break with the state or federal governments; thousands of the men had fought and died to preserve the United States only a few years back, so why rebel against that government now?

Coal companies operating in the east of the state were generally smaller and more financially precarious than TCIR, the massive company that dominated not just the coal industry but also iron ore and railroads throughout mid-Tennessee. This meant that companies in Coal Creek and Briceville had far less control over the day-to-day social lives of residents: they did not own the housing, the general stores, the churches, or the buildings in which social clubs and unions met. Workers and other citizens thus had much more autonomy in these eastern towns compared to their allies in the west, and their union membership and tight organizational structures reflected this. According to William Riley, the Black secretary-treasurer of UMWA (United Mine Workers of America) District 19, which consisted primarily of these eastern towns, membership had grown to 1,200 by July 1892. Though racism persisted in the union's ranks, the UMWA consistently organized both white and Black miners, insisting—at least in writing—on a biracial unionism highly uncommon in the post–Civil War South.

Briceville and Coal Creek boasted a number of secret or semi-secret fraternal and sororal organizations as well,

Harper's Weekly, 1892

Coal Creek miners meet to discuss the emerging struggle against the convict lease.

including two Odd Fellows, a Masonic Lodge, a Knights of Pythias, a Sons of Vulcan, and a Ladies Aid society, not to mention a number of brass bands and baseball leagues. There were also multiple Knights of Labor locals, which were affiliated with the United Mine Workers of America. Company managers and bosses often complained about these social groups, citing the fact that they used secret oaths, pledges, and rituals in their meetings, but the companies were unable to eradicate them. Towns in mid-Tennessee had fewer such groups, and those there were had significantly less autonomy from the coal companies. It is undeniable that the trust, camaraderie, and secrecy created by these many organizations laid the groundwork for the highly organized and secure actions that came about in 1891.[14]

Throughout the 1880s, miners in east and mid-Tennessee organized around a number of issues. Their largest grievances were demands for an independent checkweighman (rather than a company-appointed one, who

14 Unless otherwise noted, all of the direct quotes and references in the rest of the chapter are attributed to Karin Shapiro's *New South Rebellion*, the only full text to deal with this rebellion in depth.

under-weighed workers' coal production), payment in legal tender as opposed to scrip, and the abolition of the convict lease. Though both UMWA and Knights of Labor locals grew throughout the period, in 1887 and 1889 miners in Coal Creek led two unsuccessful strikes around the issues of checkweighmen and wage reductions.

The Rebellion Begins

It was not until the focus shifted directly onto the convict lease that the miners began kindling a deeper rebellion. On July 5, 1891, after forcing a lockout over its workers' demands, the Tennessee Coal Mining Company brought convict laborers into its Briceville mines. After a week and a half of meetings and discussions, miners armed themselves, stormed the stockades, and put the convicts on trains to Knoxville. They were assisted by many small shop owners and other sympathizers from nearby towns, who realized their livelihood would also be threatened if free miners' income suddenly vanished. Despite the miners' bold attack, they remained initially committed to dialogue with the state government, directing their grievances to supposedly sympathetic Governor Buchanan. Their telegram read,

> We the miners, farmers, merchants and property-holders of Briceville and Coal Creek and vicinity assembled to the number of five hundred, who have come together to defend our families from starvation, our property from depreciation, and our people from contamination from the hands of convict labor being introduced in our works ... do hereby beg you, as our Chief Executive and Protector, to prevent their introduction and thus avoid bloodshed, which is sure to follow if their taking our livelihood from us is persisted in.[15]

Their appeals proved to be fruitless; despite his populist credentials as a leading member of the Farmers' Alliance, Buchanan quickly ordered three military companies to accompany the prisoners back to the Briceville stockade and keep them there.

Flouting Buchanan's call for order, the miners and their allies reassembled on the morning of July 20, and again marched on the Briceville

---

15 It is unclear if by "contamination" the miners are referring to the effect of racial integration—a strange suggestion given that free miners were themselves integrated—or to the notoriously low-grade coal mined by the prisoners.

stockade. This time there were two thousand of them, including men from as far away as the Kentucky border. Armed with pistols, rifles, and shotguns, and actively excluding the participation of anyone "under the influence of whiskey," the miners once again removed the prisoners from the stockade and put them on a train for Knoxville. In keeping with a sense of propriety, the miners dispersed for a midday dinner at 1:30 p.m., and then reassembled at 2:30 p.m. to march on the stockade in nearby Coal Creek. The same actions were carried out there, once again with the aid of their more "rowdy" allies from Kentucky, where similar confrontations had occurred in 1886.

It is worth noting that, up to this point, no shots had been fired, no company property destroyed, and none of the prisoners liberated (in being sent to Knoxville or Nashville, they were generally returned to a state prison). Nevertheless, these actions cost the company and the state a tremendous amount of money—in terms of militiamen's pay, lost production in the mines, and the costs of housing and food for convicts sent to the prisons. Union leaders used the threat of these costs to force the state legislature to conduct a special session to address concerns about the convict lease. Hopeful that this session would solve their problems, the miners naively allowed the return of convicts and militia to their towns on July 24. It was the miners' representatives, along with a prominent pro-union attorney named J.C.J. Williams, who convinced many of the rank-and-file miners to negotiate. Even as Williams rose to speak at an event on July 23, he was interrupted by miners yelling, "Fight it out!" Nevertheless, the president of UMWA's local district supported calls for negotiation and peace, and the rank and file followed suit.

The miners' faith in the legislature and governor was misplaced. Despite opposition to the convict lease by Buchanan and other Farmers' Alliance Democrats, as well as opposition from the Republican minority, politicians decided the cost of breaking their lease with Tennessee's main coal company was too great. Instead of abolishing the convict lease, the legislature used the special session to make several decisions to the miners' detriment. They passed a new bill making interference with state convicts a felony, granted new powers to the governor enabling him to bypass the legislature when mobilizing troops, and appropriated an additional $25,000 of state funds to the state militia. The miners would have been better off never having called for the special legislative session; their patient attempts to negotiate strengthened their enemies and bought the state time to strategize about how to neutralize the miners' rebellion.

The Coalfields Heat Up

On Halloween night 1891, after waiting months for legislative negotiations and various court cases to run their course, one thousand masked miners held their own "special session." The Tennesseans and south Kentuckians laid siege to the stockade in Briceville, freed the convicts, and burned the buildings to the ground. This time they helped the convicts go free, providing clothes, food, and transportation to the prisoners. Some of these inmates set out for the Kentucky border, while others joined the miners in their march on Coal Creek, where they liberated more prisoners, burned company property, and looted a store owned by a mine superintendent. They freed about three hundred prisoners. As the *Knoxville Tribune* wrote, the "miners have acted for themselves and have solved the convict problem with a vengeance." All that remained after the quick uprising was a burned stockade and convict clothes "scattered for miles along the Coal Creek Valley."

In a brilliant bid to avoid incrimination, prominent leaders of the miners' campaign all resigned from their positions three days before the attack, issuing public statements that only peaceful, legislative tactics could abolish the lease. A large public dance was also organized the night of the rebellion to provide an alibi for those most likely to be targeted as ringleaders. One miner cleverly remarked, "Nero fiddled while Rome burned, but Coal Creek danced while Briceville burned." Though union leader Eugene Merrell claimed the actions were totally spontaneous, this was clearly false: in addition to arranging alibis for visible leaders, mine workers pre-arranged clothing for hundreds of convicts, cut telegraph wires to prevent outside communication, wore masks and padded clothing to hide their identities, and chose a night when Anderson County's sheriff was conveniently out of town.

Two days later, excited by their earlier success, miners attacked the stockade at the Oliver Springs mine, also burning the buildings, looting the company store of clothes, and liberating almost two hundred more prisoners. This attack effectively rid the last East Tennessee mines of convict labor. Though many of these prisoners were recaptured, it is estimated that at least one-third of them escaped completely. Given the abominable death rate of convict laborers, then, it is safe to say that the miners' and prisoners' joint actions easily saved hundreds of lives. Forty years after the rebellion, Mollie Scoggins of Coal Creek recalled the ease with which the prisoners integrated themselves into the small towns after their release. "The convicts," she said, "did not do any damage when they were turned loose, though some people were afraid they would, and when one came to my door for food and picked up my little boy I was scared and just trembled. But he petted and talked to him and I thought 'he is probably a married man with small children of his own.'" Even after some prisoners were recaptured, raiding parties of East Tennessee miners would often confront the arresting officers and reliberate the prisoners.

Arson, looting, and the liberation of hundreds of Black prisoners by mostly white miners in the post–Civil War South all created tremendous levels of tension and controversy in the Tennessee press. Some union leaders and miner-sympathizers expressed hesitation and disapproval, while the Democratic Party's newspapers directed fury and outrage against the "rampant lawlessness" of the treasonous miners. This could be interpreted as the beginning of a loss of public support, though merchants and farmers continued to aid the miners. Throughout the course of the insurrection, not one of the thousands of miners, merchants, or farmers implicated in the rebellion testified against another comrade.

More important than public appearances, the actions of October and November 1891 were extremely effective: robbed of their strikebreakers, east Tennessee coal companies were forced to hire back the very same workers who had torched their own property, and then were made to grant them all of the concessions they had previously demanded. Union organization increased drastically as well, demonstrating that at least the miners themselves were able to see through the lies hurled at them by the political press. Nevertheless, the convict lease system still existed on paper, and mines in mid-Tennessee continued to use prisoners. Inevitably, on New Year's Day 1892, Governor Buchanan sent an occupying force of eighty militiamen, along with two hundred convicts, back to Coal Creek. The troops quickly erected a fort, and "settled in for a long sojourn."

The Occupation of Coal Creek

The citizens of Briceville and Coal Creek quickly came to detest the small occupying army sent by Governor Buchanan; the drunken and disorderly conduct of the troops, along with their "molesting of citizens on public roads," infuriated locals. That one group of guards, in posing for a photograph, accidentally discharged their weapons and murdered a convict only contributed to this reputation. Their presence also increased tensions between TCIR and the state government, as the continued occupation

led to fierce debate and ultimately lawsuits over who should be financially responsible for the militia's presence. The convict lease was becoming
ever more expensive and unpopular, and arguments over the roles of public and private heated up, even as such distinctions became increasingly
meaningless. Much of eastern Tennesseans' ire became was now directed at
the occupation itself, with "indiscriminate shooting" taking place between
miners and soldiers.[16]

Things remained quiet in eastern Tennessee for the first half of 1892,
with some miners channeling their energy into a cooperative mining
venture, which in fact was largely initiated by the one-time president of
TCMC, B.A. Jenkins. It was Jenkins who initially brought convict labor to Coal Creek, and his "cooperative" venture, though supported by
many Briceville miners, also came under obvious criticism for that reason.
One Knights of Labor member remarked that he could not "find in the
prospectus anything at all concerning cooperation, it is simply a stock
company, nothing more." Representatives of capital remained totally in
control of the enterprise, meaning, in the words of one letter writer, the
cooperative basically "amounted to a hill of beans."

While some eastern miners tried their hand at "cooperative" capitalism, workers in the mid-Tennessee town of Tracy City were finally driven
to rebel. In the early morning of August 13, 1892, after a refusal on the
part of company officials to provide more work to free miners, the workers
marched on the stockades. Between 150 and 300 miners looted supplies
from the company, put the convicts on a train to Nashville, and burned
the stockades to the ground. The convict guards were totally outnumbered
and put up no resistance. Evidently the miners had plotted their action
even while peacefully appealing to their bosses for more work. Shapiro
writes:

> The preparations involved both attention to timing and mili-
> tary training. For weeks before the assault, the miners met on
> Sundays in a "holler back of a hill" to consider their options
> and eventually to set the time when they would "run the con-
> victs off the mountain." In those same weeks, the local sheriff,
> Captain Alec Saunders, "drilled the men," giving the miners
> some pointers in military comportment and discipline.

16 Soldiers were also excluded from town gatherings. One such gathering—a "grand pic-
nic" and dance held to celebrate the one-year anniversary of the attack on the stockade and militia in Briceville—clearly heightened such tensions. The dance floor and
stage for the event were intentionally built out of lumber torn from the old stockade.

News of the rebellion spread to nearby Marion County, and two days later miners marched on the nearby Inman stockade, disarming guards along the way who were being sent as reinforcements. Sympathetic to the miners' cause, the local sheriff refused to act. The Inman raid emulated earlier attacks, though due to the close proximity of a railroad, the miners chose to dismantle the stockade piece by piece rather than use fire. By the next day, TCIR's coal mines at Tracy City and Whitwell; its coke ovens at Tracy City, Whitwell, and Victoria; its ore mine at Inman; and its blast furnaces at South Pittsburgh had all been shut down.

Beyond their economic damage, these attacks signaled the spread of the coal miners' insurrection westward into middle Tennessee. Despite calls for caution from some union leaders, within two days of the Inman raid, a group of between one hundred and two hundred men assaulted the prison house in Oliver Springs. For the first time, the guards refused to release the convicts, and instead a half-hour shootout ensued. The miners chose to retreat with their wounded, but sent word throughout the eastern part of the state. Incredibly, using only the telegraph and word of mouth, they managed to return the next day 1,500-strong. Despite two military companies being sent to reinforce Oliver Springs, the workers used their numerical superiority to negotiate the removal of the convicts from the stockade and disarm the militia. After burning the stockade, they provided a train for the convicts and their guards, but forced the militiamen to walk all the way home. The miners then marched northward, determined to end the occupation once and for all in nearby Coal Creek.

Attacking the Occupation, Ending the Insurrection

On August 15, in the midst of the raids at Tracy City, Inman, and later Oliver Springs, Governor Buchanan privately concluded that he might finally end the convict lease. He threatened TCIR with this because the company had refused to pay their "rent" for almost eleven months and had not reimbursed the government for a variety of other expenses incurred during the revolts of the previous year. The rebellion of convicts and free miners was pouring salt on the open wound of tension between Tennessee's state and capital. Buchanan was furious with TCIR's refusal to pay the nearly $100,000 debt they owed; TCIR was equally frustrated with the ineptitude and incompetence of Buchanan's government in quelling the rebellion, which was in itself largely due to tensions between the rivaling Democratic and Farmers' Alliance factions of Tennessee's governing elite.

Whatever Buchanan's intentions may have been, the rebellion in eastern Tennessee had spread well beyond the containment of mediation and empty promises. On August 18, the captain in charge of the occupying militia, who was in Coal Creek to negotiate with the thousands of angry miners pouring into town, was himself taken hostage. Robbed of their superior, the superintendent and warden agreed to give the convicts up to the miners. When informed of this decision, a Lieutenant Fyffe, who was the acting commander of the fort, threatened to turn his Gatling gun on any guards or convicts leaving the fort.

Hearing this threat, the miners' patient waiting quickly came to an end. Scores of workers began firing upon the fort from positions in the surrounding hills and then charged it. Two militiamen were killed in the attack, and many others wounded, though it is unknown if any miners died. Inexplicably, despite better training and far superior numbers, the miners quickly retreated.[17] Though another company of militiamen was fired upon by miners elsewhere, the main skirmish occurred at this fort.

It is difficult to understand why the men retreated as they did. Over two thousand armed farmers, merchants, and mineworkers had gathered in Coal Creek, ready to end the convict lease and the occupation of their town. The number of militiamen present, even when counting the military companies on their way as reinforcement, pales in comparison to this force. In her book, Shapiro argues:

> East Tennesseans were acutely aware of the recent use of federal army regulars in the Buffalo switchmen's strike and of the overwhelming use of state troops in the showdown between the Carnegie Steel Company and the Homestead steelworkers. The outcome of these conflicts surely contributed to the miners' refusal to engage in pitched battle.

It may also be the case that the miners simply did not want an all-out war with the state of Tennessee. Many of these workers still considered themselves loyal patriots; they were largely pushed into their insurrection unwillingly, and they had rarely if ever articulated a vision of society so

---

17   In total, four soldiers were killed that day, and it seems that each died under suspicious circumstances: two were reportedly shot by fellow soldiers, and the other two killed when their weapons accidentally discharged. Even newspapers that were harshly critical of the miners reported upon the abominable training and conduct of the militia in comparison with the miners, who drew upon both their experience as Civil War vets as well as upon the past year's skirmishes at prison stockades.

radically different as to justify a full military campaign against state and capital. Their tactics had already gone beyond the demands they spoke of: though the struggle for independent checkweighmen and legal tender would continue for decades at some worksites, it was clear that the convict lease would soon be abolished. Their short-term goal had already been accomplished, and no larger ambitions had taken its place. Though it would be convenient to blame their retreat upon the cautious words and selfish intentions of this or that representative, in fact there is no historical evidence to suggest this. Lacking a more radical critique of society and property ownership in southern Appalachia, the miners' insurrection probably contained within it the seeds of its own decay.

After the events of August 18, hundreds of troops swept through the region, arresting several hundred miners who had chosen not to flee Tennessee. The majority of those arrested refused to show up for court so consistently that their charges were either dropped or reduced to court costs and a fine. Only two men out of the thousands of insurrectionaries were ever given prison time for their involvement: S.D. Moore received one year for conspiracy, and D.B. Monroe—notably dubbed "anarchist Monroe" by the press—was given seven years for involuntary manslaughter and interfering with state convicts.

Prisoners and miners alike continued to rebel in whatever ways they could. On April 19, 1893, almost one hundred miners attempted to liberate convicts from the Tracy City stockade only to have their dynamite rendered useless by heavy rainfall. In July 1894, prisoners from that same stockade managed to get their dynamite to work, consequently killing several guards and destroying company property. In late 1893, eastern Tennessee miners engaged in a partially successful eleven-week strike against a wage reduction, and several walkouts also occurred in 1894 as part of a nationwide strike led by the UMWA.

Unfortunately, the disappearance of hundreds of militant miners who were fleeing their court cases took its toll on rebellious activity in Tennessee. By the late 1890s, eastern Tennessee was no longer the hotbed of class war it had been. In the absence of this activity, the racism of many white miners rose to the surface, and tensions between those miners who supported the establishment of a southern (and likely segregated) miners' federation and those who did not brought organizing almost to a standstill. Though eastern and middle Tennessee had given birth to one of the most widespread, best organized, and "successful" insurrections in American working-class history, the coalfields remained quiet for the remainder of the twentieth century. About a year after the insurrection had faded, on December 31, 1895, Tennessee became the first state to abolish the convict lease. Other states, like Alabama, would continue to use the system to exploit unpaid Black labor for decades.

Lessons from the Coalfields

It would be difficult to overestimate the commitment and determination of the convicts and miners who repeatedly defied the Tennessee laws between July 1891 and December 1895. Their rebellion brilliantly combined a cunning ability to play on pre-existing divisions in Tennessee's ruling class with effective, easily reproducible tactics that brought immediate economic relief to thousands of workers, not to mention the liberation of hundreds of prisoners. Their tactics of armed stockade raids, looting company stores, and burning company property combined short-term gains like increasing the workers' striking power with the longer-term strategic value of rendering the convict lease cost-prohibitive. That the stockade raid was reproducible is demonstrated simply by the fact that some version of this tactic was used ten times in just thirteen months. Though it was an armed struggle, the battle over the convict lease remained social rather than military in nature, popular and generalized in character, and involved both waged and "nonwaged" workers in the community.

Particularly impressive was the determined refusal of the miners and convicts to acquiesce to the niceties of "public opinion."[18] The rebels continued with attack after attack, despite being bombarded with calls for caution from their own, as well as fierce condemnation from nearly every newspaper in the state. After their initial flirtation with legislative sessions, they remained resolutely committed to a course of action that accomplished its own ends without regard to editorials or public opinion polls. And, despite the presumed importance of that great abstraction we call "the public," their numbers grew tremendously with every prisoner they freed and every stockade they burned. Their primary tactic was not the

---

18 Movement leaders raised the fear of militancy alienating "public opinion" even as statistics on union membership during the rebellion point (paradoxically) to the *increased* appeal of the movement to miners. The fuel for their fear resided mainly in newspaper articles, which in the late-nineteenth century were primarily mouthpieces for the various factions of the Republican and Democratic Parties. One is reminded of the "public" referred to in newspapers today, that passive, middle-class media construction that opaquely sits as judge and jury over the actions of all the dispossessed.

generalized riot of much of that period's labor unrest, but massive and informal—albeit semi-disciplined—armed attacks on state and capitalist property (and the liberation of prisoners, who were treated as property). Ultimately, they achieved their goal of the lease's abolition, with a bit of irony that itself teaches a lesson: Much as it was the conservative hawk Richard Nixon who ended the Vietnam War, it was the racist Governor Turney (who as a judge had consistently supported the lease in court) who ended the convict lease in Tennessee. The politician in office is unimportant; it is our own capacity as a social force that matters.

Despite the incredible militancy and courage of its participants, this rebellion remained largely conservative in its aims. At least until the very end of the rebellion, free miners' external and internal dialogue continually reaffirmed the individual rights of land ownership under an agrarian commonwealth; tied the "right" to rebel with homeownership, masculinity, citizenship, and the Declaration of Independence; and articulated their rebellion as centrally driven by the single-issue of the convict lease. In demanding an end to the lease, miners often framed their demand as for the "free" competition of labor. As for the convicts who rebelled against their own regime of work and control, it is more difficult to assess their varied motives and visions. Insofar as their history continued a legacy of revolt against both work and punishment, passed down from slavery, their struggle has a clear anticapitalist and antiauthoritarian trajectory, although it may not have been articulated explicitly as such.

To judge by the explicit declarations and recorded conversations of the free miners, however, the insurrection was reformist in character and mostly driven by preindustrial conceptions of labor and politics. By 1893–1894, this dialogue had begun to shift, with workers tipping their hats to radical labor struggles in other parts of the country, acknowledging the new realities of their industrial peonage, and the true role of the political elite in Nashville and Washington, DC. But the ideas of class war present in this new discourse came too late to drive the insurrection further than it had already gone. Given the likely fact of federal military intervention and the weak labor movements in most surrounding states, it is possible that it couldn't have gone much further anyway.

A paradox exists here: On the one hand, it seems problematic to consider such a fiery and violent eruption merely from within a reformist framework, regardless of how the miners' leaders articulated themselves. On the other, militant tactics do not alone make for revolutionary content or direction. This paradox between form and content is a constant problem for the radical student of southern history, and to an extent for the American anarchist in general. In a region largely lacking in explicitly radical or revolutionary traditions—partly due to an absence of the immigration that characterized other hotbeds of labor strife, but nonetheless being an area having a vast history of inspiring homespun rebellions—it can be difficult to know how to read the intentions and desires of our southern forebears. The single-issue nature of Tennesseans' struggle over the convict lease seems fairly apparent: had the miners and convicts transcended this form, the insurrection would presumably have looked differently, or shifted in scope as time went on. But to only understand the desires and interests of the eastern Tennessee rebels in terms of the limited language and theoretical framework available to them at the time is also a mistake. We cannot believe that thousands of Black and white convicts, miners, and small shopkeepers armed themselves, attacked soldiers and property, liberated prisoners, and disobeyed strict racial codes of conduct merely for the sake of a simple policy change.

A 1915 photo of convicts leased out to timber companies in Florida. In many southern states outside of Tennessee, the convict lease system continued on for decades.

This also raises a conflict between the traditional progressive historian on the one hand—who tends to treat uprisings and class war in the literalist sense, interpreting the interests or desires of the proletariat in a strictly demand-based way—and the starry-eyed anarchist on the other, who is intent on always reading an implicit radical desire in the actions of his or her would-be comrades. The former is a conservative approach, too timid and terrified to step beyond the role of the objective historian, one that often silences history's more radical but less literate protagonists and ultimately fails to grasp larger patterns of conflict and development. With the latter we obviously hold certain sympathies, but the radical approach can sometimes be *too* anxious to read an inherent revolutionary meaning in the tactics of the historical rebel. Perhaps sometimes a tactic is just that.

We would argue that the burning of Tennessee's prison stockades teaches us less about the desires of its immediate participants and more about the larger nature of the social war in Appalachia at that time; of the limitations and possibilities of a newly industrializing proletariat in a geographically and politically isolated area; and of the importance of a socially tight-knit community that had developed a number of "apolitical" but autonomous institutions—from Elks lodges to baseball teams to women's auxiliaries to brass bands. In their Appalachian enclave, these groups were far more independent from the state than the decaying remains of civil society that surround us today, and they seemed to play a galvanizing rather than stultifying role.

In directly and immediately accomplishing the (albeit temporary) halt of the convict-as-forced-scab, the stockade attacks brought to the horizon the *possibility* of a self-directed activity driven by something other than a politics of demands and negotiation. But it never entirely reached this point, as the cessation of hostilities remained conditional on a policy change from Tennessee's state legislature. The struggle remained demand-based, and its participants remained *subjects* of the regime they attacked. Our contemporary situation pushes us to ask: what could have driven this insurrection further, beyond the scope of demands or the role of the citizen-subject?

Beyond the Stockades

Following the stockade wars in Tennessee, miners in Appalachia continued to struggle around a wide range of specific grievances and general conflicts. Wages, safety issues, independent checkweighmen—as well as broader struggles around liberty and autonomy in communities where, increasingly, The company controlled every aspect of social life—continued to be issues for decades to come. Capitalists would arrive at the conclusion that the best way to prevent labor unrest was to control not just the factory floor but every aspect of daily life, from housing and food to religious worship, gender norms, and recreation.

Given the reality of a more rural population, a long history of agrarian servitude, and the popularity of the lucrative convict lease, the forms of class conflict in the South in the decades after the 1890s look very different than those in the rest of the country. Because the economy, alongside social hierarchies around gender and race, developed so uniquely in the South, resistance developed differently as well. Struggles that challenged the power structure in the southeastern United States therefore very quickly came to challenge a number of basic assumptions about what it meant to organize and rebel as a class. In retrospect this might be understood to have been an advantage at least as much as a detriment. By this we refer to the possibility of wildcat strikes that have no clear demands at all, and also to the inclusion into the struggle of unwaged segments of the population and concerns around everyday life that have little or nothing to do with immediate workplace conflicts.[19] In our region, the workplace has often not been the center of class violence at all, a trait that southern history now shares with the contemporary United States as a whole. The lack of unionism here is certainly (and painfully) evident in the low wages we're paid, but equally evident is the conservative role such unions play in shoring up the power structures of democracy and capital. When riots break out down South, at least the state has one less institution with which to reliably negotiate a return to social peace.

That class rebellion in the South centered so clearly around resisting regimes of punishment and state control remains an important marker for the country as a whole. The "loophole" of the Thirteenth Amendment, which would allow for involuntary servitude as a form of punishment, provided a vital pool of virtually-free labor for the national economy. It was to the detriment of the labor movement as a whole that it ignored this fact, as a well as a testament to that movement's racism. This intersection of race and violence never ceases to haunt us.

---

19   We would also point out that challenging what it means to rebel as a class requires recognizing the role that ecology and wilderness have played in many of the struggles of our region, and how the destruction of certain wilderness areas has functioned to discipline the poor while reproducing a class forced to sell its labor.

History can have a strange way of spinning full circle. As a tactic, the burning of prison stockades and liberation of prisoners in small backwoods towns like Coal Creek and Briceville was once so peripheral to mainstream organized labor that historians barely gave it a nod. Now, as traditional organized labor goes the way of the dodo—and as the United States creates more economically redundant populations and in turn incarcerates and tortures more people per capita than any nation on Earth—we can fully appreciate the relevance and brilliance of a class struggle that directly linked itself to a generalized attack on prisons. What was once peripheral has now become central. We need a "stockade war" now more than ever.

The emergence of textile mills in the South in the early-twentieth century followed closely behind the building of railroads and the harnessing of rivers, the felling of timber and the enclosure of pastures along the Blue Ridge Mountains and across the Piedmont plateau. Northern industrialists were no strangers to the bounty of natural resources, raw materials, free land, and cheap labor that awaited them in the southern states after the Civil War. The end of an agrarian capitalism based in slave labor forced a new class of southern merchants, bankers, investors, and landowners to learn from their northern invaders (some of whom were already familiar business partners) and embrace the possibility of industrialism.

While the convict lease temporarily helped solve a labor problem in certain industries, cotton became another solution to the crises of power and capital that the white southern business and political elite shared. Sharecropping, or tenant farming, focused on cash-crop production and the crippling debt of its tenants to the landholder, while industrialization, in the form of textile production, served to put to work the increasingly vast reserve of landless laborers and precarious farm families who grew tired of tending others' land or who found no hope in the crop lien system.

Wherever landless farmers found themselves in debt due to the forced planting of cash crops like cotton or tobacco, they also discovered new forms  of resistance in an isolating environment. The burning of barns that stored cotton before market and other forms of property destruction aimed at the landlord or the merchant were rampant at the turn of the century. In a time when rural alliances between Black sharecroppers were threatened by the terror of Jim Crow and white vigilantism, arson in particular provided a relatively safe and effective means of enacting revenge or attacking profits. So ubiquitous that it became the center of a William Faulkner story, barn burning as a tactic was used by Black and white sharecroppers alike as a defense against the otherwise omnipotent will of large landowners.

On the production side, southern merchants invested first in mills—often from capital they accumulated through their tenants and sharecroppers—in order to attract foreign owners to towns that were already well acquainted with cotton production. The Piedmont, a plateau range that extends from the Appalachian Mountains to the Atlantic coastal plain, as wide as three hundred miles in North Carolina, became the prime target for textile mill construction. With plentiful rivers and coal supplying the power, and an infrastructure that supplied raw materials, tax-free land, and ample pools of cheap labor, the industrialization of the Piedmont was a dream come true for bankers, merchants, lawyers, speculators, developers, and investors up, down, and across the Atlantic.

But by the early 1920s, in the years before the Depression, textile shares were already falling and payouts in stock dividends were scarce. The fickle nature of the new market economy was intensified by the constant overproduction of raw cotton and textile commodities. Mill owners looked to northern and European economists, management specialists, and labor scientists to solve the problem of falling profits. The *stretch-out system*, as workers came to call it, was introduced. New management teams forced workers to produce more for the same (or less) in a shortened amount of time, while intensifying the phenomenon of "night work," which simply meant keeping the machinery running twenty-four hours a day. These new techniques of extraction plagued workers and quickly inflamed tensions in the mills between workers, superintendents, managers, and owners.

It was not merely the working conditions and the abysmally low wages that drove millworkers to revolt. The generation of millworkers who had grown up on the farm but recently entered wage work were not disciplined in the ways of the clock and the whistle. Young, often single women were the first to fill the new factories and the first to strike. Millworkers, young and old alike, maintained strong bonds of kinship and traditions of mutual aid that were passed down in the foothills or the mountains, before the emergence of the "welfare capitalism" of the mill village. Beyond maintaining this sense of identity and community, many millworkers and their families still lived on land that they owned, at most just one generation removed from the experience of creating their own means of survival and their own customs of care. These bonds would form the basis of a rebellion that spread beyond Appalachia into the heart of the Piedmont, the most profitable textile region in the country.

"The strike was a spontaneous demonstration of unorganized workers, with those most warlike members of the human race, enraged girls, in the vanguard."

—Irving Bernstein, labor historian

"Well, we had some that was just, you know, daredevils like me. I guess I was a daredevil, because I went several times.... I was arrested once. I got away before they got me in jail.... While they were arguing about taking us, two or three truckloads of us, why, I saw a chance to slip out. There was a friend of ours from Hampton that drove a taxi, and he'd pulled up to the side. I was a'standing up in a truck and my sister was with me, and I said, 'Let's get out of here.' And she said, 'They'll kill us if we do.' And I said, 'I'm agoing.' And I jumped out and she did too, and we got in that car."

—Bessie Edens, striker

"Anarchy threatened to overwhelm law. Borders were constantly in danger of transgression. All these unruly women, fascinating as they might be, were also terrifying. They were the ones who constantly threatened to transgress one of the most emotionally charged of all frontiers, that of gender."

—Robert Whalen, journalist

WILD HEARTS IN THE SOUTHERN MILLS:

Women in the Strike Wave Against the Textile Industry, 1929–1930

EVERYONE TRULY BELIEVED THAT THE SOUTH WAS, ONCE AGAIN, ABOUT TO explode. That was the common warning found in the scores of scholarly articles and books, local newspapers and bulletins, and labor movement journals that chronicled the massive strike wave that hit Tennessee, North and South Carolina, and Virginia from 1929 to 1930. Metaphors invoking uncontrollable elements, especially fires and storms, were woven alongside the well-worn verbiage of war.[1] A second migration to the south occurred, this time not of industrial investors, but of academics, journalists, authors, politicians, trade unionists, and Communist organizers. Lines in a turf war about who would represent the interests and image of the opposing forces were already being drawn before the first walkout in Elizabethton, Tennessee, on March 12, 1929.

Anne O'Hare McCormick, a reporter with the *New York Times* who covered southern labor conflicts, wrote in 1930 that the strike wave

---

1   Did these illustrations sensationalize the situations or reflect a true image of class war erupting on the assumed "peace" of the industrially blooming, postwar South? This era was much less afraid to use terms of class war, as Anne McCormick from the *New York Times* proved, but the southern media's role in maintaining the myth that labor and capital should have the same goals (progress), and thus exist harmoniously, is exhibited in how "shocked" the southern press was to discover that there were tensions in the mills.

"involved 17,000 workers and was characterized by savage violence, murders, kidnappings, evictions, military intervention everywhere and white-hot partisanship. There were no bystanders in this conflict; it had all the elements of class war."[2] Tom Tippett, a northern labor riot tourist who spent the summers of 1920 and 1930 in Elizabethon, Gastonia, and Marion claimed that, "17,000 or 18,000 workers rebelled by walking out on strike in at least fifteen different communities."[3] The foremost historian on Gastonia writes, "In South Carolina alone some eighty-one strikes involved 79,027 workers."[4] From the perspective of individual actions, historian Allen Tullos believes there were 175 strikes in the Piedmont textile mills from the late 1920s to the early 1930s.[5] The bureaucrats of industry and labor had their own numbers, as did the local press in each uprooted town. But more poignant and pressing than any sum of numbers and figures of mere "people on strike," is that the walkouts, blockades, occupations, conspiracies and attacks on infrastructure and management were spontaneously initiated by women and men and youth, pulling on their ties of kinship and friendship to counter the cotton empire.

The people of the southern textile mills were crudely and simply interpreted by most of the northern writers that flocked there. The typical male millworker was written as a backwards, ignorant, moonshinin' patriarch who ruled his household with force and cowered in the face of his employer. The women were barefoot and pregnant, with no options and no voice. The families lived "timelessly" as if they "belonged to the past" and knew nothing of the outside world, lost in the smoke of the Blue Ridge Mountains or trapped in the time capsule of the mill village. They were illiterate and superstitious; they distrusted foreigners and understood nothing of politics. They were walking cartoons whose accents and colloquialisms made them difficult to translate and whose close-knit customs made them awkward to interpret. Whether these characterizations drawn by northern writers were the results of intentional sensationalism or a lack of intelligibility, the result is that a grotesque stereotype of white, poor southern people was reproduced by the first and second wave of writings about millworkers from the strikes. It would not be until the end of

---

2   Robert Weldon Whalen, *"Like Fire in Broom Straw": Southern Journalism and the Textile Strikes of 1929–1931* (Westport: Greenwood Press, 2001), 2.

3   Tom Tippett, *When Southern Labor Stirs* (Huntington: Appalachian Movement Press, 1972).

4   John Salmond, *Gastonia, 1929: The Story of the Loray Mill Strike* (Chapel Hill: University of North Carolina Press, 1995), 9.

5   Whalen, *"Like Fire in Broom Straw,"* 8.

the twentieth century that a new generation of historians who sought to understand the complexities of the cotton mill world would find the survivors of this strike wave and listen to their stories, which deeply contradicted the virulent myths perpetuated by journalists a generation earlier.[6]

Many reporters and labor historians projected the monotonous and miserable situation of factory work one-dimensionally onto the people who performed those tasks. However, the tens of thousands of individuals across hundreds of miles, who participated and supported one another in these struggles, cannot be represented simply by their wages or their output, or the hours they worked. Nor can they be easily summarized by a series of observable traits simply because they shared a common experience of mill "life." Work was simple to explain. Life was what they fought for outside the shadow of the mill.

Finding Themselves at the Mill

For the majority of the textile mills located in the Piedmont region, "the mills were cornerstones of the South's class and race architecture."[7] The intentionally segregated industries of tobacco, for Black workers, and cotton, for white workers, assured that a cross-race solidarity among the poorest workers in the country would be difficult to achieve. Active recruitment by the cheerleaders of these industries of white tenant farmers, sharecroppers, and subsistence farmers from the mountains of Appalachia promised a new, comfortable modernity—where one could live in a brand new house with electricity and running water, walk to nearby stores, or use the mill's transportation services to stay on one's land.

The centralization of working families in towns and cities coincided with the rise in sharecropping and tenant farming as the dominant mode of agricultural production in the southern states. For landless farmers, enclosure and subdivision of large tracts of land for cash crop production forced many into a debt-bond with landowners, or pushed them to try a life in the mills in hopes of saving up money and returning to the land.

For the descendants of the Scotch-Irish settlers of eastern Tennessee, the landing of textile mills followed decades of resource extraction in the great conifers and hardwoods of the Blue Ridge Mountains and their mineral rich valleys, where many men left family steads to follow the railroad, timber,

---

6   Even authors whose firsthand accounts and early studies of the strike wave, like historian Irving Bernstein and labor movement advocate Tom Tippett, presented these types of narrow understandings of millworkers.

7   Whalen, *"Like Fire in Broom Straw,"* 84.

Gaston Gazette

Mill women were often grossly represented if they were unaware of the outside world. Here we see a line of women in the inspection department at the Loray Mill in the late 1920s with flapper haircuts, sailor shirts and dresses, all styles that were popular (and controversial) in that era all over the country. In Elizabethton, historians report that the girls and women were hyper-aware of the newest fashion trends, which was perfectly logical considering they were making the very fabric that revolutionized the fashion industry in the 1920s.

and coal expeditions. A generation earlier, some of these families would have fought against the coal companies and the convict lease; the textile mills represent another step in their proletarianization. While over 80 percent of families still owned their own land in the 1920s, the average homestead acreage was rapidly shrinking in size. Ecological destruction in the mountains forced families to sell their labor: "By the time Carter County was 'timbered out' in the 1920s, farm families had crept upward to the barren ridge lands or grown dependent on 'steady work and cash wages.'" Many mountain folks who entered mill life did so at a distance, attempting to retain as much autonomy on their land as possible while constantly adapting to new opportunities to make ends meet outside of the home.[8]

The City of Power

The spark that ignited a surge of wildcat strikes in the heart of the cotton empire was not set off along the cluster of textile towns in the Piedmont

8   Jacquelyn Dowd Hall, "Disorderly Women: Gender and Labor Militancy in the Appalachian South," in *Half Sisters of History: Southern Women and the American Past*, ed. Catherine Clinton (Durham: Duke University Press, 1994), 184.

of central North Carolina, but from the peripheral mountains and hollers in the southern Appalachian mountains. Elizabethton, dubbed "The City of Power" after construction of the state's first hydroelectric dam on the Watauga River in 1912, was a burgeoning industrial city along two rivers in Carter County in the Blue Ridges of East Tennessee. In the early 1920s, talk of a textile mill arriving in the town generated much excitement in the area. As rumors settled into official plans, Elizabethton tripled in size, from about two thousand residents to just around eight thousand during the decade that two German-owned textile mills opened downtown. The Bemberg mill, the smaller of the two, opened first, in 1926, already world famous as a "manufacturer of high-quality rayon yarn by an exclusive stretch-spin process."[9] The larger Glanzstoff plant opened two years later, introducing their new "viscose" process to make rayon yarn. Together they employed between 3,200 and 5,500 men and women and youth, as young as fourteen, in to order to convert wood and cotton byproducts into this new synthetic "silk" called rayon.[10]

The city of Elizabethton offered the parent company of both mills, J.P. Bemberg, free land to build on and ten years of tax exemption.[11] This type of courting by the southern business class was commonplace at the time; most northern and European mill owners were not interested in moving their operations to the South until a solid local financing of the project existed, alongside a promise of continued lower production costs. The agreement by local merchants and investors to donate tax-exempt land and guarantee low wages was common knowledge. A young worker in the mills, Bessie Edens, remembered hearing these terms directly from the German mill-owners: "In fact, one of them [German owners or managers] told me what these people [local merchants] told them when they first mentioned coming here. They're the ones that caused them to pay low wages, the people here in town. Said women wasn't used to working, and

---

9   Ibid., 183.
10   "The post-World War I fashion revolution, combined with protective tariffs, spurred the American rayon industry's spectacular growth.... Dominated by a handful of large European companies, rayon spinning mills clustered along the Appalachian mountain chain." The exact number of workers at the mills is difficult to assess because of a fire that destroyed records. Jacquelyn Hall quotes the number as 3,200 active employees before the strike, while union organizers and labor movement witnesses on the ground frequently quote 4,000–5,500 (Jacquelyn Dowd Hall et al., *Like a Family: The Making of a Southern Cotton Mill World* [Chapel Hill: University of North Carolina Press, 1987], 246).
11   Hall, "Disorderly Women," 184; and Irving Bernstein. *The Lean Years: A History of the American Worker 1920–1933* (Boston: Houghton Mifflin Company, 1960), 14.

they'd work for almost nothing, and the men would work for low wages. *That's the way they got the plant here.*"[12]

The religion of free labor that northern industrialists proselytized, and to which southern merchants were converted by necessity (rather than morality) after the Civil War, rested on an orthodox belief that work was defined as the exchange of labor for wages. As industrial work strengthened its hold in the South, the class that controlled these mills increasingly understood all forms of life that existed outside the factory as merely sites to reproduce the labor force, rather than as places where labor was also performed. The invisibility of women's unwaged work of caring and tending to a household and family—whether it be their parents, extended family, or their own children—contributed to the myth that "women weren't used to working." Mountain women in the 1920s, whether single or married, young or old, were experts at keeping plants, animals, and humans alive and healthy in what amounted to a lifetime of labor invisible to those who believed that work was defined by a wage. Many women were also accustomed to balancing their expected duties at home with what they called "public work," or various precarious and flexible jobs performed outside the home in exchange for money.[13]

It was men who traveled from the surrounding hills and mountains to build the giant mills and outfit them with spindles, reels, looms, chemicals, and clocks. It was also men who performed the incredibly dangerous roles in the chemical divisions of rayon production, which involved soaking the cellulose from wood and cotton in an acid bath to produce the "viscose" solution that would be spun into a soft, silk-like yarn. But women in southern Appalachia were certainly used to working, and they filled the mills—accounting for 44 percent of the workforce at the Glanzstoff mill and 30 percent of the Bemberg mill by 1929. Men and women were initially coerced to work "for almost nothing," but the German owners and locals who were invested in the mill did not receive the docile and malleable workers they expected.[14]

Even with the one thousand newly constructed Watauga Development Corporation homes paid for by the mills, a true company town or "mill

12 Bessie Edens, interview, Southern Oral History Program Collection, Louis Round Wilson Special Collections Library, University of North Carolina (our italics).

13 Hall, "Disorderly Women," 186–187.

14 The Bemberg and Glanzstoff mills were not exemplary in their low wages: women's wages usually ranged from $6–9 for over fifty hours a week, depending on their skill level, while men's ranged from more often from $10–12 a week. Fifty-five to sixty-hour work weeks, including overnight shifts and half-Saturdays, were commonplace (Tippett, *When Southern Labor Stirs*, 25); Hall, "Disorderly Women," 185.

village" like those of the Piedmont never emerged in Elizabethton. This was due, in large part, to the decision of workers who came from the highlands and hollers outside of town to not leave their family farms, the majority of which were shrinking but still owned by a family member. This goes for many, but not all, of the single girls and women who chose to commute into work with other family members, neighbors, and friends, instead of making the move into downtown boardinghouses. The connection that these folks retained to traditional ways of living and supporting one another, customs that did not centralize the cash exchange or wages of mill and town, emerged as a unique and crucial resource during the upheavals to follow.

The "rugged individualism" that mountain people were accused of in their choice to live in difficult to access places, often far from neighbors, also created refuges away from the mill-controlled town, where plans could be made and actions strategized away from company spies, national guardsmen, union officials, and the courts.[15]

The Misery of Work

What began as a demand for increased wages quickly came to include all aspects of the drudgery of mill work: hard rules, speed-ups, pay cuts, encroachment on the weekend, and injuries from dangerous tasks. While men were still paid more on average than women for comparable labor, the shared reality—that no one was able to make the living they expected in the new industry—created solidarity across divisions of labor and lower hierarchies of position.

Margaret Bowen and Bessie Edens, two of the most dedicated and radical strikers, were technically "foreladies" in their section. Management at the mill promoted young women to positions of authority, perhaps hoping to train them from a young age to be sympathetic to the mill and enforce evolving tactics of efficiency and control. They failed to predict that women, like seventeen-year-old Bessie Edens, who was "supervising" seventy-five other friends, relatives, and neighbors, would strengthen their collective opposition against management by defending these relationships over symbolic positions of power.[16]

---

15   Unionists frequently blamed the failure of labor organizing in the mountainous South on rural southerner's "pioneer roots" and their disinterest in working with outsiders. The opposition to centralization and representation were translated as "rugged individualism." However, these unionists failed to understand the mutual aid that was at the core of mountain life, because it was based on kinship and bioregion rather than ideology.

16   Hall, "Disorderly Women," 187; Bessie Edens, interview, Southern Oral History

As extensive interviews through the Southern Oral History Program and Jacquelyn Hall's work have shown, there were a wide range of experiences that led women to seek work outside of the home and wind up at the factory gates in the late 1920s. While many young women decided to live in the communities that they were raised in, this did not imply that young women lived uncritical, traditional lives or did not aspire to lives beyond both the holler and the mill. Girls, like fourteen-year-old Nettie Reece, frequently lied about their ages to get accepted at the new mills, eager to work alongside the friends who they grew up around and to escape judgmental fathers. Other women were looking for an alternative to domestic and service labor for Elizabethton's wealthy classes, of which they spoke with even more disdain than mill labor. In two sentences, Bessie Edens explains the expectations of young women around her: "The girls were supposed to do housework and work in the fields. They were supposed to be slaves." Many of these women were leaving behind a harsh life at home (or a boardinghouse), where paternalistic structures attempted to control their entire lives, only to find a different set of parents at the mill with a new set of "hard rules."[17]

Constantly evolving regulations and punitive processes were an expected feature of industrial work in Europe and the United States. However, innovative theories in the emerging fields of biometrics (studying the worker's movements in the factory) and scientific management (applying new methods of discipline and reward to workers) were adopted by mill owners in response to the industry's falling profits in the postwar economy of the 1920s. Owners would outsource the introduction of new processes of work and discipline by hiring management teams to come to the mills to assess their efficiency and train in new practices, which often involved timing workers and creating new patterns in the work day. The intensification of work at the mill, coupled with techniques aimed specifically at controlling women's movements, resulted in immediate backlash in Elizabethton.

Hard rules were introduced that targeted women: some to do with traditional patriarchal obsessions with gender presentation, such as regulations on clothing and make-up, and others that were aimed at reducing the amount of time women went unsupervised in the mill. Washroom visits required a ticket from a supervisor and were strictly timed; each tardy resulted in a dock of pay, and multiple infractions would get a woman fired. But these washroom rules were particularly hard to enforce given

---

Program Collection.

17   Historian Jacquelyn Hall takes this term from the young women who used it themselves to refer to new regulations introduced at the mills (Hall, "Disorderly Women," 187).

that management men were not allowed in women's bathrooms.[18] When Christine Galliher was asked about the extensive washroom regulations, she responded: "I went to the washroom when I wanted to. I went by my own rules, if you needed to go to the washroom."[19] The bathroom became an obvious and necessary space to spread subversive gossip. When Dr. Hall interviewed Nettie Reece about how she knew a strike was impending she cited "bathroom gossip." One can only imagine one of the questions circulating in the washrooms on those early days in March: *Why do we work for nothing in a mill when we already do that at home?*

Walking Out

On March 12, 1929, Margaret Bowen asked for a raise for herself and her section in the inspection department at the Glanzstoff mill. Margaret had asked the foreman previously for a raise, but it went nowhere. She reiterated

18 Hall, "Disorderly Women," 189.
19 Christine Galliher, interview by Jacquelyn Hall, *The Southern Oral History Program Collection*, August 8, 1979.

In both Elizabethton and Gastonia, women were on the front lines harassing and fighting armed national guardsmen, most of whom were men in their communities and some of whom they could convince to join the strikes. Women in Elizabethton de-armed guardsmen on the roads leading into town, while these women in Gastonia fought in front of the mills on their picket lines.

Gaston Gazette / Edward Levinson Collection at Wayne State University

that she only made ten dollars a week and her coworkers made $8.96 for over fifty-five hours of work a week, imploring that they could not survive on those wages after the cost of boarding or commuting. His response was clear: He did not intend to ever give her or the other inspectors a raise; they made enough money and should consider "getting a bank account." The insinuation that they were not underpaid, but were merely reckless girls who did not know how to manage money, sent Margaret Bowen's department over the edge. Within moments and with only a few whispers, work stopped in her department for the morning. By lunchtime the work refusal was spreading. "The manager came in and asked me and two other girls if we were planning on a strike. Nobody said anything." Again the manager repeated the rumor and nobody said anything. While he was interrogating the women in inspection, other women in other sections were gathering. By the end of lunch, between three hundred and five hundred girls and women, all but seventeen in their sections, walked out.[20]

For the rest of the day, the inspectors-turned-strikers staged themselves around the factory to communicate what was happening at various shift changes. Scuffles broke out with company police when a security guard named "Buck Little" hit one of the women with a billy club. Male workers showed up with lead pipes and began attacking security guards and machinery. In an ironically titled piece called, "Sheriff Sees No Violence," the *Elizabethon Star* claimed that the acting president of the Bemberg and Glanzstoff mills, Dr. Arthur Mothwurf, was attacked when a "flying rock hit him in the head." This report was the first of many in which local press struggled to maintain a façade of social peace in their cracking industrial utopia.[21]

The following day, the first wave of women strikers returned to the mill to encourage everyone to walk out. They ran through the plant, hooting, hollering, and singing, pulling people off of their jobs, and shut the entire mill down by the afternoon. That same day, Mothwurf secured a sweeping injunction on the strikers that immediately banned them from picketing on or near mill property. When the strikers ignored the court's decree, town officials responded quickly with Mothwurf to urge the governor to send in the state militia. Just days later, by March 18, the Bemberg operation was shut down by the combined force of workers at both mills. Meanwhile, state militiamen swarmed the town to protect the mills and the frightened uptown business class. With upwards of five thousand on strike, production at a halt, and militia forces

---

20   Bernstein, *The Lean Years*, 14–15.
21   Whalen, *"Like Fire in Broom Straw,"* 17–18.

accumulating, spring appeared to be forcing its way out of a long and oppressive winter.

The Union Steps In

Between March 18 and March 21, the American Federation of Labor (AFL) sent United Textile Worker (UTW) organizer Al "Tiny" Hoffman to represent and negotiate the interests of striking millworkers.[22] Direct participation in or even awareness of this process by the strikers is dubious at best. Fifty strikers organized a local chapter of the UTW only days before negotiations began on March 22. Some sources believe that a local carpenter named John Penix, who had been involved with union organizing in eastern Tennessee in the past, used his connections to get in touch with AFL or UTW affiliates after millworkers reached out to him for support. Other theories tend to believe that the AFL simply saw an opportunity to stake a claim in southern labor organizing, and were well aware of tensions at the mill prior to the first walkout.[23]

For those strikers whose voices made it into written history, opinions about unions varied widely—from disdain to disinterest to dedication. In a practical sense, many strikers believed that unions arrived to help them secure demands and offer material support during strikes, and so they were interested in their ability to support when it was helpful, and disinterested or spiteful when it wasn't.[24] Without claiming knowledge of how thousands of strikers related to the presence of union organizers in their struggle, it seems that in the case of Elizabethton, unionism began as one tool of many to collectivize resources and try out various strategies. Decisions about when to strike, what tactics to employ, and who was to act were not routed through a centralized body, and the majority of activity

---

22 By this point, the American Federation of Labor was the governing body of the most powerful national trade unions in the United States.

23 Hoffman was not a new figure in southern mills; he appeared across the Piedmont in 1927 and 1928, including in Durham, North Carolina, where he helped start the Piedmont Organizing Council, which promoted unionization through UTW. Hoffman was also at the scene when workers walked out of a textile mill in Henderson, North Carolina in 1927, signing up eight hundred workers during the small strike. He was a charismatic and complex organizer who understood southern millworkers better than most outside organizers, but also continuously took orders from national union bureaucrats who sold out workers during the height of their struggles in the mills (Hall, *Like a Family*, 218).

24 Some, like Margaret Bowen and Bessie Edens, would make longstanding relationships with union people they met through the strike, although their identities as workers and radicals were not defined solely through their union activity or experience.

was self-directed by strikers in smaller groups, often connected by geography, gender, and kinship.

Meanwhile, striking workers paraded around downtown in fast and loud motorcades with "hundreds of girls" hanging out of cars, buses and taxis, yelling at Guardsman, singing together, "shouting and laughing at people who watched them from the windows and store-fronts," and generally horrifying the bourgeois sensibilities of uptown residents. Mass assemblies, speeches, and musical events took place day and night at a tabernacle that had been built for President Hoover's visit the year before. Pickets turned into skirmishes with Guardsman on a daily basis.[25]

A secret hotel meeting was arranged for March 22 between Bemberg and Glanzstoff president Mothwurf, Al Hoffman of the United Textile Workers, an official from the Tennessee Department of Labor, the captain

Edward Levinson Collection at Wayne State University

of the Tennessee National Guard, and the sheriff of Carter County. The talks ended in a "gentlemen's agreement" with a host of negotiations between the mill owner and Hoffman who represented the unionized workers. The mill agreed to not discriminate based on union membership but also would not recognize the organization, they would even out wages between the two mills, and offer "good girl help" raises to an ambiguous set of female workers. None of this was in writing, and immediately after,

The tactic of "Picket by Dancing" as depicted here in the 1934 General Textile Strike at a thread mill in Austell, Georgia, first emerged in the Elizabethton strikes in 1929 and quickly spread to subsequent strikes across the south. Using string bands, automobiles, and dancing crowds, strikers blocked entrances to roads leading into the shut-down mills in order to keep scabs from arriving as well as blocking armed forces from the area.

Mothwurf publically denied meeting with the other parties, claiming that he had no interest in negotiating with striking workers.[26]

When strikers heard Mothwurf's public denial, the immediate response was a mass assembly. The captain of the Tennessee National Guard

---

25　The state militiamen were many strikers' brothers, future husbands, and friends. Tactics of teasing and taunting encouraged some Guardsman to take off their uniform and join the revolt (Hall, "Disorderly Women," 199; Whalen, *Like Fire in Broom Straw,* 17–18).

26　Hall, "Disorderly Women," 190.

arrived at the meeting and tried to blame Mothwurf's denial on his German mother tongue and a poor use of the English language. Regarding the unions, one observer wrote, "the union officials naively acquiesced in the settlement." Most strikers that attempted to go back to work, hoping for a change, were either discharged for alleged union involvement or they realized that nothing new was in store for them and left over the course of a few days or weeks. Those who re-entered the factory gates could have guessed that nothing had improved as guardsman were stationed behind machine guns on top of the plants.[27]

"It Was Kind of Rough, Some of It."

Mass assemblies, joyous parades, and street battles between guardsman and picketers continued throughout March as workers gained collective power outside of the mill. April and May's actions transitioned toward underground organizing, strategic secrecy, autonomous blockades of scabs, acts of collective and individual self-defense, and wildcat walkouts. Some of this new militancy blurred with the ongoing union organizing in town, while other aspects occurred completely beyond the bounds of the UTW. New enemies, loyal to the mills, assembled to combat those who represented dissent to the social order, while women continued to violate the behaviors that northern unionists and the southern press expected.

Late in the night of April 3–4, three cars containing merchants, doctors, lawyers, and ministers loyal to the mill attempted to abduct three men they believed represented the evil that had descended on their town. Hoffman and Ed McGrady were both kidnapped separately by the vigilante restorers of order. Hoffman was driven to North Carolina, forced out of the car and told if he ever returned they would "fill him with bullets." McGrady was taken to the town of Bristol, Tennessee, and also warned that he would be killed should he return. Allegations circulated that one of them was also tarred and feathered, an archaic form of torture that white vigilante mobs across the south continued to use well into the twentieth century.[28]

The third car never completed its mission. Bessie Edens's version of the story speaks eloquently to what happened to the mob that attempted to kidnap local carpenter and old radical John Penix:

27 Tippett, *When Southern Labor Stirs*, 60–62.
28 Bernstein, *The Lean Years*, 17; and Bessie Edens, interview, Southern Oral History Program Collection.

One night there was a car drove up (the man [John Penix] lived with his sister, his old maid sister), and [a] man got out and knocked on the door. The man went to the door, and the sister, of course, got up. They started to take him, to put him in the car— they was going to tar and feather him, they thought. But sister just walked back to her bedroom and got a gun, and she shot through that car. She was the cause of one man's death, but that never was proved either and never was told too much. But one of them died right after that, and he was a doctor. And another one that was a merchant got it in the arm, and they sent him to Kentucky to a hospital. I think they was the only two that was hurt in the car. But they didn't take the man. I guess I told something about that in the school, about that woman.... She didn't work there [at the mill] and neither did her brother. They just sympathized with the union. They had moved here from some other place, I think, and they was just friendly with it. But they was going to take him because he was friendly with them, I guess; it was pretty rough on them. The people, now, in town was doing that; and it was the leading people in town. Of course I know a lot of stuff I can't tell. I wasn't in that; I didn't do it. But there is a lot of things you can't tell, you see. It was kind of rough, though, some of it.[29]

It was common knowledge around the strikes that John Penix's sister saved his life and shot at his abductors with their rifle. Accounts of that night other than this one do not make a direct correlation between the killing of a wealthy doctor and the woman's defense of her brother. What stands out besides the brave actions and impressive night vision of the carpenter's sister are the reminders from Bessie that "there is a lot of things you can't tell." Throughout the long interviews with Bessie Edens, Christine and Dave Galliher, and Robert Cole—all proud strikers in 1929—are carefully answered questions or sensitively told stories that let their interviewers know when they don't think they should be talking about a person or an action. The warnings, silence, allusions to secrecy, and strategic forgetting that appear in these interviews are often due to obtaining sensitive knowledge about illegal acts during the strike, while at other times they are reminders of the fear and trauma that the threat of vigilante justice instilled in strikers during that time.[30]

29 Bessie Edens, interview, Southern Oral History Program Collection.
30 Also in early April there was a vigilante raid on Communist headquarters in Gastonia during the Loray Mill strike. Following the attack, North Carolina's governor

Strikers stood resolute against the fear mongering of the merchants and ministers. The day after their kidnapping, Hoffman and McGrady reappeared in Elizabethton with an armed motorcade of strikers by their side. Robert Cole became an armed bodyguard for Hoffman and never left his side, always carrying his favorite nickel-plated .38 Special with him. At one point, the courts issued eighteen warrants for his arrest after a particularly rowdy day at the picket line when strikers jumped the fence and raided the plants.[31] When Cole was accused of owning and using high-powered rifles to snipe at scab buses, he directed his Johnson City lawyers, who had no faith in his case, on how to navigate the local court system. Cole denied all charges until it came to his .38, which he admitted to the judge with pride that he owned and brandished. Cole was later responsible for tracking down Hoffman's car when it was stolen, and the thief, a private company spy named "Slick," fired twice at Cole, but was disarmed and run out of town.[32]

Stories like these became marginal notes in the histories of the Elizabethton strike, written as they were by labor historians who preferred to focus on the micro-details of trade union negotiations or the ongoing drama between Communists and trade unionists in simultaneous strikes happening in Gastonia. While Dr. Hall and her direction of the Southern Oral History Program's documentation of the cotton mill world and strike wave did not shy away from the dynamics of violence in the strikes, what emerges is a segregated view of the roles women played in relation to strikers use of violence:

> As far as can be determined, no women were involved in barn burnings and dynamitings—what Bessie Edens referred to as the "rough … stuff" that accompanied the second strike. Men "went places that we didn't go," explained Christine Galliher. "They had big dark secrets … the men did." But when it came to public demonstrations, women held center stage.[33]

Gardner sent an undercover detective to try and gain information about the raid. In his findings, the detective reported that the strikers were "scared to death," but also that "it is an impossibility, it seems, to get anything worthwhile direct from any of these mill workers. They are simply *NOT* going to talk to anyone" (Whalen, *"Like Fire in Broom Straw,"* 84).

31   These warrants were actually intended for his brother; both men were involved in the strike and the courts often confused them.

32   Robert Cole, interview by Jacquelyn Hall, Southern Oral History Program Collection, May 10, 1981.

33   Hall, "Disorderly Women," 91.

While both women admit that they were often involved in different actions than the men around them, there was respect and trust across marriages, family members, and friendships to engage in autonomous decision making and action without the pressure to needlessly disclose information to loved ones. There are many ways to engage in and support a clandestine action; one person might light the match, but an entire network of people makes this possible through their affinity, conspiracy, and silence.

On Cursin' and Scabbin'

By April 15, those who went back to work after the botched March 22 negotiations had finally had enough. Bessie Edens remembered that when she a blew a whistle in her section that day, some didn't know what was going on, but others began to "stir" and knock spindles of yarn over. In a phone call between Hoffman and the head of the federal Labor Department's Conciliation Service on April 16, Hoffman proclaimed, "two union boys were fired at the Glanzstoff ... the workers got together.... They telephoned [Mothwurf] every hour [but he] refused to talk with them.... The people just walked out. A complete walkout, 5,500 workers of both plants.... They have just revolted and came out on their own." Hoffman went on to warn the Federal labor men that if the company hired scabs and tried to start the plant back up, he couldn't say what would happen.[34]

Immediately following the April 15 walkout, Tennessee's governor, Henry Horton, ordered eight hundred state police and deputy sheriffs to the area, on top of the hundreds of guardsmen that were already deployed. A combination of these troops were ordered to protect buses that would now be coming in from cities, towns, and faraway hollers to transport strike-breakers so the plants could reopen.[35]

Striker Christine Galliher also remembered that the strike took a serious turn once national guardsmen started protecting scabs:

> I suppose what caused that violence was that they brought strike-breakers in here—I don't remember where they came from—who would work at the plant. I don't know how they got them, unless they advertised for them, but they brought people in here that went to work, and of course that took the jobs of the people that were striking. But they got to keep those

---

34 Whalen, *"Like Fire in Broom Straw,"* 19.
35 Bernstein, *The Lean Years*, 18.

Aerial image of the North American Rayon Corporation in 1947. During World War II, the German-owned mills were taken over by the government and began producing for the war. The German surname of "Glanzstoff" was removed and replaced with the patriotic title of "North American Rayon Corporation" while the Bemberg mill became the "American Bemberg" mill.

jobs, and they got the benefits of what the other people were striking for. And it's always been that way, and it'll always be that way.[36]

Since the buses had to travel through many of the hollers that strikers were from, like Gap Creek and Valley Forge, thousands of strikers set off to block roads that would bring the buses full of scabs. Others took a different route, and from hideaways in the hills with high-powered rifles began to shoot out the tires of the buses as they drove by. In the end, the blockades created more drama than the sniper's bullets. Women amassed at Gap Creek were met by hundreds of guardsmen who ordered them off the roads and back to town. A defiant woman sat on the road in protest of walking hours back to town, and immediately all the other strikers sat with her. The troops then tear-gassed the crowd and ordered buses to pick them up. In the confusion back at the courthouse, a few keen arrestees like Bessie Edens were able to slip away and escape when the Guards' backs were turned.[37]

Women picketers at Valley Forge cursed and waved weapons in the Guardsmen's faces. The American flag apparently made a big hit with young

36 Christine Galliher, interview by Jacquelyn Hall, Southern Oral History Program Collection, August 8, 1979.
37 Bessie Edens, interview, Southern Oral History Program Collection.

women on strike, both in fashion and function: some women in town would march up and down the "Bemberg Highway ... draped in the American flag," so that every time they passed Guardsmen the men would be forced to present arms. The *Elizabethton Star* complained of female strikers out in the streets protesting and partying in "men's trousers." Another woman, Trixie Perry, a single mother that traveled frequently, showed up to court with a handmade outfit and cap that consisted of a cut-up and refashioned American flag, outraging the prosecutor and bourgeois courtroom attendants. Women's antics in the courtroom for the 1,250 arrested over the course of that spring became such a mockery of law and order that a union official jumped over a bench during a trial, making a desperate plea for strikers to "have some respect" for the courts.[38]

In a revolt that involves thousands of young women, there is much more on trial than what appears on the docket. Prosecutors did not attempt to hide their assumptions about the moral character of women like Trixie Perry or Texas Bill, a person who was female-assigned but whom other strikers remembered as always having worn a cowboy get-up. The gender performance and sexuality of these women were obsessed over in the public sphere, whose symbolic order was carefully managed by the bourgeois class of Elizabethton. Mill women were well aware of the stereotypes that circulated behind their backs, even when a strike was not exploding on the front page of the newspapers. Poor women in the mill towns were always in excess or lacking in the proper—and thus hyper-managed and rehearsed—performances of femininity and sexuality that bourgeois women embodied.

Unfortunately, the UTW carried with it this same bourgeois sensibility. The union itself compromised the autonomy of young female strikers, for example when they ordered a large percentage of young women strikers to "go home" in the active spring period of the demonstrations. "Instead of capitalizing on women's contributions, UTW organizers yielded to middle-class fears of sexual misbehavior; at the height of the strike, they sent a quarter of the picketers back to their hillside homes, 'chiefly young single girls whom we want to keep off the streets.'"[39] This was not a particularly surprising move for Hoffman to make on behalf of the UTW, or for Matilda Lindsay, who traveled down from the National Women's Trade Union League. Both organizations capitulated to the conservative politics of AFL president William Green, who staunchly believed that the way

---

38   Whalen, *"Like Fire in Broom Straw,"* 19, 73.
39   Hall, *Like a Family*, 219.

toward spreading trade unionism in the country was through a compromise-based approach, focusing more on the management and ownership of the mill than the interests or needs of the workers themselves.

This is confusing, given the resources and risks that individual UTW organizers invested in the Elizabethton strikes. However, from a politically and economically strategic perspective, showing up for Elizabethton and Marion was essential to the UTW if they wanted to get their foot in the door of the hundreds of other "unorganized" southern mills. When looking closely at correspondence between Hoffman, McGrady, UTW officials with federal labor conciliatory parties, and the workers themselves—whether in Elizabethton, Marion, or Danville—it was clear that the union wanted strikes to remain as manageable as possible, so they could remain visible but controllable bargaining chips in the game of reconciliation between labor and capital. The UTW did not have to worry about the consequences of their actions for real millworkers in the South, because they had few ties to the region and, if need be, could simply leave.

On May 16, saboteurs struck at the heart of the infrastructure of Elizabethton and the rayon plants when they dynamited a water main that supplied the town and plants. It was a heroic attempt to shut down the scab- and loyalist-filled rayon plants. Little remains to piece together what effects the attack had on the plants and city inhabitants, and whether that played into the federal intervention to come. Barn burnings of company-owned machinery and attacks on strikebreaker's houses may have continued well into 1930, but such attacks often did not make headlines when the press was determined to restore order and generate baseless speculation about the excellent economic prospects for the upcoming year.

Bitter Concessions

Officially, the Elizabethton strike ended when Anna Weinstock, a young federal labor negotiator, arrived in town and secured the final round of agreements between Mothwurf and Hoffman on May 26. Almost immediately, the impotent changes that the parties agreed upon, along with the continued fight by blacklisted men and women to reveal these contradictions, faded out of view. Local and national headlines were eager to announce that the strike was "SETTLED BY A WOMAN!"—as though her gender added a victory of social progressiveness to the declared peace between classes.[40]

---

40 Hall, "Disorderly Women," 193; Whalen, *"Like Fire in Broom Straw,"* 74.

The great "settlement" that Weinstock was credited with "single handedly achieving," was more due to the fact that Hoffman knew the AFL was no longer planning on investing resources or commitment to the strike. On top of the national abandonment of the millworkers, the local branch had exhausted its resources over the six weeks of relief funding and was in debt. At the May 26 negotiation, Hoffman agreed to a settlement that made no mention of wages, working conditions, or hours for the millworkers. The mill admitted two concessions: one clause that assured they would not discriminate based on union affiliation and another that promised if an employee was not reinstated they could file a case with the mill's new personnel officer. After two and a half hours of debate at a meeting called for by the union and Weinstock, the settlement was accepted by strikers in attendance, although it is unclear what portion of the 5,500 workers on strike were in attendance and what position those not in attendance held on being represented by local union organizers.[41]

Union activity would continue for a few months, and some workers traveled alongside those who were blacklisted to lend support to the Marion strike across the mountains in North Carolina. A year after the first walkout, in March 1930, millworkers held a demonstration in solidarity with those who were blacklisted, but in general, the rayon plants went back to business as usual and any strength that remained in unionized workers was recuperated by new strategies in management. The new personnel officer immediately set up a company union in order to capture and redirect workplace organizing. Company unions were a popular response by mill management in the South after the wave of revolts that awoke them to the strengths and limits of workers. Company unions produced their own internal newspapers, set up sports and cultural events, and improved mill welfare programs, all of which created the illusion that working and living conditions around mills improved when workers collaborated with management to their mutual benefit.[42]

On October 1, 1930, the new acting president of the Bemberg and Glanzstoff mills, known as Consul Kummer, was found dead in his bedroom with both wrists slashed. News reports in the region mentioned that a window in his room was found open with a flowerpot smashed beneath. Sheriff Moreland reported a portion of the note, written in German, to an official at the mill's German headquarters, which read: "I can't wait further

41   Hall, "Disorderly Women," 193; Tippett, *When Southern Labor Stirs*, 72–73.
42   Tippett, *When Southern Labor Stirs*, 73–74.

for the rayon people." The Sheriff then refused to make the rest of the note public and ruled the death as a suicide. When Bessie Edens was asked about Kummer's death, she immediately responded that she couldn't talk about it, has never talked about it, and asked the interviewer where she heard about it. After being asked whether people in the union knew what happened to him, Bessie said, "I think some of them did. But they was afraid to say anything and they're still afraid to say anything, everybody.... You never hear it mentioned. But at that time it was suspicious looking, things were." The mystery remains as to whether Kummer was killed in retaliation by blacklisted workers, by union forces, by industry men who lacked faith in his leadership, or if it was in fact a suicide.[43]

As for the lasting legacy of the strike wave in Elizabethton, Bessie Edens believed:

> Well, we all knew that we couldn't go back. There was ninety of us that they never called back because we was leaders of it. I knew I wasn't going to get to go back, and I didn't care. I wrote them a letter and told them I didn't care whether they called me back or not. (laughter) I didn't! If I'd starved I wouldn't of cared, because I knew what I was a doing when I helped to pull it. And I've never regretted it in any way, only just losing my job; of course, I would have liked to have kept it, but you can't do everything. And it did help the people, and it's helped the town and the country. We have better homes here, and people have had better living than they've ever had in their lives around in here.[44]

Not all were as hopeful. Christine Galliher presented a more stark material outlook when asked how she survived being blacklisted during the Great Depression: "I don't know how people survived. I supposed it's just your spirit or something, because I don't believe young people today could survive. We're just survivors, I guess. It boils down to that.... [Back then] you could fend for yourself, now there's not much way you can fend for yourself." When asked if things got any better after the strike she replied, "Well things couldn't have gotten any worse."[45]

---

43 Associated Press, "President of the Rayon Companies Commits Suicide," *Kentucky New Era*, October 1, 1929; Bessie Edens, interview, Southern Oral History Program Collection.
44 Bessie Edens, interview, Southern Oral History Program Collection.
45 Christine Galliher, interview, Southern Oral History Program Collection.

Both women attribute the millworkers' lack of continued organized resistance to the fact that, soon after the strikes, the mill ended up raising wages and shortening hours, thus giving workers what they initially fought for. As Christine insinuated, those who were blacklisted from the mill and other opportunities in town returned to what they knew best—surviving.

Some women went back to domestic service; men traveled like their fathers had across borders, looking for seasonal work, while families and friends shared shelter and resources. Many strikers, like Bessie, knew that they were not going to return to the mills and were prepared to make a living off their land again, defiantly saying that they knew how to take care of themselves before the mill and hadn't forgotten their ways.

Industrial postcards, like this one of American Bemberg in Elizabethton, were a way of showing the country (and the world) an image of the "New South," one that was eager to attract northern and European investment with its abundant natural resources, tax-free land, and (so they believed) the promise of a passive workforce.

The Strike Rolls Over the Piedmont

Throughout the summer, as the fires of Elizabethton were dying out, hundreds of textile mills between North and South Carolina popped off into strikes like firecrackers. The stretch-outs and hard rules that Elizabethton workers fought to abolish were industry-wide practices that generated massive resentment and unrest in nearly every textile mill in the South. While sharing common grievances, the strikes in North Carolina, in comparison to Tennessee, illuminate the different tensions and consequences that existed for millworkers and owners in the Piedmont than those in the mountains.

The stories that unfolded in Gastonia have been told many times and very poignantly, largely due to the famous Communist intervention in the militant strike at the Loray Mill. Loray was the largest textile mill in the "City of Spindles," and the literal center of textile production in the Carolinas, with fifty-two mills in the county. The appalling working conditions inside the mills were reinforced by the double bind of debt and welfare that virtually imprisoned workers on the "mill hills," the textile industry's version of company towns in the steel and mining industries.[46]

---

46   Tippett, *When Southern Labor Stirs*, 76–78.

In April 1929, a month after the initial walkout in Elizabethton, tensions exploded when workers struck after the mill fired all workers they suspected of initiating a union backed by Communist organizers. Of the 2,200 workers, 1,800 went on strike, but management was able to keep the machinery running with scabs who fought their way to work through picket lines every day. The conflict lasted well into October, and generalized into a revolt against work, housing "welfare," debt, and segregation, largely due to the influx of Communist support around the country and influence of local worker, mother, and strike-songstress Ella May Wiggins.[47]

The workers' rebellion climaxed in May when mill owners evicted nearly a hundred families from company houses. The workers responded by erecting a tent village on a free strip of land near the mill and forming an armed guard to protect themselves against state and mob violence. When Gastonia police attempted to enter the occupied land and destroy the tents, a fight broke out in which an armed worker shot and killed the police chief. The resulting trial was the largest and most expensive up to that point in North Carolina history, ending with two Communist organizers fleeing to Russia to avoid imprisonment.[48]

Little research or writing has emerged about the often short-lived South Carolina strikes, probably due to the fact that the majority of mill towns resolutely declined invitations by outside organizers and gained local support in their leaderless strikes. In many instances, the strikers were able to force the abolition of the stretch-out system—a major victory that other mills would not achieve until after the General Textile Strike of 1934. Yet in some of these situations, the spurning of "outsiders" and the local support for the workers' demands coincided with Klan endorsement of the strikes, which strengthened the power of segregated industry, acting as a peace treaty between classes in the name of white solidarity.[49]

White supremacy directly accounted for the lack of meaningful connections between white and Black workers within the textile industry, as well as the neighboring tobacco industry and sharecropping fields. The hundreds of arson attacks by both white and Black sharecroppers on barns in the cotton industry, well documented in Georgia but occurring

---

47 Wiggins's vocal antiracism actually predated any Communist influence, and was based partly on living in one of the only nonsegregated mill villages in Bessemer City.

48 One of the two organizers, Fred Beal, became so disillusioned under Stalin's regime that he returned to the United States to try to live underground, but was caught in 1934 and spent eight years in a North Carolina prison (Bernstein, *The Lean Years*, 28).

49 Ibid., 33.

throughout the South, attest to a mostly ungrasped potential, whereby workers in similar situations found a common wisdom in attacking an industry they shared, but did so secretly and in isolation. It is also important to remember the moments where these borders did begin to break down, for instance in the life of infamous striker-songwriter Ella May Wiggins and in the virulent propaganda and speeches of the Communist organizers at Gastonia. Whites who profited from the textile mills attacked white strikers and organizers in vigilante mobs generally reserved to terrorize Black southerners. The segregation of the mills was key to maintaining a strictly racialized social order that southern capitalists knew was their strongest antidote to an impending class war.[50]

For its part, the middle-class Black press in Charlotte maintained a precarious distance from these mostly white strikes in nearby Gaston County. On the one hand, they encouraged readers not to become involved, but on the other declared that:

> If whites who are poor and disadvantaged have no rights to self-defense and no rights to legal procedure, the blacks will know where they stand.... They who produce the wealth of the world are entitled to its enjoyment. And the wealth of the nation should not be controlled by a small factional part of it. As long as it is so controlled and men and women are compelled to labor for a pauper's wage, there will be discontent, strikes, which neither threats nor violence, bayonets, nor bastilles can suppress.[51]

Another obstacle that strikers would attempt to overcome and transform was the mill village, the company housing they often referred to as "the jail." Control over every aspect of daily life—housing, food, clothing, social outlets—gave both the state and mill companies a potent weapon in defusing and destroying strike activity. While both the rebellious eastern Tennessee free miners of earlier years and the mill women of Elizabethton still held a connection to land and family yet unsubsumed by work and the wage, the social life of millworkers in the Piedmont was suffocated

---

50   After the 1929 Loray Mill strike was effectively over, Wiggins was murdered in an act of revenge for her fierce efforts to overcome the racist indoctrination of her fellow millworkers. Ella May's murderer was acquitted, as were the vigilantes who shot eight Marion strikers in the back for blocking scabs from entering the mills (Tippett, *When Southern Labor Stirs*, 106).

51   Whalen, *"Like Fire in Broom Straw,"* 89–90.

by these forces. Due to this architecture that enforced debt and welfare, workers in Gastonia and Marion did not have sustainable networks of support outside of the mill, and many were literally starved into crossing the picket line. Nonetheless, the resistance that formed in those spaces of misery and confinement led, in the decades to come, to the abandonment of the company town and mill village as a form of social control.

Back in Elizabethton, the stability of the rayon plants would wax and wane with the Depression years until World War II, when government forces seized control over the German-owned mill and began producing rayon yarn for tire cord and parachutes to be used for the war. After the war, women's jobs were increasingly phased out in favor of specialized training for male workers to adapt to new processes of production. Meanwhile, technological innovations were introduced continuously up through the seventies across the textile industry, replacing workers with machines at a staggering rate. The Bemberg plant closed in the seventies, unable to keep up with a growing international market. North American Rayon Corporation (previously Glanzstoff) limped on until the North American Free Trade Agreement and a massive fire destroyed their operation for good.[52]

A Crisis of Representation

Across the board in the southern mills, owners would make concessions months after strikes had ended, when collective strength had been beaten down by hunger, repression, and the union's pressure to compromise. While many workers knew that their sweat and blood did, in fact, change the future of life in the mills, the tensions that remained were not resolvable by quantitative shifts of wages or hours in the workers' favor.

The Depression that swept the country in the wake of the stock market crash in October 1929 forced mill owners to increase their adaptive capacities to extract value from workers, while also having to navigate national legislation reform. The economic crisis also intensified conditions that had started the initial influx of landless laborers and struggling farmers to the mills in the first place. Merchant class land ownership, cash crop competition, debt, and enclosures made a retreat to subsistence farming nearly impossible for industrial workers who found no hope in the mills. Leaving was one form of refusal that landless people had access to in this moment, and increasingly white and Black sharecroppers and millworkers took their chances on west- and north-bound highways.

---

52 Hall, *Like a Family*, 354.

Strikers in caravan outside of the shut down American
Glanzstoff mill in Elizabethton, spring 1929

For millworkers who stayed on to fight for better conditions, the
UTW's platform was seen as a way to force some changes, but beyond its
temporary interventions like the strike revolt of 1929, and its success in
spreading the General Textile Strike of 1934 from Alabama up through
the Carolinas, trade unionism never gained a stronghold in the South.
There was a kind of mutual rejection of unionism, by both northern national organizers who refused to lend infrastructure to long-term support
of southern causes, and by southern workers who refused to organize on
behalf of a union that left after moments of crisis.[53]

Simply speaking, union organizers were not interested in adapting
their organizing methods and applying strategies that were generated from
southern workers who knew their territory better than educated outsiders.
Women in the mills were simultaneously ignored and manipulated by
southern organizing drives.

---

53   There were notable exceptions to this rule in various towns and industries, for example in Durham, North Carolina, with its tobacco and textile industries. However, the
union never penetrated the worker's identities in the South to the extent it did in the
Northeast, Northwest, and other regions where unionism, masculinity, job security,
and professionalization in industrial sectors were deeply embedded in a culture of
work.

To most UTW officials, the South was a foreign land; they paid attention to southern workers only sporadically and then primarily as a low-wage threat to the union's strongholds in the Northeast.... The union sent few female organizers to the region, framed its strategy around the demand for a "family wage"—that is, a wage that would enable a man to keep his wife and children at home—and made no attempt to address working women's needs.[54]

Edens was one of the first to sign up with the local in Elizabethton. Her courage, wit, and sharpness led to her recruitment by National Women's Trade Union League organizers who started a southern summer camp to educate and train young women in the mills. She was invited back a few summers in a row, and offered scholarships by northern philanthropists from whom she was required to request funds. Her secretarial and organizational leadership in the union went unpaid, but Edens began working as a cook and cleaner during the day in order to be able to afford to stay at the camp, attending night classes with her friends who were also millworkers turned domestic workers. They would have to leave their children with family members while they worked and attended classes.[55]

Their lives working for the union increasingly mirrored the limited options they had before: domestic and secretarial work supplemented their unwaged labor as mothers and caretakers in their homes and communities. Edens was frequently encouraged by women unionists who were unmarried and had no children to apply to a northern college on the promise of scholarship. She declined the offers multiple times and explained that she could not and would not leave her kids with her mother alone. But for Edens, and her southern coworkers and comrades at the summer camp, their commitment to their family was treated as an unimportant and expendable part of their time by unionists. No one understood the caring labor they performed on a daily basis, which went uncompensated and thus unseen by a labor movement that defined work through the wage. The experiences of radical strikers like Bessie Edens speak to the reality that union involvement in the South amounted to a sociological experiment for academics and organizers rather than an invested relationship based on reciprocity; learning based on experience, creative fashioning and sharing of resources, and sharing the responsibilities of care were never the

---

54   Hall, *Like a Family*, 219.
55   Bessie Edens, interview, Southern Oral History Program Collection.

foundation of these professionals' presence. Edens sums up the contradictions in her relationship to the Northern unionist women best, "I would have liked to have gone and studied them.... I might have got more out of them than they would me.... But they'd have never known it."

The primary form of caring or resource sharing that unions knew was fundraising and donations, which was important when hunger was on the line, but did little to support the long-term self-directed activity of workers in an environment where mill owners controlled most of the area's cash flow and resources. Union activity did not prioritize the spontaneous and creative fashioning of resources that southern workers excelled at—as is exemplified by activities like looting vegetable gardens of the rich, or building relationships with store owners to ignore company-owned debt.[56]

Unions may have been able to look the other way while saboteurs and looters got the goods in the first three decades of the twentieth century, but Roosevelt's signing of the Wagner Act in 1935 signaled a new phase of their institutionalization. This legislation both legalized and formalized unions, eventually resulting in strict rules surrounding who they were allowed to organize and what such a process would look like.[57] Trade unions in the United States quickly came to be dominated by bureaucracy and political motives that turned workers' needs into something to be wagered, manipulated, and exchanged.

This institutionalization proceeded with few hiccups, largely because it merely formalized bureaucratic structures already inherent to the vision and scope of American trade union politics.[58] With a few notable exceptions, the union has always been something separate and distinct from the

---

56   In Kentucky coal country, in 1931, Harlan County mine workers looted from vegetable gardens and stores when the United Mine Workers organizers failed to provide the food that was promised to encourage miners to strike. A battle cry of the strike, "We starve while we work; we might as well starve while we starve" rang with self-aware humor at the pointlessness of work when you couldn't even feed yourself (Bernstein, *The Lean Years*, 378).

57   The passing of the Taft-Hartley Act in 1947 made it illegal to conduct solidarity strikes between industries, and prohibited domestic, farm, or public workers—most of whom were predominantly Black or Latino—from organizing. Additionally, workplace organizing was rerouted into a slow, procedures-driven process of elections, which was easy for employers to manipulate and more manageable for a state worried about unpredictable eruptions of class violence.

58   This is particularly apparent with the anti-radicalism of the AFL, as well as in the highly elitist craft unionism of the previous century. The AFL even supplied scabs to help break other strikes organized by the sometimes-anarchist Industrial Workers of the World (Louis Adamic, *Dynamite: The Story of Class Violence in America* [Oakland: AK Press, 2008], 65.).

self-driven activity of workers themselves. As soon as this is understood, it becomes clear that the union is in essence an alienated form of our own resistance, torn from our own desires and strictly limited in scope to one aspect of oppression under capitalist life. If work is our own productive or creative capacities alienated from us by capitalism, then the unions are our own capacities for resistance alienated from us by representation and democracy. This does not mean that we will never benefit materially from their existence or that no inspiring resistance has ever happened under the shadow of union organizing, but in the final judgment, the union as an institution can only be an enemy, and the more institutionalized it is, the more monstrous that enemy shall be.

The union arrived in Elizabethton when that community was on the edge of revolt, in a context where the fuel for class struggle was not union elections or government-approved pickets, but arson, work refusal, street battles, and communal structures of care and support. These were some of the final years when unions could feasibly tolerate a struggle that was largely outside of their own control. Through further institutionalizing this apparatus, the state managed to script and choreograph these struggles. This process resulted in tremendous concessions for a certain minority of America's working class, but also forced the dispossessed to find new avenues to assert their own power, vision, and defiance.

The 1920s and '30s saw some of the most violent and bitter class strug-
gles ever to shake the United States. From sanctioned, union-organized
strikes to spontaneous wildcats, arson, and sabotage, American workers
had to fight desperately for every inch of ground that they gained. Individual battles were lost more often than won, but the larger lesson was clear:
American capitalism could not continue in its present form. In this sense,
the Great Depression of the 1930s was as much a crisis of government and
social control as it was of finance and economics. The country's entry into
World War II was a short-term solution to this dilemma, but the larger solution was to bring well-disciplined representatives of the working class into
democratic government.

So, while the struggles of the Depression brought victories for certain
segments of America's working class, the decade ultimately ended with a
peace treaty between the appointed representatives of capital and labor.
Legislation like the Wagner Act legalized private sector union organizing,
while excluding most public workers, domestic workers, and farm workers,
and established official channels for mediation to help avoid the more uncontrollable elements of the previous decades' clashes. This peace treaty made the trade union a partner in government and social control while
bringing stability for capitalists on the eve of World War II; it also further
institutionalized hierarchies of race, gender, and class within America's oppressed. Postwar struggles reflected this betrayal, often adopting a direct
focus on the identities with which these hierarchies were established.

In particular, a new wave of Black struggle highlighted age-old in-
tersections of race and violence. Unlike much of the Black rebellion of the previous two hundred years, many movement leaders sought to understand and constrain this struggle within
the framework of rights and citizenship, particularly in the
South. The limits of such an approach quickly became clear,
however, as Black veterans defended their communities
from white vigilantes, teens fought back against
police, and the words of Frantz Fanon on colonialism and violence reached a new generation of ghetto residents. The freedom struggles of the period exploded beyond their own
boundaries, raising new and old questions of
identity, authority, and legitimacy that have
yet to be answered.

The Uncle Toms, the Judases, the Quislings of the black "elite" would deny this rising consciousness. They do everything possible to make white Americans think that it is not true, while apologizing for us to the very people who oppress us. Some of these "responsible" Negroes are afraid that militant action damages "amiable race relations." They complain that race relations may deteriorate to a point that many Negroes may lose jobs. What they mean is that they may lose *their* jobs.

—Robert F. Williams, *Negroes with Guns*

In the final analysis, the state can recognize any claim for identity—even that of a state identity within itself. But what the state cannot tolerate in any way is that singularities form a community without claiming an identity, that human beings co-belong without a representable condition of belonging (being Italian, working-class, Catholic, a terrorist, etc.).

—Giorgio Agamben, "Marginal Notes on Commentaries on Society of the Spectacle"

I seen a lot of shit in 22 years
It's like a tour of duty
Life is booby-trapped, it's hard to see the beauty…
You gotta think like a soldier
I'm training myself to snatch pistols outta holsters.

—Dead Prez, "Psychology"

FROM REBEL TO CITIZEN AND BACK AGAIN:

Civil Rights, Black Power, and Urban Riots in the New South

IN THE LATE 1960S THE UNITED STATES EXPERIENCED A MASSIVE, WIDE-spread series of rebellions in dozens of urban centers around the country. Catalyzed by both the failures and limited successes of the Civil Rights movement that began a decade earlier, and driven by a centuries-old culture of Black resistance, these uprisings shook America to its core. In 1964, the year of the first Civil Rights Act, there were an estimated four-teen Black uprisings, but from 1965 to 1968, according to a study by the US Senate Committee on Government Operations, there were a total of 166 major instances of Black urban violence. Looting became common-place, and occurred in 107 of these instances, and street-fighting with projectiles, the firebombing of stores, and armed sniping from rooftops were standard.[1]

Contrary to dominant media representations and sociological theories of the time, the rioting was often celebratory and infectious, but also con-tained a certain political wisdom. Looting was typically targeted at expen-sive, white-owned, or affluent Black stores. Street-level violence focused

---

1   Other studies that included a wider variety of disturbances put the number even higher; one study cited nearly three hundred disturbances in 1967 and 1968 alone (Daryl B. Harris, *The Logic of Black Urban Rebellions: Challenging the Dynamics of White Domination in Miami* [London: Praeger, 1999], 48).

on policemen and national guardsmen attempting to enter insurgent territory, and only rarely extended to white civilians. Participants reported the experience as having both a general insurrectionary character as well as a specific focus on pressuring city officials to provide some kind of immediate relief for poor residents (in which the rioters were often successful).

The impressions of one participant, who joined the massive August 1965 uprising in South Los Angeles out of passive curiosity and immediately recorded his feelings afterward, are instructive and worth quoting at length:

> A brick came out of nowhere and smashed through the window of a hot dog stand across the street. Someone yelled: "That's Whitey's, tear it down." A number of people from both sides of the street converged on the stand and began breaking all the windows. Several men climbed into this stand and began passing out Cokes and other beverages to the people outside.... As they passed a small gas station, several people wanted to set it afire. One of the people standing nearby the station told them: "Let it stand. Blood owns it." A liquor store and a grocery store were the next targets.... Next to the liquor store was a meat market. These windows were also smashed and people in cars drove up and began loading meat into the trunks of their cars. Two young boys ... came running out of the store...carrying a side of beef. The crowd roared its approval and greeted the boys with laughter and cheers. Several men came walking toward me laden down with liquor. One of them paused in front me and asked: "What do you drink, brother?" He and the other stopped right here on the street to have a drink. My reply was: "Whiskey." They opened a bottle of whiskey and handed it to me. I drank a large swallow and handed it back. Twice around and the bottle was empty. We laughed and they continued down the street.... A cry went up the street: "One-Oh-Three. Hit the Third!" It referred to 103rd Street, the business center of Watts (a mile to the east and the north). The people piled into cars and headed for 103rd Street. Others followed on foot. As I was getting back into my car to drive to "One-Oh-Three," several men jumped into my car and said: "Let's make it, baby."[2]

2   Quoted in Anthony Oberschall, "The Los Angeles Riot of August 1965," in *The Black Revolt: The Civil Rights Movement, Ghetto Uprisings, and the Separatism*, ed. James A. Geschwender (Englewood Cliffs, NJ: Prentice-Hall, 1971), 279–280.

Tampa residents jeer and scream at national guardsmen as they patrol the area during three nights of rioting.

The standard interpretation of these urban rebellions portrays them as irrational and highly divorced from the organized and politically legible activity of the Civil Rights movement. At best, they are seen as understandable but unfortunate outbursts, to be prevented through better policy making, better communication between city officials and Black community leaders, and better government practices. These riots are typically understood through a regional lens to be a strictly northern (or western) phenomenon.[3] From California and New Jersey, we are given pictures of buildings on fire and Black teenagers fighting police; from Alabama and North Carolina we are fed pictures of calm "Negro" students sitting in at lunch counters or being peacefully pounded down the street by six-hundred-pound water cannons.

While it is true that some of the largest and most destructive of the urban uprisings of the 1960s occurred in Watts, Newark, and Detroit, this narrative obscures the numerous, tumultuous rebellions that did occur in the South, often in direct conflict (though sometimes also accidental cooperation) with the Civil Rights organizations that predominated there. Part of the reason we inherit this regional perspective is that massive studies of the riots were done in the aforementioned cities, while most of the rebellions in the South received no such published attention.

---

3   The term "New South" has been used in many ways, sometimes as a reference to the post–Civil War period, but for our part we use it to refer to the Civil Rights period and beyond, when the country's political structure was permanently changed by the growth and development of an increasingly important Black political class. The term has obvious cosmetic significance as well, as the South sought to reshape its image for reasons of commerce and population management.

This regionalized dichotomy played a political role as well, however, giving politicians and activists a supposedly pure (southern) model of nonviolent protest to impose upon their constituencies. But the model was a myth: the riots of Atlanta, Tampa, Augusta, Louisville, Orangeburg, Memphis, Birmingham, Greensboro, and many other southern cities all told a different story, a story about the millions of Black people whose anger could not be contained by the political reforms or preferred methodology of Civil Rights leaders, whose dreams of freedom from a century earlier had been ignored but not forgotten.

The Coming Storm

Southern power structures—media, government, property owners, and businessmen—were inconsistent on the question of Black rebellion: they maintained brutal standing armies of police and vigilantes to suppress locals' efforts toward freedom, seemingly acknowledging an irreparable tension, while at the same time forever blaming "outside agitators" for riling up the supposedly content locals. For many white people across the South, the struggles of the 1950s and '60s thus came as a surprise. For them, the façade of the "southern Negro"—who would passively accept the segregation, exploitation, and indignity of white supremacy—was suddenly shattered.

Cracks in this façade had long been visible for those who were paying attention. The scattered but militant struggles of earlier decades prophesied the urban rebellions of the late '60s, and as the history of struggle against the cotton industry in Georgia's Black Belt attests, sabotage and self-defense were consistent features of black survival and political struggle. Community defense against lynch mobs, cross-burnings, and KKK and police terror was also a constant reality, predating any debates over violence or nonviolence that emerged in the 1950s and '60s.

In particular, there was the powder keg that was the Black veteran: made to experience innumerable indignities in the United States armed forces during a purported war against fascism, he returned angry, trained, and defiant. In Columbia, Tennessee, on February 25, 1946, for example, an everyday dispute between an older Black woman and a white business-owner over a radio repair resulted in a large armed clash. The woman, Gladys Stephenson, felt cheated by the owner, who charged her double the price though the radio remained broken. In the midst of the argument the man threatened Ms. Stephenson, at which point, her son, James, a

Navy veteran and former boxer, stepped in to deescalate the situation. As they left the store, James was sucker-punched in the back of his head by the white store owner. In the ensuing brawl, the veteran defended himself against several white employees and onlookers while his mother used shards of glass to slash at their attackers.[4]

The act of a Black family defending itself from white attack caused an immediate scandal among Columbia's white supremacist establishment. By that afternoon, word had spread that a white lynch mob had gathered and surrounded the jail where the Stephensons were being held, and veterans and civilians from the Black community organized themselves and stationed snipers with shotguns, pistols, and rifles on rooftops. The snipers took shots at the mob when it approached, wounding four policemen. In the words of one historian, "This is 1946. You had veterans up on those roofs. They had taken down the Nazis. They weren't having it. For them, this was a new day." The following day, state troopers and national guardsmen, armed with machine guns, combed Black neighborhoods beating residents, firing shots randomly into homes, and arresting over one hundred people. Police murdered two of the arrested at the jail, reportedly for attempting to steal the sidearms of white officers. Due to a lack of evidence, only twenty-five Black arrestees were ever tried. A clever legal defense by the NAACP resulted in the acquittal of twenty-three men, only one of whom ever did time.[5]

The importance of the veteran experience reappeared several years later in Monroe, North Carolina with the unique NAACP chapter led by Robert F. Williams. Monroe was a small town of about eleven thousand at the time, which bordered South Carolina and was home to the regional headquarters of the KKK. Returning home after serving as a marine, Williams was driven to organize an NAACP chapter in 1955 after experiencing discrimination in the armed forces. This, combined with his participation in armed defense during a race riot in Detroit, gave him the basic knowledge to start organizing.[6] As Williams wrote several years later,

---

4   Carol Anderson (Emory associate professor of African American Studies), Emory University, Podcast Video, March 13, 2012, http://news.emory.edu/stories/2012/03/hidden_history_of_civil_rights_movement_tennessee_riot/campus.html.

5   Carol Anderson, Podcast Video; Caroll Van West, "Columbia Race Riot, 1946," http://tennesseeencyclopedia.net/entry.php?rec=296.

6   Speaking about his earliest experiences of Black consciousness, Williams recounted witnessing as a child the vicious beating of a Black woman by a white police officer named Jesse Alexander Helms. The officer was none other than the father of the later famous Senator Jesse Helms, who once observed with admiration that his father "had the sharpest shoe in town and didn't mind using it" (Timothy Tyson, "Robert

We began a recruiting drive among laborers, farmers, domestic workers, the unemployed, and any and all Negro people in the area. We ended up with a chapter that was unique in the whole NAACP because of the working class composition and a leadership that was not middle class. Most important, we had a strong representation of returned veterans who were very militant and who didn't scare easy.[7]

The chapter quickly grew from two to over two hundred members, and immediately set out to start desegregating public facilities. They succeeded with the public library, but received a violent push back when attempting the same with the public pool. The Klan began holding increasingly massive rallies, calling for the ouster of the NAACP leaders and driving through Black neighborhoods firing pistols.

The NAACP chapter armed itself in defense, getting a charter from the National Rifle Association and using funds donated by a northern church to buy rifles. Their guns were quickly put to use: in the summer of 1957 an armed motorcade of Klansmen attacked the house of the chapter vice president, which was defended successfully by NAACP members.[8]

The struggle to integrate the swimming pool continued, with "stand-ins" and pickets. Williams and several youth were at one point attacked on the roadside by white vigilantes and police; they defended themselves with carbines and .45-caliber pistols, holding off the vigilantes and disarming the police until they were allowed to leave. No blood was shed. Like so many other public facilities in the segregated South, the town of Monroe closed the pool to avoid it being integrated.

The most immediate consequences for the Monroe chapter's militancy came not from the KKK but from the NAACP hierarchy, who, upon hearing of William's advocacy of direct action and self-defense, suspended his membership. Mabel Williams soon took over leadership of the chapter. Foreshadowing the direction of later groups like the Black Panthers, the chapter shifted to reflect the analysis and needs of its members, focusing more on economic exploitation, as well as the political and symbolic struggles of public integration campaigns. They developed a ten-point program and began to press for its implementation, but before they could

---

F. Williams, 'Black Power,' and the Roots of the African American Freedom Struggle," *The Journal of American History* 85, no. 2 (1998): 540, http://history.msu.edu/files/2010/04/Timothy-Tyson.pdf).

7   Robert F. Williams, *Negroes with Guns* (Detroit: Wayne State University Press, 1998), 14.

8   Ibid., 10.

Black teenagers struggle against water cannons during protests and rioting in the downtown area, April 1963.

make much progress, Williams was framed for kidnapping two prominent white racists who had been driving through his neighborhood with a banner on their car that read "Open Season on Coons."[9]

The federal charges forced Williams to flee Monroe, and he successfully escaped to Canada and then Cuba, where he continued to support the Black freedom struggle through a newsletter, *The Crusader*, and later a radio program called *Radio Free Dixie*. The radio show could be picked up in the United States, and years later Harlem residents recounted passing around tape recordings of his shows as teenagers.

The Bricks and Bottles of Bombingham

A final precedent is worth contemplation in considering the southern origins of the late 1960s urban rebellions. In the spring of 1963, a large campaign of direct action emerged in the deeply segregated city of Birmingham, Alabama. Known to Black people as "Bombingham" for the vicious brutality with which its racial hierarchy was defended, Martin Luther King, Jr., and the Southern Christian Leadership Conference (SCLC) chose the city as a strategic site in which to attack segregation. Their organization joined with the local group, Alabama Christian Movement for Human Rights, which had organized an ongoing, highly effective boycott of segregated white-owned stores since 1962.

The campaign in Birmingham was a test case for the application of King's philosophy of nonviolence, in a context where not just a single

---

9   Ibid., 31.

public institution but instead the entire citywide reality of segregation and racial hierarchy was being targeted. Secretly dubbed "Project C" by organizers, to avoid any detection of the planning by city officials and police, the campaign began on April 3 with sit-ins staged at lunch counters, and pickets outside of white-owned stores. These continued for several days until the second phase of the project began with street demonstrations. On April 6, a group of thirty demonstrators was mass arrested on a march, and the following day policemen, led by the notorious white supremacist Eugene "Bull" Connor, attacked a crowd with night sticks and dogs.[10] By April 10, a circuit judge had passed an injunction against the participation in or encouragement of any kind of protest activity. King, who drafted his famous "Letter from Birmingham Jail" after his subsequent arrest, promptly defied this.

Demonstrations continued, with "kneel-ins" at white-only churches in addition to more pickets and sit-ins around the city. Until the third phase of the campaign—the controversial introduction of large numbers of child demonstrators—the pickets and marches were small, typically numbering about thirty or forty people. But after weeks of nonviolence trainings for schoolchildren by SCLC members, thousands of children were organized. On May 2, the first contingent of three hundred young people marched in waves out of the 16th Street Baptist Church into downtown. Police arrested them en masse over a period of four hours.

The same tactic was employed the following day: this time Bull Connor ordered police to attack the children with fire hoses, dogs, and clubs. Quoted as saying, "I want to see the dogs work.... Look at those niggers run," police behavior galvanized both national attention as well as the immediate anger of onlookers and parents.[11] The fragile approach of strict nonviolence fell apart: upon seeing cops attack children, the crowds of onlookers began hurling bricks and bottles at the police. An interview

---

10 For the duration of the direct-action campaign in Birmingham, the city was technically (and bizarrely) under the control of two separate governments. Only shortly before the beginning of the campaign, voters had elected to replace the three-man City Commission, led in part by Bull Connor, with a Mayor-Council structure. The commission refused to leave office, however, and despite both administrations meeting in the same buildings during these months, Connor maintained total control over the police force. While both administrations were racist and pro-segregation, the obvious confusion and division between the two structures played into the hands of the demonstrators.

11 Lee E. Bains, "Birmingham 1963: Confrontations over Civil Rights," in *Birmingham, Alabama, 1956–1963: The Black Struggle for Civil Rights*, ed. David J. Garrow (Brooklyn: Carlson Publishing, 1989), 180.

conducted years later with Washington Booker, a high school freshman at the time, is telling:

> It was inconceivable [to us] that people would go down and put themselves in the positions to fall into the hands of the police. We thought that was the dumbest thing.
>
> The first day that we actually went down to observe a demonstration, we kind of hung around in the crowd, watched what happened. It pissed us off—excuse me—as we watched.... The police were waiting. The police were everywhere. They were waiting for them. They pounced on them and the crowd started screaming. Of course we did what we did. We got back in the crowds and started throwing bricks at the police. That was our thing. The police would run into the crowd. For a long time one of the proudest things that I was ever proud of and I talked about it for a long time, that somebody threw a brick and the police ran into the crowd and the guy ran and I was like right here. And as the policeman came running the crowd kind of split, and I just fell in front of him and he fell over me and the guy got away.... I'll never forget that. It was right there on that corner.... That was our contribution at that point.[12]

A magazine correspondent reported the outbreak of rioting during a youth march in this way:

> Connor's cops were relaxed, eating sandwiches and sipping soft drinks. They were caught by surprise when the doors of the 16th Street church were flung open and 2,500 Negroes swarmed out. The Negroes surged across Kelly Ingram Park, burst through the police line, and descended on downtown Birmingham. Yelling and singing, they charged in and out of department stores, jostled whites on the streets, paralyzed traffic.
>
> Recovering, the police got reinforcements. Firemen hooked up their hoses. Motorcycles and squad cars, sirens blaring, rushed into the area. Two policemen grabbed a Negro, shoved him against a storefront—and found themselves caught inside a glowering circle of 300 Negroes. A voice growled menacingly:

---

12 Washington Booker, interview by Willoughby Anderson, Southern Oral History Program Collection, November 17, 1991.

"Let's free him." But demonstration leaders quickly broke into the circle and managed to save the policemen.

The riot ebbed—and then, an hour later, exploded again. In Kelly Ingram Park, hundreds of Negroes began lobbing bricks and bottles at the lawmen. A deputy sheriff fell to the pavement, shouting "Those black apes!"

For two hours, the battle raged, but slowly, inexorably, in trucks and cars, the police closed in on the park. The Rev. Fred Shuttlesworth, one of King's top advisers, yelled helplessly at rioters from in front of the church.[13]

SCLC organizer James Bevel ordered parents and onlookers to leave, saying, "Everybody get off this corner. If you're not going to demonstrate in a nonviolent manner, then leave." SCLC called off the demonstration for the day. The demonstrations continued in the following days, however, ultimately filling Birmingham's jails with some two thousand protesters. Feeling the economic boycott, the bad publicity, and the threat of another outbreak of Black violence, white businessmen started meeting with each other to discuss the possibility of negotiations. At the same time, Alabama's racist governor George Wallace sent in six hundred National Guard to suppress the rebellion. Despite SCLC's attempts to calm the demonstrations, King was quoted as saying, "We will turn America upside down in order that it turn right side up." The county sheriff threatened to impose martial law.[14]

As a complete breakdown of order seemed imminent, the Birmingham's business class finally agreed to all four major demands of the campaign: a desegregation of downtown facilities, placement of Blacks in clerical and sales jobs, release of prisoners in jail on low bail, and the establishment of permanent communications between white and Black leaders.

An announcement of the successful negotiations didn't stop the violence: After a large KKK rally on May 12, two bombs struck the Black community in retaliation for the campaign, one targeting the hotel room where campaign organizers had been meeting. Riots immediately broke out in the area, with men and women throwing projectiles at police and national guardsmen, un-arresting fellow rioters, and attacking white stores.

---

13   "Freedom Now," *Time*, May 17, 1963, http://cgi.cnn.com/ALLPOLITICS/1996/
analysis/back.time/9605/15/.

14   Bains, "Birmingham 1963," 181.

Outlined against the flames that shot 150 ft. in the air, there was the mass of Negroes barring with their bodies and with a rain of rocks, bottles and bricks the firemen who had rushed to save a white man's store.... And Birmingham went to war.... Thousands of enraged Negroes surged through the streets, flinging bricks, brandishing knives, pummeling policemen.[15]

After consistently refusing Civil Rights leaders' requests for protection from KKK terror all over the South, President Kennedy finally sent in federal troops, not to protect protesters but to guard against the possibility of a Black uprising. King returned from Atlanta to speak out against further rebellion, and the fires died out. Birmingham slowly established a new normality, gradually integrating the Civil Rights negotiations into its economic and racial hierarchies. Despite an obvious breakdown in the strictly nonviolent approach, and the fundamental role that rioting played in forcing the hand of city officials, media generally portrayed Birmingham as a victory for the Civil Rights mainstream.[16] This helped to repair Martin Luther King's reputation while undermining any alternatives to the political model represented by the SCLC.

On-the-ground experiences told a different story of Black self-defense and rebellion in Bombingham, and this story would spread throughout the South. Years later, participants like Washington Booker would point to these riots as a fundamental moment that pushed them in a revolutionary direction.[17] Accounts by participants like Booker are a reminder that

15 "Freedom Now," *Time.*

16 The entire juxtaposition between nonviolent demonstrators and "extremists," as two supposedly distinct groups, was largely a myth created by leaders and media at the time and perpetuated by certain historians ever since. As Birmingham shows, the majority of Black rank-and-file protesters were willing to use nonviolent means when they worked, and could and did transition with ease to both self-defense and attack when that felt appropriate. Proponents of armed struggle like Robert F. Williams themselves advocated mixing these approaches, and it was not uncommon for protesters to carry guns to nonviolent protests, with the understanding that this was acceptable as long as they were used only in self-defense. The elevation of non- or less-violent tactics to the pedestal of unquestionable ideology was accomplished by a rising Black political class and its allies in the white media, who saw this rigid distinction as useful to their own ends. In our time, nonviolence has become a kind of orthodoxy; in this former period, its meaning was up for debate and its proponents' dogma far less hegemonic.

17 Booker went on to organize with the Alabama Black Liberation Front, an autonomous group in Birmingham modeled largely after the Black Panthers. The Panthers were significantly less active in the South, where Student Nonviolent Coordinating Committee (SNCC) groups or other grassroots organizations often functioned as

only a small minority of Birmingham's Black residents were ever "trained" in nonviolence, that for many residents such passive methods felt very foreign and even suicidal, and that the Black population as a whole was more than capable of alternating flexibly between one model and another, depending on circumstance. According to multiple accounts, at least as many people participated in the street battles as offered themselves up for passive arrest, and in all likelihood many participated in both.

Nevertheless, the national media insisted on painting nonviolence advocates as the mainstream, and rioters as a small minority of extremists. The media's framing of mainstream protest and its presentation of public opinion were based on a political prerogative to place boundaries around the possible meaning and tactics of Black protest, while still supporting a liberal "modernization" of the South.[18] Soon, however, the popular cries of "Black Power!" would break through these boundaries, as massive urban rebellions challenged nonviolence's monopoly on legitimacy.

We Are Not Concerned With Peace

Atlanta

The relatively minor skirmishes of violence in the midst of organized, planned campaigns like Birmingham 1963 forecast similar future disturbances if the Civil Rights movement was unable to contain the anger and political ambition of the Black poor. In August 1965, the Watts neighborhood of South Los Angeles exploded in this direction after a small conflict between a Black family and a policeman. The riots lasted about a week, and resulted in thirty-four deaths, over one thousand injuries, three thousand arrests, and $40 million in property damage. Watts was preceded by a six-day rebellion in Harlem in July 1964, sparked by the police murder of a Black teenager. These incidents left local politicians

---

de-facto Panther chapters. ("Interview with Lorenzo Komboa Ervin," *Black Flag* 206 (Autumn 1995), http://libcom.org/library/interview-with-lorenzo-komboa-ervin-from-1995); Robert W. Widell Jr., "The Power Belongs to Us and We Belong to the Revolutionary Age: The Alabama Black Liberation Front and the Long Reach of the Black Panther Party," in *Liberated Territories: Untold Local Perspectives on the Black Panther Party*, eds. Yohuru Williams and Jama Lazero (Durham: Duke University Press, 2009).

18   *Time* magazine, for example, reassured its readers that those who "look with eagerness to a militant solution" represented only a small fringe, compared with the nonviolent mainstream, even after quoting direct observation of hundreds upon hundreds of rioters looting, burning, and street-fighting with police ("Freedom Now," *Time*).

and movement organizers anxious about the possibility of such rebellions spreading through the South, which partly encouraged white officials to preemptively negotiate with moderate Civil Rights leaders in order to avoid similar events.

Their fears were confirmed in September 1966 in Atlanta, Georgia, when years of antipoverty and tenant organizing in Black neighborhoods finally spilled over into riots. Labeling itself "too busy too hate," the city was proudly considered progressive by its media and politicians for its "Atlanta Style" of interracial mediation, and the riots took most leaders by surprise. Unlike some southern cities, Atlanta had a politically active and long-established Black elite that maintained communication with the city's white politicians. For decades the entire city's Black population had been spoken for by a small handful of wealthy Black men via the Atlanta Negro Voters League, who facilitated white management of the Black population and got out the Black vote for white politicians.

Atlanta's Black elite was both reinforced and challenged in various ways by the emergence of the Civil Rights movement, which on a local scale manifested with struggles around segregated neighborhoods, welfare, policy brutality, tenant organizing, recreational facilities, and municipal

A crowd of rioters stream past a smashed police cruiser in the Summerhill neighborhood of Atlanta, 1966.

services. More radical local organizations, like the Vine City Council—a multiracial grassroots group that fought evictions and organized a rent strike in early 1966—worked off and on with regional groups like the increasingly militant and nationalist Student Nonviolent Coordinating Committee (SNCC).[19] The Black middle class remained largely ignorant of these struggles, comfortable in their own neighborhoods and loyal to the white mayor, Ivan Allen. For his part, Mayor Allen supported the courts' eviction of rent strikers even while he cleverly offered to move the tenants into public housing as an alternative. He also built a massive stadium adjacent to several poor neighborhoods, displacing hundreds and maybe thousands in the process. With a progressive veneer, the administration used public infrastructure and development projects to break up social ties in poor areas, and thus disrupt, divide, and deny any attempts to change conditions.[20]

This strategy could delay but not prevent the conflicts of the late '60s. On September 6, 1966, police gunned down a Black man fleeing arrest in the Summerhill neighborhood, in the shadows of the new stadium. A contingent of Black police was sent in to disperse the angry crowd that was quickly gathering, but they failed to do so. Neighbors began to organize a demonstration for the afternoon, and two SNCC members supported it by driving around in a sound truck. These two men were arrested after refusing to turn off the sound system, and the neighborhood erupted as residents threw projectiles at police and flipped or burned police cars. One account by an Atlanta historian describes the scene as such:

> Accompanied by two police officers, Mayor Allen arrived at the scene. He began walking back-and-forth through the crowd urging residents to leave the area. Allen struggled to the roof of a police car which was parked in one of the area's intersections. When he tried to address the crowd, residents began to heckle him and rock the car. Allen lost his balance and fell into the arms of the police officers. Bottles and bricks once again began to fly.[21]

19 The group's name can be misleading. Though initially invested in a tactical (rather than ideological) nonviolence, SNCC radicalized throughout the 1960s, eventually rejecting nonviolence as impractical and dangerous. They also expelled whites as the group moved in a more nationalist direction.

20 David Andrew Harmon, *Beneath the Image of the Civil Rights Movement and Race Relations: Atlanta, Georgia, 1946–1981* (New York: Garland Publishing, 1996), 199–204.

21 Ibid., 205.

Due to a series of roadblocks set up by police and the political maneuvering of Allen and the Black elite, the riot in Summerhill failed to extend beyond the first night. At that point, there had been just seventy-five arrests and a single building set aflame, but just four days later, a new series of conflicts erupted, this time in Northeast Atlanta. The riot was again catalyzed by police conduct: after a white motorist shot two Black youth on Boulevard Avenue, a police officer who arrived on the scene was injured by a projectile of some kind. The first ambulance took away the cop, who was only mildly injured, while the teenagers were left bleeding on the pavement. As a result, and because the nearest hospital was whites-only, one of the youths died in transit.

An enraged crowd gathered and immediately began to attack police with sticks, bottles, and bricks. Leaders from Martin Luther King, Jr.'s SCLC showed up to calm the crowd, but were arrested by police. Over the next three days, residents would fight the police with Molotov cocktails and burn down four white-owned businesses.

Before the riots, Allen had prepared a list of twenty-five Black ministers who he would contact in the event of a disturbance, including Reverend Martin Luther King, Sr., who described the rioters as, "not my people." Other Black religious leaders condemned the uprising on behalf of Mayor Allen, criticizing "those who would initiate disorder and disrupt the city's peaceful racial climate."[22] Black workers employed in a government antipoverty program formed "Good Neighborhood Clubs" to preserve law and order as the white media joined the Black elite in placing the blame on the agitation of Stokely Carmichael and SNCC. Only a small minority of the Civil Rights community defended SNCC or drew attention to the deplorable slum conditions in the affected neighborhoods. Grassroots neighborhood organizations that had attacked these conditions with strikes and eviction defense supported the accused and refused to condemn the rioters, but were left isolated.[23]

An opportunity for building on Atlanta's riots of 1966 soon presented itself in the Dixie Hills neighborhood in June 1967. A minor arrest of a Black teen by a white officer at a shopping center attracted a crowd

22 Ibid.
23 Several radical religious groups played an interesting role here. A network of Mennonite houses rooted in the affected neighborhoods, for example, published statements supportive of the riots and encouraging their white constituency to show solidarity with rioters. The mostly Black Vine City Council was actually cofounded by a radical white Catholic Worker named Hector Black. Despite various racial tensions with nationalists, these groups at least had the benefit of being autonomous from Atlanta's political establishment, unlike many Civil Rights organizations.

when the teen's sister attacked the cop with her purse. After police arrested her as well, a crowd of hundreds gathered to discuss a possible protest and the many grievances facing poor neighborhoods, including unreliable trash pickup, police brutality, and unemployment. A call for petitions from moderate leaders was ignored, while a cry for "making the police work until they fall in their tracks" was met with cheers. Stokely Carmichael was quoted as saying, "It is not a question of law and order. We are not concerned with peace. We are concerned with the liberation of Black people."[24]

As the crowd poured into the street, its numbers grew to over one thousand. Residents threw projectiles and firecrackers at police while smashing police car windows. The city responded the next day by sending in crews to work on municipal services and clean the streets, while also organizing Black teenagers into youth patrols to stop the violence, people whom SNCC referred to as "Black traitors."[25] A demonstration several days later had fewer residents than police present, and despite efforts to fight anyway, the police brutalized the protesters. The dividing lines of class and power that would complicate such rebellions in the future began to appear in earnest that day: One group of policemen fired on retreating youths, in the process killing a middle-aged man and critically injuring a nine-year old boy watching from their front porch. The cops were Black.[26]

The neighborhood calmed after the shootings by those whom they considered their own. A local Black state senator petitioned for Carmichael's exile from Atlanta and received over one thousand signatures in the Dixie Hills neighborhood. Massive media attention on "outside agitators" and a loyalty to newly elected Black politicians undermined possible relationships between angry neighbors and autonomous groups like the Vine City Council or SNCC, disrupting their day-to-day organizing efforts and limiting their influence during spontaneous bursts of outrage.

Despite politicians' rhetoric about outside agitators, the riots clearly had local roots, and city officials were forced to at least appear to respond to certain grievances. For instance, new recreational facilities were built (a demand once made by Civil Rights leaders but long ignored); municipal

---

24 *Report of the National Advisory Commission on Civil Disorders* (New York: Bantam, 1968), 55.

25 Initially proposed by a Black senator named LeRoy Johnson, who had been elevated to his position largely by the Civil Rights movement, these youth patrols were consciously modeled after the "White Hats" used to quell the rebellion that shook Tampa earlier that week (*Report of the National Advisory Commission on Civil Disorders*, 56).

26 Ibid.

services were immediately improved in affected areas, though reportedly discontinued after a month and half; and Mayor Allen promised seventeen thousand new low-income housing units within five years, via a new federal program.

Unfortunately the housing initiative actually worked backwards: due to the demolition of older housing, after nine years there were actually 20 percent *fewer* low-income housing units than before, with numerous vacant lots dotting the neighborhoods. The loss meant even further displacement of poor residents, disrupting the networks of grassroots groups, families, and neighbors that had catalyzed the urban rebellions of 1966 and 1967.[27] Atlanta's stadium and public housing projects both provide excellent examples of how social control evolved during and after this period. No longer the strictly *negative* force of prohibition and repression, the state adapted to use social democracy and infrastructure development to physically and psychologically maneuver, manage, and police oppressed populations.

Tampa

Just six days before the uprising began in Atlanta's Dixie Hill neighborhood, Tampa, Florida, erupted into three furious days of arson, looting, and street-fighting.[28] At 5:30pm on Sunday, June 11, 1967, three Black youths broke into a photo supply warehouse. After a delay of about forty-five minutes, several groups of police officers gave chase through the alleys and streets of the neighborhood of the Central Park Village Housing Project. Once they caught up to one of the boys, a white cop named James Calvert pulled his .38 revolver and fired a single shot into the teen's back. The nineteen-year-old's name was Martin Chambers, and he died almost instantly.

In less than an hour, over five hundred people had gathered in the immediate area of Central Park to spread the news and discuss the shooting. Residents began talking about other grievances, including the sexual assault of neighborhood women, constant police harassment, unemployment, and general patterns of discrimination. One of the few Black officers on the police force begged the crowd to disperse and explained there would be an investigation. As the Kerner Commission reported:

---

27   Harmon, *Beneath the Image of the Civil Rights Movement*, 209.

28   Though some may debate Tampa being a "southern" city, we highlight this episode because the precedent set in Tampa for Black-led recuperation is absolutely crucial to understanding how southern Civil Rights leaders worked to contain and prevent Black rebellion throughout the region (and nation).

This time the maneuver did not work. From nearby bars and tawdry night spots patrons joined the throng. A window was smashed. Haphazard looting began. As fluid bands of rioters moved down the Central Avenue business district, stores whose proprietors were particularly disliked were singled out. A grocery store, a liquor store, a restaurant were hit. The first fire was set.[29]

Both Governor Claude Kirk and the chief of police were away from the city at the time, and it took officers until nearly 11 pm to enter the area. Police and rioters clashed as residents threw Molotov cocktails and other projectiles, and during the fighting one officer died of a heart attack, while another was badly injured when struck by a fellow officer's tear gas canister. The rioters also attacked white motorists in the area, though some neighbors intervened to allow the motorists to leave. The National Guard was called in to replace local police.

The rioting died down by 1:00 a.m., and Governor Kirk returned to Tampa ready to act. Kirk set up a meeting the next day in a nearby school to placate residents' anger; both white and Black speakers were booed off the stage. Government-employed antipoverty workers went door to door all afternoon asking people to "stay off the streets," while teens instead used the time to build up arsenals of bottles, bricks, and homemade incendiary bombs behind buildings.[30] By 9:00 p.m. some residents were exchanging gunfire with national guardsmen, while others attacked buildings and businesses with Molotov cocktails. The authorities contained the rebellion inside a perimeter, but could not regain control.

The following day, an inquiry into the murder of Martin Chambers reconvened. Investigators and media visited the scene of the shooting, questioned three youths who witnessed it, and heard the testimony of Officer Calvert. The NAACP appeared at this inquiry, visibly frustrated with the unruly Black residents of the housing project, and stated that if they couldn't bring evidence of police misconduct to the hearing, then "they need to shut up."[31]

29 Also called the "US Riot Commission Report," the Kerner Commission published a widely disseminated, massive, and thorough social study of the wave of riots that struck the United States from 1964 to 1967. Though tied explicitly to efforts to better govern and manage the population, it is a highly useful and at times deeply insightful look at the demographics and circumstances of these uprisings (*Report of the National Advisory Commission on Civil Disorders*, 44).

30 Ibid., 46.

31 Joey Machado, "The 1967 Central Park Riots in Tampa," http://jam1592.blogspot.

Besides the limited role of the NAACP, both grassroots and more institutionalized Civil Rights or Black Power groups were basically nonexistent in the Tampa conflict, which initially left city officials clueless about how to communicate or negotiate with Central Park residents. A solution soon presented itself though, when several teens who attended the inquiry volunteered to spread word through the housing project that officials were "doing their best." Perhaps eager for something to contribute, these youths agreed to police their own streets if national guardsmen were pulled back. While the violence continued with various firebombings and small attacks, the patrols of youths, identified as "White Hats" for their shiny city-supplied helmets, replaced police on the streets of the Central Park area. According to one study:

> Many riot leaders agreed to join the volunteer youth patrols and stop rioting. The patrol units, shaped into a makeshift paramilitary organization, received their uniforms with white helmets and took up positions in the Black Central Avenue project community. Some youths were named captains and lieutenants while given the responsibility of patrolling hot areas in squads to convince the rioters, often friends, to cease the looting and arson. Sheriff Beard kept the National Guard and police out of these areas except when called by the volunteer patrols. The White Hats were credited with dispersing various crowds on the brink of violent behavior. By Thursday morning, the worst appeared to be over.[32]

One has to admire the brilliance of the youth patrol concept developed by Tampa's authorities. Acknowledging that both local police and the National Guard could contain but not stamp out the rebellion, and undoubtedly under national pressure to end the conflict before it spread further, Governor Kirk and other officials counterintuitively turned to the community in rebellion to police itself. The concept worked because it combined certain aspects of the Black power struggle—the desire to control one's own neighborhood or territory and a paramilitary structure that mimicked the militancy of groups like the Black Panthers—in a superficial, ultimately reactionary manner that was more than palatable to the power structure.

---

com/2008/02/sample-3-1967-central-park-riots-in.html.
32   Joey Machado, "The 1967 Central Park Riots in Tampa."

In replacing the hated presence of the police with local youths (albeit ones inflated with their own self-importance while bedecked in pseudo-military finery), the state gave residents "control" over their own neighborhood. Simultaneously, the most immediately present symbols of the larger oppressive system were removed. Neighbors would not attack their own teens, and were prevented from taking their attack elsewhere by the lingering presence of the National Guard at the perimeter of the territory. At 9:00 a.m. on Wednesday morning, less than seventy-two hours after the murder, Florida's state attorney general exonerated police officer James Calvert in the shooting of Martin Chambers. This was a flagrant insult to the residents of Central Park, but instead of it sparking a second round of rebellion, by Thursday the conflict had fizzled out.

In its admiration for community self-policing initiatives, the Kerner Commission described the demographic of the likely "counter-rioter" in the following terms:

> The typical counter-rioter, who risked injury and arrest to walk the streets urging rioters to "cool it," was an active supporter of existing social institutions. He was, for example, far more likely than either the rioter or the noninvolved to feel that this country is worth defending in a major war. His actions and his attitudes reflected his substantially greater stake in the social system; he was considerably better educated and more affluent than either the rioter or the noninvolved.[33]

The youth patrols would represent a major turning point, not just in ending the Tampa conflict, but also in developing a whole new method of policing and population management in the United States. The White Hats model, whether acknowledged as such by name or merely by form, would spread all over the country and play a crucial role in preventing or containing numerous civil disturbances. Published in early 1968, the Kerner Commission—which became virtually required reading for mayors, police, and other authorities—heavily emphasized the emerging importance of citizen patrols and self-policing institutions, pointing out that these methods often succeeded where the National Guard failed. A horizontal administration of the state, always present but usually behind the scenes, was taking center stage.

---

33   *Report of the National Advisory Commission on Civil Disorders*, 129.

Louisville

While the state was attempting to study, manage, and suppress these riots, uprisings continued to occur with increasing frequency in 1967 and 1968. In the first nine months of 1967, there were 164 civil disorders, and in 1968 there were 110 incidents of unrest occurring in the weeks immediately after the assassination of Martin Luther King, Jr., alone.

As it became clear that the nonviolent-direct-action campaign model of the Civil Rights era was ineffective against the range of fundamental oppressions—slum housing, failing schools, abject poverty, drug abuse, unemployment—experienced by the Black poor of America's cities, the rhetoric and ideas of Black Power spread. It would be a mistake, however, to see this shift as the sole cause of the uprisings of the late 1960s. Though both were related to the failure of the Civil Rights movement and the persistence of racism, the spread of these uprisings was not just the result of Black Power, but also of a broad range of changes in the American political landscape, in which resistance via spontaneous, demandless rioting replaced the semi-scripted class battles of the 1920s and '30s. To the extent that Black Power did play a role in the uprisings, it was much more one of uneven ideological influence than active organizational direction.

By the end of the decade, in fact, many militant groups like the Black Panthers argued that such insurrections—spontaneous and uncontrollable—were counterproductive to building the kind of political power that those cadre organizations desired. These groups sometimes even helped to prevent such conflicts, as the Panthers did on April 9, 1968 in Oakland, California, after the death of Martin Luther King, Jr.[34] Growing organically out of the social life of the ghetto, these rebellions were typically kicked off by bands of politically educated but organizationally unaffiliated youth, spread by impromptu gatherings of angry residents, and sustained by the casual mutual aid that results between neighbors in such crisis situations.[35] Political militants sometimes participated and were often blamed, but never controlled this activity.

Nowhere was this complicated interaction between movement organizations—both liberal and radical—and the spontaneous activity of a

---

34 "Black Panther Party Pieces of History 1966–1969," *It's About Time*, http://www.itsabouttimebpp.com/chapter_history/bpp_pieces_of_history.html.

35 According to demographic studies of those arrested in riots around the country, the typical rioter was "proud of his race, extremely hostile to both whites and middle-class Negroes and, though informed about politics, highly distrustful of the political system and of political leaders" (*Report of the National Advisory Commission on Civil Disorders*, 111).

rioting population better exhibited than in Louisville, Kentucky, in 1968. Known as the "Gateway to the South" for the fact that Black passengers traveling south by train would have to switch from integrated to "colored only" cars there, Louisville had a complicated history of southern, white-supremacist cultural norms and northern-style industrial development existing side by side. It was not uncommon for Black workers to labor alongside white workers as part of an interracial union, only to go home to violently segregated neighborhoods.

In 1954, for example, two couples trying to break that housing segregation were viciously attacked. A radical white couple named Anne and Carl Braden helped a Black family, the Wades, to move into a white neighborhood by buying the house and then immediately turning it over to them. Both the Wades and the Bradens were the subject of harassment, death threats, foreclosure from the bank, vandalism, and ultimately a bombing. Segregationists raised the red flag, asking, "Is he really looking for a house or is he a pawn for the cause of communism?" The Bradens and Andrew Wade ultimately faced charges of sedition, winning in court but losing their employment in the process. Half of the house was destroyed in an incendiary attack.[36]

Anne Braden went on to join neighbors in founding a group in 1963 called the West End Community Council (WECC). For many years, the interracial group was an important force in the local Civil Rights struggle on a number of fronts, in particular for housing integration in Louisville's West End. The campaign for integrated housing eventually stalled and failed to reverse the trends of white flight and slum housing, and WECC declared its support for Black Power, all the while maintaining multiracial leadership and membership. A uniquely local interpretation of this national phenomenon developed, with integrationists and white radicals remaining highly involved in the support of Black militant groups, for instance helping others to found the Black Student Union (BSU) and the Black Unity League of Kentucky (BULK). For their part, these new groups fought evictions, conducted radical education efforts, fought against drug abuse and drug dealers in Black neighborhoods, defended Black workers on the job, and opened Black social and cultural centers.

On May 7, 1968, little more than a month after the assassination of Martin Luther King, Jr. in Memphis, a series of events would seriously challenge these bonds. That day, police pulled over a Black teacher on

---

36 Tracy K'Meyer, *Civil Rights in the Gateway to the South: Louisville, Kentucky 1945–1980* (Lexington: University Press of Kentucky, 2009), 67.

suspicion of robbery. When a businessman named Manfred Reid approached, thinking his friend had been hurt in an accident, policeman Michael Clifford assaulted him. As is often the case when police attack a civilian, the victim was charged with assault. Black leaders were furious, and the city initially fired Clifford.

Thirteen days later, in the midst of this controversy, the SCLC's Poor People's Campaign made a stop in Louisville. During a rally calling for the dismissal of Clifford, the crowd clashed with police and smashed a store window. Tensions continued to escalate, in particular when, on May 23, after protest by the Fraternal Order of Police and a white segregationist group, Clifford was reinstated.[37]

BULK soon called for a demonstration against the reinstatement for the following Monday, promising speeches by Stokely Carmichael and James Cortez of SNCC. At 7:30pm a crowd assembled at 28th St. and Greenwood Avenue, listening to local militants give speeches from the hood of a car. One member of BULK pointed out that the mayor owned a furniture store in the area, declaring, "I ain't preaching no violence. So don't quote me. If it was me I'd turn it over, I'd turn it over!"[38] Cortez, a SNCC organizer from out of state, spread a rumor that Carmichael's plane was unable to land due to intervention by white officials, urging the crowd to disperse peacefully and return later.

After just forty-five minutes, gangs of teenagers assembled on rooftops attacked a bus passing through the area with rocks and bottles. A lone patrol car showed up, and was attacked by the crowd with more projectiles. A riot began that lasted throughout the week. It quickly spread beyond the initial rallying point, enveloping the downtown shopping district. Within several hours, Black snipers were reportedly on rooftops, firing at police, while rioters set police and civilian cars on fire, firebombed a business, and looted weapons from pawnshops.

National guardsmen were patrolling the streets by the next day, but this did not stop the rebellion. Black residents taunted and hurled stones at the soldiers, and attacks continued. Black leaders, including A. D. King (Martin Luther King, Jr.'s brother), and SNCC's James Cortez, urged rioters to stop. The strategy of youth patrols emerged again:

> During the day on Wednesday, members of KCLC [the Kentucky branch of the SCLC], including Reverends Leo Lesser

---

37 Ibid., 187.
38 Ibid., 188.

and King, successfully negotiated with city hall an agreement to pull back the National Guard and the police and let a group of young Black marshals keep order. King announced the agreement at a "cool-it" rally organized by WECC chair Eugene Robinson, urging people to show calm now that Blacks were "patrolling the area."[39]

A member of BULK, Robert Sims, showed less restraint at the rally, refusing to call for peace and stating, "I hope you'll tell the white man that you won't accept any more crumbs.... I won't tell you to stop rioting. I tell you to do whatever is necessary."[40]

On Wednesday night, two Black youth were murdered: one gunned down by a police officer while at a vending machine, the other shot by a white shop owner on the sidewalk outside his liquor store. After these shootings another surge of rioting erupted on Thursday and Friday, but died down by the weekend. The final toll was 119 fires set, 472 arrests, two people killed, and $250,000 in property damage.

In spite of the obvious disagreements over agitation versus recuperation, with some leaders trying to stop the rebellion while others encouraged it, the resulting arrests brought together the broad and divergent milieu of Black struggle in Louisville. A group of around eighty white people protested at city hall for the release of those arrested during the conflict, and eventually formed the White Emergency Support Team to join with WECC, BULK, and the Black Student Union in defending those facing charges. Ultimately, the city arrested and charged six known activists, including Sam Hawkins and Robert Sims of BULK as well as James Cortez, with conspiracy to destroy private property. Rather than distance themselves from the would-be rioters, however, the Black and white antiracist groups of Louisville understood the arrest of the "Black Six" to be an attack on militancy generally, and in turn rallied around them, linking previously disparate organizations to provide legal support and solidarity demonstrations. The support teams kept up the pressure with petitions, protests, and fundraising for nearly two years, and in July 1970 the judge ordered a verdict of not guilty for lack of evidence. The only defendant of the six to do time was James Cortez, who faced an additional charge of illegal possession of a weapon after a shotgun was found in his car.[41]

<hr>

39   Ibid., 190.
40   Ibid., 191.
41   On the other hand, some of the 472 arrested during the riots likely did time, but no statistics on the charges or verdicts is immediately available, making the success of the

Many years later, it came to light that James Cortez, the out-of-town SNCC activist who attempted to prevent the riot, was actually an undercover FBI agent named Peter Cordoza.[42] According to an autobiography of a fellow agent, Cordoza had infiltrated SNCC and left for Louisville without permission from the Bureau. Cardoza was eventually arrested as a conspirator after fumbling his attempts to calm the rioting crowds. He told the Louisville police that he was working for the FBI, but the Bureau refused to vouch for him. The unregistered shotgun the police found during his arrest, for which he did several years in prison, was in all likelihood issued to him by the federal government. The activists who did passionate support for this relative stranger for two years never knew his background.[43]

Despite the victory in court, fighting the charges took time away from struggles on the ground against the police, drug addiction, slum housing, and other issues. As most whites fled the areas of racial conflict and poverty, the circumstances changed and WECC's long-term vision of multiracial neighborhood organizing failed. Louisville's Black militant organizations recognized the change in context, and accomplished notable things like the creation of community-run drug treatment centers and the introduction of African and African American studies at the university. The larger conditions they struggled against, however, were a different beast than the earlier, more limited integrationist campaigns, and encompassed the entirety of Black oppression under capitalism—in which capital could easily flee unproductive, conflict-ridden areas with little consequence. In this context, it is clear that no activist campaign or separatist community organizing in isolation could possibly tackle the systems responsible. Civil Rights activism no longer felt relevant or viable, while, as the ghettos became more isolated and whites turned ever more reactionary, the social context for a more systemic rupture in the American landscape seemed to disappear.

---

support work done for the rioters difficult to determine.

42   This is one more small piece of evidence to counter the bizarre pacifist illusion that suggests the government *wants* us to riot to "ruin" our movements. In fact, government agents sought to prevent such outbursts, for obvious reasons, at every turn, while repressing those like BULK member Robert Sims who risked publicly supporting them.

43   In fact, a former Louisville resident who moved to Atlanta to join SNCC recalled asking her friends in the group to see if they knew who Cortez was. No one knew him, but this information, along with the suspicion that he was an agent, unfortunately never reached comrades in Louisville (K'Meyer, *Civil Rights in the Gateway to the South*, 192–193).

Postscript: A New Class Takes Control

As the 1960s came to a close, urban rebellions remained common but isolated, and though they sometimes succeeded in forcing action by city officials, they failed to permanently hold territory or spread beyond their own neighborhood or city borders. Meanwhile, the US government led a brutal campaign of violence against Black militants, assassinating leaders of groups like the Black Panthers and jailing hundreds across the country. Groups like SNCC and the Panthers were either brutally repressed, faded away, or became more like political parties, reshaping their image to engage in electoral campaigns. This further isolated rioters, strikers, and others whose rebellion was inconvenient for a newly rising Black political class.[44]

In retrospect, the differences between the Civil Rights and Black Power tendencies in this time appear to shrink. While the vague cries for Black Power that began in the South and spread across the country certainly represented a radicalization of Black political thought, organizations in both the Civil Rights and Black Power camps aimed to *politicize* the social discontent of poor Black people, to render the potential self-activity of an angry population into an actionable political program. Nowhere was this more evident than in these groups' dealings with the riots that erupted in their cities; the conduct of institutionalized Civil Rights groups was often traitorous, and that of many Black Power groups unreliable at best.[45] One sociological study of the time noted, "Such militants have been influential in 'cooling' their communities during periods of high riot potential. Theoretically oriented Black radicals see riots as spontaneous mass behavior which must be replaced by a revolutionary organization and consciousness."[46] Groups from both the moderate and radical camps tended to see such spontaneous rebellions as unintelligible and secondary to their political task of movement or

---

44   An excellent book that explores the Panthers' transition to electoralism is Elaine Brown's autobiography *A Taste of Power* (New York: Anchor Books, 1993). Other examples of Black Power's political drive can be found in SNCC activist Julian Bond's campaign for state representative in Georgia, or the many years of governance of Winston-Salem, North Carolina, by former BPP members.

45   One further illustration of the Civil Rights betrayal: To gain support for the 1968 Civil Rights Act, liberal legislators agreed to a provision that allowed for five years in prison for anyone found guilty of traveling or using a phone across state lines "to organize, promote, encourage, participate in, or carry on a riot," which was defined simply as an event with three or more people and the threat of violence. The first person to be prosecuted under this Civil Rights Act was a Black SNCC leader (Howard Zinn, *A People's History of the United States* [New York: HarperCollins, 2003], 461).

46   Robert Blauner, "Internal Colonialism and Ghetto Revolt," in *The Black Revolt*, 239.

party building, only rarely expressing explicit support for the rebellions and often hesitant to provide immediate material infrastructure or coordination in the midst of the insurrections themselves.

To make this critique is not to argue the revolutionary credibility or desires of many courageous rank-and-file Panthers, SNCC members, and other grassroots militants, nor is it to dispute their personal feelings of affinity with the ghetto rebels. It is also worth noting that those party militants who did express public support for the riots often faced severe consequences. But there was also a political basis for their ambivalence. The traditionally statist orientation of much of Black Power, and the false alternative of a strictly identity-based focus on cultural activity, laid the groundwork for many organizations' recuperation.[47] That which was palatable in militant groups' platforms—the Panther's free breakfast programs, or BULK's drug treatment centers, for instance—was often swallowed up by the state and spit back out as government clinics or Headstart, while many Black Power leaders ended up invested in local power structures alongside former Civil Rights activists and white business leaders.[48] An investment in such legitimized structures, even from a "radical" position, was totally at odds with active participation in urban riots.

In this way, organizations from both camps contributed, whether intentionally or not, to a multiracial reconstitution of the liberal political class in the United States. Particularly in the South, this was no minor achievement; it represented a massive, fundamental shift in how southerners approached the democratic state. However, what it ultimately achieved was a strengthening of those structures at the basis of state, capital, and white supremacy, improving their ability to withstand rebellion from below. For many in the Civil Rights movement, this was in fact their conscious intent: to fulfill the promise of democracy.

---

47   Though outside the scope of this chapter, it is worth mentioning that the influence of anticolonial struggles in other countries was of major influence on militants in the United States. Those struggles presented a political model that helped explain the role of police and white commerce in Black neighborhoods, while encouraging a praxis of aboveground party building alongside underground guerilla warfare. The latter was generally isolated and brutally suppressed, while the former integrated into the state apparatus in the ways we discuss here. It does seem worth noting as well that, similar to the way that the American Black political class was elevated to its position by the struggles of the 1960s, the successful African anticolonial struggles typically resulted in governments run by Black elites on behalf of global capitalist interests, represented by institutions like the World Bank and International Monetary Fund.

48   K'Meyer, *Civil Rights in the Gateway to the South*, 210.

Perhaps no example could better illustrate this than the illegal strike of Atlanta's sanitation workers in 1977.[49] Pitting the almost entirely Black workforce of trash collectors against the city's first Black mayor, the struggle was representative of the new kinds of social conflicts that could erupt in the post–Civil Rights era, and would demonstrate the kinds of betrayal Black workers could now expect from the political class newly constituted by the gains of the previous decade's freedom struggles.

Atlanta's sanitation workers had previously organized an illegal strike in 1970, against the white mayor Sam Massell, who had attempted to break the strike by firing the workers and replacing them with prison labor. The specter of racism in a white mayor firing Black workers loomed large just two years after the Memphis sanitation strike, in which Memphis's mayor had tried the same tactic prior to the assassination of Martin Luther King, Jr. Atlanta's new liberal class of Civil Rights leaders and white progressives turned against Massell. Ambitiously capitalizing on this opposition, Massell's own vice-mayor, a Black political figure and former National Labor Relations Board lawyer named Maynard Jackson, criticized Massell's tactics and called the workers' wages "a disgrace before God." Jackson's intervention, along with possible fear of another outbreak of riots, pushed the mayor to negotiate, to rehire all the fired workers, and to give them a significant raise in pay.[50]

Riding his popular handling of the strike controversy and boosted by a newly powerful alliance of Black civic groups, churches, and white progressives, Jackson was elected Atlanta's first Black mayor in 1973. Four years later, Atlanta's sanitation workers went on strike again, first as a wildcat action in January and February, and again on March 28, this time with all 1,300 members of Local 1644 and official support from their union, AFSCME.

But unlike 1970, the political support expected by the strikers never appeared. No longer seeing the strike as a Civil Rights or "Black" issue, middle-class Black organizations and churches remained steadfastly loyal to their new political representative Mayor Jackson, who, despite garbage collectors still subsisting on below-poverty wages, passionately opposed

---

49   US labor law prohibits a strike by public employees; nevertheless, strikes by public employees, both wildcat and union-sanctioned, increased tremendously in the '60s, a trend that was not reversed until political winds shifted in the mid-'70s with mayors' use of the replacement tactic.

50   Joseph A. McCartin, "'Fire the Hell Out of Them': Sanitation Workers' Struggles and the Normalization of the Striker Replacement Strategy in the 1970s," *Labour: Studies in Working-Class History of the Americas* 2, no. 3 (2005): 69–70.

the strike on budget grounds. The Chamber of Commerce and the Atlanta Business League—as well as the Atlanta Baptist Ministers Union, the Urban League, and the Southern Christian Leadership Conference—supported Jackson. White liberals turned a blind eye, while most of Atlanta's poorer Black residents stayed on the sidelines, perhaps sympathetic to the strikers but also steadfast in their support for Atlanta's first Black mayor.

Jackson even went a step further in his opposition: with enthusiastic support from both the Black and white press, he threatened to fire all striking workers if they did not return to work within forty-eight hours. On April 1, when the strikers refused to return to work, Jackson started hiring permanent replacements. Hundreds of Black and white workers showed up to take the strikers' jobs. To drive home the betrayal, there were two separate Martin Luther King, Jr., memorials dedicated on April 4 that year: at one ceremony, the strikers attempted to remind the crowd of Memphis and the connections between labor and Civil Rights; at the other, Martin Luther King, Sr., defended Mayor Jackson's actions and, on the anniversary of his son's death, told the Mayor that he should "fire the hell out of them."[51]

The strikers fought back anyway, picketing to prevent the hiring of scabs, unfurling a huge banner at an Atlanta Braves game ("Maynard's Word Is Garbage"), and brilliantly dumping trash on City Hall's front lawn.[52] But isolated from their main support base and lacking even basic solidarity from other parts of working-class Atlanta, they had lost before they even began. By the end of April, most of the workers had reapplied for their old jobs at lower pay; others remained unemployed. As one labor historian wrote,

> When the dust from the 1977 strike settled, it was clear that Maynard Jackson had done something that perhaps only a popular Black mayor with a strong labor and civil rights record could have accomplished. He had made it permissible to use a tactic that AFSCME had once associated only with white "southern-type city officials." He had fired and replaced strikers. Soon other municipal employers would follow suit.[53]

---

51 Ibid., 68.
52 David, "A Disgrace Before God: Striking Black Sanitation Workers vs. Black Officialdom in 1977 Atlanta," http://libcom.org/library/disgrace-god-striking-Black-sanitation-workers-vs-Black-officialdom-1977-atlanta.
53 McCartin, "Fire the Hell Out of Them," 87.

The tactic of permanently replacing striking workers, often associated with President Reagan's 1981 en masse firing of air traffic controllers, was actually pioneered in 1977 by a Black civil rights mayor of the New South. The strategy spread from the public to private sector, and has drastically reshaped labor struggle in the United States since that time. Bound by obedience to the law and their own political reformism, institutionalized labor unions have not adapted, and the number of strikes in the United States has decreased nearly every year since the early 1980s. Big Labor remains wedded to electoralism, even as the Democratic Party seeks a suitable dumping ground for its corpse.

The racial reconstitution of the local and national political class, heralded by many as the major victory of Black struggle of the 1960s, stabilized the power structure in a way that no amount of national guardsmen or crowd control tactics ever could. Fresh from the experience of managing a social movement, and having taken what benefits it could from that struggle, the Black political class proceeded to help police any oppressed populations who resisted its paternal influence. In a piece written after a wave of rebellion hit Cincinnati in 2001, former SNCC member and Black Panther Lorenzo Ervin mentioned the role of this class in parroting white narratives of recuperation:

> I have heard this garbage for years. Going back to the 1965 Watts rebellion, when Black folks rebelled after years of LAPD racist brutality, it was a line put forth by the white ruling class and its Negro spokespersons that we were "torching our own neighborhoods." Never mind that we didn't own a damn thing in the ghetto, that it was the cops themselves shooting and torching Black homes, and that this was clearly a struggle with deep roots in historical oppression, the government's line was duly picked up by the Negro bourgeoisie, and passed off as "truth" along with "the police right to stop looters" and "we need peace."[54]

During and after the 1970s, the institutional role of this new political class grew ever more crucial. Even so, Black leaders have been unable to stop the ghetto riot from continuing to be a viable strategy for the poor. Uprisings continued to resurface over the next twenty years: Elizabeth,

---

54   Lorenzo Komboa Ervin, "Black People Have a Right to Rebel," in *How Fast It All Blows Up: Some Lessons from the 2001 Cincinnati Riots* (One Thousand Emotions, 2001), 3.

New Jersey, in 1975; Miami in 1980, 1982, 1984, and 1989; Queens in 1986; Brooklyn in 1989 and 1991; Washington, DC in 1991; Manhattan in 1992; and most famously, alongside sympathy riots in cities all over the United States, Los Angeles in 1992.[55] These riots were increasingly characterized by a lack of organized activist influence or stated political demands, and began to include white protagonists alongside Black and Brown ones, as urban conditions worsened and antagonism toward police increasingly crossed racial boundaries.[56]

From Rebellion to Citizenship

Sympathetic histories of this period have often discussed the Black freedom struggles of the 1950s and '60s in terms of gradualism: an impatience with the modest gains of the Civil Rights movement led to a dangerous rejection of nonviolence, white liberalism, and integrationist policies, all characterized generically by a transition to extremist Black Power rhetoric and organizations. The riots of the late '60s tend to be vaguely folded into this historical narrative, represented as a sad departure from the words and deeds of heroic leaders like Martin Luther King, Jr.

While certainly Black Power's grasp on the younger generation increased with the failures of Civil Rights, a larger view of Black struggle in this country would position much of the sentiment of Black Power— emphases on self-defense, community autonomy, and oppositional cultural development, for example—not at the fringe of this process of '60s radicalization, but rather at the center of centuries of pan-African and

---

55 The level of popular participation and destruction from the 1992 Los Angeles Riots was immense, trumping even the most devastating riots of the 1960s: ten thousand businesses were destroyed, seventeen thousand arrests were made, and two thousand people were deported, with property destruction estimated at $1 billon. These statistics do not include the solidarity protests and rebellions that happened in forty-four different cities around the country. All of this occurred in the absence of a cohesive Black social movement at the time (The Chicago Surrealist Group, "Three Days That Shook the New World Order," *Race Traitor* 2 [1993]: 10).

56 Recent examples of these multiracial moments include the riots in Toledo in 2005, which were sparked by a neo-Nazi march; the 2009 and 2010 riots in Oakland after a transit officer shot an unarmed Black man named Oscar Grant; and the massive wave of looting and rioting that shook the United Kingdom over nearly a week in August 2011 after the police shooting of Mark Duggan. 1992's Rodney King riots in LA also had a multiracial component, with crowds frequently featuring Black, white, and Brown cooperation, and police records showing over one thousand whites arrested (Johann Kaspar, *We Demand Nothing* [Everywhere: The Institute for Experimental Freedom, 2009], 23).

Black political struggle. From the maroons of the Great Dismal to the slave insurrections and guerilla fighting of the Civil War, from community defense against state terror to arson attacks on the cotton industry, even a brief survey of Black struggles would place many of the radical ideas associated with the late 1960s and early '70s firmly in the popular mainstream of Black history. The practice of communal self-defense, in particular, is historically so ubiquitous as to hardly count as a political position at all, but rather is a simple fact of everyday social life.

In this long view, it becomes clear that the historical outlier in Black struggle was not the various grassroots sentiments of Black Power, but rather the positions of Civil Rights leaders considered mainstream at the time. Nowhere could this be more clear than in interviews like the one with Washington Booker, who along with his high school friends reacted with dismay and confusion at the absurdity of Black children laying themselves down to be beaten by white police in Birmingham. The only way to explain the anomaly of the Civil Rights moment is that, after World War II, for just the second time in American history, there arose the prospect of Black political leaders being seriously integrated into a white state.[57] The result of this betrayal has been made fairly clear.

The historical anomaly represented by Civil Rights' strategies includes the use of *rights* as a political framework for understanding liberation. For much of American history, Black rebellions and social movements appear more as a path to exerting or seizing *power*, in contrast to pressure placed upon the state to recognize certain *rights*.[58] There are certainly exceptions to this pattern: numerous Black leaders and white abolitionists of the nineteenth century discussed an end to slavery from within the rights framework, for instance. Their rhetoric, however, comes off more as a gesture to white supporters than as a genuine reflection of slave revolts at the time: A slave is not a citizen and is not bound by the rules of good behavior when she asserts her humanity. The abolition of slavery by the state was a way to introduce new forms of control via citizenship. Civil Rights leaders of the 1950s and '60s, not unlike northern Republican activists during Reconstruction, were tasked with making postracial citizens out of

---

57   The first time this prospect occurred, during Reconstruction, the opportunity was extremely brief, and largely overshadowed by the nonelectoral battles being waged by Black communities in the South. Additionally, there was virtually no Black middle class in the South at the time, for obvious reasons, making difficult the development of a Black political class that could permanently impose its will on larger struggles.

58   To be clear, in this case our use of the word "power" does not refer to a coercive *power-over*, fundamentally at odds with freedom, but the *power-to* of an active community of liberated human beings.

rebellious Black bodies. One becomes a citizen not by achieving freedom but by trading in its possibility, relinquishing the aspiration to power and autonomy for the right to be policed, to vote, to sign a labor contract, to be free from involuntary servitude "except as a punishment for crime whereof the party shall have been duly convicted."[59]

Black Power, though, cannot be understood simply as the contemporary philosophical antithesis to the Civil Rights mainstream, but rather is an extremely varied concept that is itself full of inconsistencies and competing trajectories. As an expression, the term "Black Power" was first coined by Stokely Carmichael in 1966 during a speech in Greenwood, Mississippi, but what followed was vague and its meaning up for heated debate. Anything that empowered Black people could be and often was included: armed defense groups, free food programs, eviction defense, the growing popularity of African culture and fashion, and a renewed interest in Black and African history—all would fit the bill, but so too would the election of Black politicians, a popular investment in Black capitalism, and even the increasing numbers of Black cops on the force. Pro- and anticapitalists, revolutionaries and politicians, women challenging male authority and proud male heads of family, cop haters and cops all contributed to the meaning and practice of the term. The difficulty in defining this concept naturally came along with the heterogeneous (or nonexistent) nature of any single Black community, which even on a local level would include starkly contrasting political visions and violently conflicting class interests.[60]

Black Power thus represented a variety of only partial rejections of the discourse of Civil Rights and its attempt to grow citizens out of Black rebels. We say partial because it generally remained wedded to certain structures or forms of life under state and capital, represented, for example, through the nuclear family, the creation of Black-only business groups, or the election of so-called revolutionaries to city councils. Though isolated, temporary, and incomplete, the urban riots of the period deserve to be understood as a distinct phenomenon that represented another kind of rejection: these moments effectively transcended the activism and party building of both Civil Rights and Black Power. If Black Power represented a threat insofar as it might destabilize the specifically white-led construction of a new Black political class, seeking instead to build that class on strictly

---

59 We are quoting here from the glazed-over portion of the Thirteenth Amendment that effectively excludes prisoners from the abolition of slavery and indentured servitude.

60 This is an irresolvable problem that continues to this day to confront those who adopt the model of the white ally.

Black terms, the urban riots threatened to tear apart this class entirely, and perhaps the very fabric of daily life under capitalism. Even as Civil Rights, Black Power, and the urban rebellions shared certain constituent elements, the hostility or ambivalence of the former two to the uncontrollability of the latter helps to explain the betrayals and missed opportunities of the late 1960s and '70s.

This being said, it is certainly unfair to blame local militant organizations alone for rebellions' failure to spread or hold territory more permanently. Central blame must be placed on the persistent racism of the white poor and working class who—though exploited, debased, and attacked in myriad ways—as a majority refused to see their own struggles reflected in the fires of Atlanta or the looting of Louisville. This was not for lack of rebellion by white people in the period, as is exemplified by everything from radical feminist and antiwar movements to the growing practice of illegal strikes by public employees and wildcat strikes in the coalfields of Appalachia. Yet the political control over these possibilities usually remained firm, and their sequestration into specific issues solid, with the solidarity between something like a miners' strike intentionally timed with a ghetto rebellion never materializing. Whiteness accomplished its historical task.

The other explanation for the riots' limitations, already discussed at length, was the active role in recuperation played by Civil Rights leaders themselves. This soon-to-be-powerful class played its position perfectly, aiding police efforts to stop rioters, isolating or condemning any organized political support for the rebellions, and strategizing with city officials about how to best keep rebellions from spreading. The strategy of youth self-policing, so dramatically employed by Tampa's White Hats, could not have occurred in cities across the country without the active negotiating efforts of this new political class. It was their coup d'état.

Nevertheless, questions remain: Why did the rioters of Tampa stop when Black youth with made-up titles, white helmets, and silly armbands asked them to do so? Why did anyone in Dixie Hills care what Senator LeRoy Johnson had to say, when he so clearly didn't care about Dixie Hills? More broadly, why would the skin color of the police matter? Black leaders' successful management of these rebellions speak to the Achilles heel shared by many of the freedom struggles of the 1950s and '60s. Black identity, the source of the movement's unification, also proved its ultimate limitation. This identity urgently accomplished the seemingly necessary task of unifying a disparate group for the sake of struggle, but in the process obscured the vast array of experiences, contradictions, and interests of

Black communities in favor of the myth of a single Black consciousness. Unfortunately, but not surprisingly, Black politicians, paid government antipoverty activists, and businessmen were able to push their own interests by securing the racial loyalty of the Black poor. In the streets of Atlanta, Tampa, Louisville, and other cities, Black identity was a tool for rebellion, but also for management and policing.

Then and Now

The constant reconstitution of democracy allows it to swallow new identities while resisting any kind of structural change. This presents the would-be rebel with a serious problem. The struggles we participate in seem to inevitably coalesce around the subjectivities to which we are assigned in this society—the supposedly common experiences of class, race, gender, sexuality, and so on—in a way that proves initially to be a source of needed unity. It is a paradox that the basis of our struggle would be given to us by the structures we struggle against, that "the class exploited by a common structure of domination is unified *on the very basis* of that domination."[61] We cannot avoid this paradox simply by refusing to address the various hierarchies that confront us. Nevertheless, at some point this paradox comes to a head as these categories of experience and unification become a limitation, and it becomes our task to transcend them entirely. Along with the basic principles of an antiauthoritarian sensibility, we are reminded that revolution requires new processes of self-abolition as much as self-definition.

To acknowledge these limitations pushes us to engage earnestly with those situations where we find the gathering of various identities and interests somehow resistant to external institutionalization or a forced unification. This is one way to understand the importance of the demandless riot in the decades since the Civil Rights era. Even as an act that can start from the place of a single shared experience of oppression, rooted in a specific identity, the riot is often a space where multiple groups or identities can freely appear, intersect, dissolve, reappear, and in the process become less distinguishable. As an opening move in an insurrectionary situation, the riot becomes unmanageable not just because of its fierceness, but precisely to the extent to which it achieves this state of transcendence. As a tactic it can be used by the enemies of freedom as well as by freedom's proponents, but as a form the riot holds the potential for a unique wisdom and collective force that can resist managers' calls for political unity-for-its-own-sake.

---

61   Kaspar, *We Demand Nothing*, 28.

For all their reformist impulses and political naiveté, the public occupations and encampments that spread in waves throughout Africa, the Middle East, Europe, Asia, and North America in the last several years speak to this potential as well. The exciting prospect was not the revolutionary nature of the individual identities present but the occupations' occasional refusal to focus on unity for its own sake, and the opportunity for diverse and even contradictory elements to swirl, converge, and react.[62] The extent to which these movements were able to contribute to any revolutionary momentum was directly related to this refusal.

A related observation leads to a call for a reorientation from identity to affinity, to shift the definition of *we* from shared factors like race, sexual orientation, or even a certain style of dress or rhetoric, to one of shared antiauthoritarian desires. Rather than automatically assuming that those with similar experiences of oppression share a political vision, the center of gravity shifts directly to the desires of the subjects themselves, allowing the diversity of lived experience to emerge. In this concept, groups of would-be rebels are likely fragmented over a variety of factors while overlapping where possible, which reflects a more accurate picture of real social life and undermines the process with which the state establishes and manages politically legible constituencies.

We must distinguish this proposal from one that reverts back to a narrow reliance on presumed class interests, a project that also relies on a false and forced unification. The failure of the white worker in the American South, and the more general failure of the supposedly revolutionary subject of the industrial proletariat, all speak to the dead end of this classical determinism. Affinity cannot be determined automatically by a calculus of interests *or* identity, but only chaotically through the risks and conversations shared with those one meets in active struggle. These encounters are not an activist specialty but rather a potential aspect of everyday life of the oppressed under capitalism.

We recognize that pointing out the strategic limitations of identities will not stop the role they play in cultures of resistance; along with class composition they will necessarily continue to shape the form and content of our revolt. In grasping at the truths and lessons of Black struggle in the 1960s, we can offer no simple answer here, but would echo the insightful words of former Black Panther Ashanti Alston:

---

62   This being said, some participants' near obsession with the processes and legitimacy of Occupy's general assemblies clearly point to the opposite trajectory.

The Black community is often considered a monolithic group, but it is actually a community of communities with many different interests. I think of being Black *not so much as an ethnic category but as an oppositional force* or touchstone for looking at situations differently. Black culture has always been oppositional and is all about finding ways to creatively resist oppression here, in the most racist country in the world. So, when I speak of a Black anarchism, it is not so much tied to the color of my skin but who I am as a person, as someone who can resist, who can see differently when I am stuck, and thus live differently.[63]

---

63 Ashanti Alston, "Black Anarchism," http://prisonbookscollective.files.wordpress.com/2011/03/Blacktotal.pdf, 4 (our italics).

The state changed, or perhaps rather its most self-aware actors began to understand it differently, as the tumultuous 1960s came to a close. Classically understood as a fundamentally repressive or negative engine, the state came to use the positive of social programs and federal funding to better discipline and manage potentially troublesome populations. Alongside this approach, a new horizontalism was coming, as civic participation, police review boards, community policing, and voluntary neighborhood watches took hold. The full citizenship promised by Civil Rights implied the state's evolution to more efficient and effective forms of social control. The state was no longer above the citizen; it *was* the citizen. Despite all the gains of the 1950s and '60s, this would not have been possible were it not for the Civil Rights movement and the introduction of its most well-positioned business- and politics-savvy actors into power.

In reaction to the revolts of the late 1960s, the logical accompaniment to new horizontalist methods of control was a massive buildup in the prison and policing-industrial complexes. This was first a response to the political radicalism of national and local groups like the Black Panthers and SNCC, as well as to the uncontrollable riots in the inner cities. Frustration and dismay at these rebellions helped galvanize support for the formation of the Law Enforcement Assistance Administration (LEAA) in 1967, which kicked off a decade of massive funding efforts to help "reshape, retool, and rationalize" policing.[1]

Part of this involved technologically militarizing America's police forces, but it also involved improving coordination and communication between

1   Christian Parenti, *Lockdown America: Police and Prisons in the Age o*

agencies and jurisdictions that were poorly trained and totally ignorant of counterinsurgency tactics. Stereotypically localized, nonprofessional, "good-ole-boy" police departments, so predominant especially in the South, slowly started to give way to a nationally coordinated, increasingly centralized and rationalized apparatus. Liberals, academics, and the emerging Black political class assisted this transition, in return for concessions such as community policing initiatives and "alternative sentencing," by signing onto things like the LEAA and participating in government reports like the National Commission on Civil Disorders of 1968.

The increased focus on prisons and policing was also the result of changing social norms and the breakdown of civil society. Much like how the private discipline of the plantation gave way to the public discipline of the convict lease a century earlier, now-private methods of social control such as the church and the family were losing power and credibility. Public institutions like the mental hospital and the prison stepped in to fill the roles of discipline and punishment accordingly. Though prison populations themselves did not explode in size until the late 1970s, all of these developments set the stage for a new phase in the social war, which would center on prisons and punishment.

The women say they have learned to rely on their own strength. They say they are aware of the force of their unity. They say, let those who call for a new language first learn violence. They say, let those who want to change the world first seize all the rifles. They say they are starting from zero. They say that a new world is beginning.

—Monique Wittig, *Les Guerilleres*

Is it surprising that the cellular prison, with its regular chronologies, forced labour, its authorities of surveillance and registration, its experts in normality, who continue and multiply the functions of the judge, should have become the modern instrument of penalty? Is it surprising that prisons resemble factories, schools, barracks, hospitals, which all resemble prisons?

—Michel Foucault, *Discipline and Punish*

Sistas, let us take the blindfold from our eyes, lay down those weighted scales, and pick up the sword!

—Suzan Stuart, North Carolina Correctional Center for Women (NCCCW), 1976

"WE ASKED FOR LIFE!"

On the 1975 Revolt at the North Carolina Correctional Center for Women

THERE ARE TIMES WHEN CERTAIN OBJECTS MAGICALLY TRANSFORM. SOME-times the pole of a volleyball net becomes a battering ram, the scales of justice become an ice pick, and chunks of concrete grow wings to help shake the very foundations they constitute. This comes from the special mix of solidarity and love found in unexpected places, hardened by rage at intolerable circumstances.

In mid-June 1975, the prisoners of the North Carolina Correctional Center for Women (NCCCW) found this magic, and gained new insight into the use of broom handles, dining room silverware, and baseball bats, as well as into the possibilities of sisterhood behind prison walls.[1] Sparked by a spontaneous sit-in over a range of grievances, the women refused all prison activities and engaged in pitched battles with guards and state police for five days in an ultimately successful attempt to shut down the prison laundry where they were forced to work. Though typically overlooked in favor of larger or more well-known men's prison struggles, this explosion was nonetheless a lightning rod for both the (anti)prison movement of the time as well as feminist politics and the local lesbian counterculture.

---

1   This facility is now known as the North Carolina Correctional Institution for Women (NCCIW).

Importantly, the rebellion also occurred on the eve of the massive boom in prison populations and prison construction that continues to this day, as America's complex of state and capital sought to manage the decline of profits in the early 1970s with new forms of surveillance and control. Prisons and policing have been the answer to the increasing numbers of desperate American poor in this precarious service economy. The uniformed men who fled under a hailstorm of rocks and concrete on the NCCCW yard were the new keepers of an entire economic order, and their retreat, however temporary, on the eve of this transition, inspires a reflection on how future rebellions might take root.

"A Common Treatment for Any Female Trouble"

In order to understand the 1975 uprising at NCCCW it is necessary to consider both the history of earlier prison resistance in the state and the institutional context in which it occurred. Prison populations remained relatively small until the massive boom starting in the late 1970s, but myriad other forms of social control were also available, from the authority of the church pastor and social worker to that of the employer, doctor, and racist vigilante. It is important to consider these others, because they constituted the foundation of social life upon which incarceration was originally built, and because they represent the complicated array of forces with which rebellious women had to contend.

It is impossible to exhaustively discuss all the aspects of social control women faced in the period leading up to the 1975 revolt, but it is worth drawing attention to at least one method of repression that integrated the many figures of gendered authority of the time: North Carolina's abhorrent sterilization program. The program began in 1919 with the General Assembly's "Act to Benefit the Moral, Mental, or Physical Conditions of Inmates of Penal and Charitable Institutions." Similar programs were common across the South, but North Carolina was unique for continuing the practice until at least 1977. The stated purpose of this practice was to enhance the State's "gene pool" by selectively sterilizing the abnormal, unintelligent, or mentally disabled, though it was justified in a number of other ways as well. The law stated that,

> The governing body or head of any penal or charitable institution supported wholly or in part by the State of North Carolina, or any subdivision thereof, is hereby authorized and directed to

have the necessary operation for asexualization or sterilization performed upon any mentally defective or feeble-minded inmate or patient thereof.[2]

Thus institutions were not only allowed to force surgery upon certain prisoners, but in fact were *directed* to do so. Those not living in institutions were also often coerced into the procedure by various State agencies.

Sterilization laws reached the US Supreme Court in 1927, where they were upheld as constitutional. In his decision, Justice Oliver Wendell Holmes words were telling:

> It is better for all the world, if instead of waiting to execute degenerate offspring for crime, or to let them starve for their imbecility, society can prevent those who are manifestly unfit from continuing their kind. The principle that sustains compulsory vaccination is broad enough to cover cutting Fallopian tubes. Three generations of imbeciles are enough.[3]

For at least four more decades the State of North Carolina continued to forcibly sterilize thousands of people, predominantly the young and poor. For the first several decades of the program, the percentage of whites to Blacks violated was roughly reflective of the North Carolina's population. The state began to sterilize increasing numbers of Blacks in the late 1950s, however, and this pattern continued into the 1970s. From the very beginning, women made up 80 percent of those targeted by the program, and by the late 1960s this had increased to about 95 percent.[4] The number of noninstitutionalized people being sterilized increased in this period as well.

Reform groups like the Human Betterment League of North Carolina, who argued that "Feebleminded girls are particularly in need of the protection of sterilization since they cannot be expected to assume adequate

---

2 Daren Bakst, *North Carolina's Forced Sterilization Program* (Policy Report), The John Locke Foundation, 2011, http://www.johnlocke.org/acrobat/policyReports/NCeugenics.pdf, 5.

3 This particular case involved a woman named Carrie Buck who was raped and impregnated at the age of seventeen. To save their reputation from the stigma of an unwed mother, her family institutionalized her for "incorrigible behavior and promiscuity" at the Virginia Colony for Epileptics and Feeble-Minded ("Carrie Buck," http://en.wikipedia.org/wiki/Carrie_Buck; Bakst, *North Carolina's Forced Sterilization Program*, 3).

4 Bakst, *North Carolina's Forced Sterilization Program*, 8; Office of Justice for Sterilization Victims, http://www.sterilizationvictims.nc.gov/aboutus.aspx.

moral or social responsibility for their actions," actively defended the practice.[5] Morality was a key theme, as those women who had become pregnant outside of marriage, even if due to rape, were found to be of "loose
morals" and would often be suggested for sterilization by family members,
neighbors, or other community members. One study illustrates how this
played out in practice:

> In 1962, a father admitted to his wife that he had incestuous
> feelings for his 14-year-old daughter. The parents went to the
> Eugenics Board seeking to have their daughter sterilized out
> of the fear that she would become pregnant—the mother had
> learned from taking her to the doctor that the daughter had
> already engaged in sexual intercourse with someone. The board
> approved the sterilization. The father who admitted to his in-
> cestuous feelings provided the consent.[6]

The same study points out how the threat of institutionalization could
be used to coerce the surgery: "Elaine Riddick was only 14 when she was
sterilized after just giving birth to a child. A social worker pressured Riddick's grandmother to 'consent' to have Riddick ster-
ilized or else Riddick would be sent to an orphanage.
The grandmother, who was illiterate, signed an 'X' on
the consent form."[7]

Economics was also an important theme for sterilization advocates, specifically in rationalizing the
practice to budget-conscious politicians; lobbyists
were adamant that sterilization could help lower the
number of people on welfare. In addition to printing colorful, child-friendly pamphlets that explained
sterilization in vague euphemisms, the Human Betterment League even drafted an economically themed
poem to such an effect, which argued that not sterilizing "morons" forced the welfare department "to pay

At the Dark End of the Street Photo Gallery

Protesters picket outside the
Raleigh courthouse during
Joan Little's trial.

5   The Human Betterment League drew its foot soldiers from the good citizens of the
    white middle class, but was funded by powerful companies like Procter & Gam-
    ble, Hanes Hosiery, and R.J. Reynolds Tobacco (Julie Rose, "A Brutal Chapter in
    North Carolina's Eugenics Past," NPR, December 28, 2011, http://www.npr.
    org/2011/12/28/144375339/a-brutal-chapter-in-north-carolinas-eugenics-past;
    Bakst, *North Carolina's Forced Sterilization Program*,10.

6   Bakst, *North Carolina's Forced Sterilization Program*, 10.

7   Ibid., 10–11.

the family more of the taxpayer's money." Welfare and other social services were used to force noninstitutionalized individuals into the surgery. For one victim, Nial Cox Ramirez, the state "forced her to make an impossible choice in 1965. If she did not 'consent' to be sterilized, welfare payments would be denied to her family. She chose to be sterilized."[8]

Many women were sterilized as minors, with the cooperating institutions being state-run reformatories for working-class delinquents or the mentally disabled, and later ended up incarcerated at NCCCW.[9] Though neither NCCCW nor the Office of Justice for Victims of Sterilization maintain statistics on the exact number of sterilizations performed at this adult facility, available case records at a variety of both Black and white girls' reformatories, such as the North Carolina Farm Colony, paint a picture of administrators commonly using the surgery, in particular upon "troublesome individuals."[10] Institutions were given wide berth in applying the practice, and it was well within the power of state-appointed doctors to judge which inconvenient or rebellious inmate fit the category of mentally incompetent. One can imagine the chilling effect of this program: Beyond the thousands of actual victims, there would have been tens of thousands of women floating through the rosters of various social services, agencies, schools, mental hospitals, religious charities, and prisons who faced the threat of forced surgery were they to step out of line at any moment.[11]

By the 1960s, this weapon of state violence and control was especially being leveled against Black women, though it remained a threat that all poor women faced.[12] Despite the absence of statistics specific

8   Ibid., 22.

9   These reformatories and mental sanatoriums were themselves subject to rebellion. In March 1931, for example, two residential buildings at North Carolina's Samarcand Manor, a training school for delinquent girls in Moore County, went up in flames. The state arrested for arson sixteen young women, who went on to stage two jail uprisings while awaiting trial. (Susan K. Cahn, *Sexual Reckonings: Southern Girls in a Troubling Age* [Cambridge: Harvard University Press, 2007], 12).

10 In the aftermath of the NCCCW riots, one participant commented that, "hysterectomy is a common treatment for any female trouble" (Susan K. Cahn, *Sexual Reckonings: Southern Girls in a Troubling Age* [Cambridge: Harvard University Press, 2007], 166–168).

11 In fact, this very strategy of diagnosing rebellious prisoners as mentally incompetent was used against the repeatedly disruptive prisoner Eleanor Rush, who was forced into a mental hospital on two occasions before dying at the hands of NCCCW's abusive staff. Media accounts of her death consistently drew attention to her institutionalization in these hospitals, subtly justifying her murder as a necessary act of disciplining the insane. Her fellow (rioting) prisoners didn't swallow the justification.

12 In a reminder that the inheritance of history never ceases to haunt its heirs, Tennessee recently passed a law charging substance-addicted women who carry their

to NCCCW, one can infer that most women at the facility would have known someone who had been assaulted by this government practice. As a program that relied on the authority of so many structures—the church, the state, the hospital, the family, the economy—to repress and manage the bodies of poor women, sterilization was symbolic of patriarchal authority in every sphere.[13]

A Regional Legacy

Despite institutional practices that resembled late 1930s Germany, by 1975 the women and men in North Carolina's prison system had already created a notable legacy of revolt.[14] Of course, as long as there have been prisons there has been prison resistance, but most of this does not take on spectacular or necessarily even collective forms, and rarely rises to the headlines of the mainstream press. The flooding of individual cells, small unknown acts of sabotage, one-on-one fights with guards, escape attempts (and successes), study groups and jailhouse lawyering, small acts of friendship across prison-engineered boundaries of race or sect—all these things are hidden but often daily occurrences in every facility. Even setting aside

pregnancies to term with misdemeanor assault.

13   Of course, the other aspect of forced sterilization is the denial of access to free and safe abortion and contraception for those who want them. There has sometimes been a racial dynamic implied here internal to feminism, with white-dominated reproductive struggles disproportionately focusing on abortion, while Black women are left earnestly reminding their white sisters of the hidden racist history of sterilization. Both the denial of abortion and forced sterilization fundamentally rest on a coercive relationship between society's institutions and women's bodies, and both are best understood not as the denial of natural or state-guaranteed "rights" but as part of a larger strategy of managing and disciplining the bodies of poor women. This strategy changes over time; it doesn't seem a coincidence that forced sterilization ends roughly in the same period that abortion becomes legal, as new forms of repression and control come to take their place.

14   Actually, the US practice of sterilization didn't just resemble Nazi eugenics practices: *it inspired them*. California sterilization advocates in particular, funded and encouraged by corporate philanthropies like the Carnegie Institution, the Rockefeller Foundation, and the Harriman railroad fortune, sent eugenics literature to German scientists and actively encouraged the practice by Nazi doctors. These advocates also proposed in their literature "euthanasia" by way of a "lethal chamber"—a chilling fact given the Nazi's later-preferred method of mass execution. Rockefeller himself personally funded hundreds of German researchers and Nazi doctors. Less than a decade later, Nazis on trial for crimes against humanity would quote Justice Holmes's 1927 decision in their defense. (Edwin Black, "Eugenics and the Nazis: The California Connection," *SF Gate* November 9, 2003, http://www.sfgate.com/opinion/article/ Eugenics-and-the-Nazis-the-California-2549771.php).

this reality, however, a brief survey of early prison disturbances reported in North Carolina's newspapers is illustrative of the many precedents for the 1975 revolt at NCCCW.

On June 15, 1952, for instance, fifteen male prisoners in Lincolnton, North Carolina, assaulted and took a guard hostage in order to force a meeting with the state prison director over grievances. One of the men involved was also credited with starting a six-hour riot at Raleigh's Central Prison a year before. The meeting was granted and the guard released.[15]

Two years later, setting a clear precedent for women's solidarity at the facility, 350 women rioted at Raleigh's NCCCW after learning of the death of one of their own, at the hands of guards and nurses. The woman, a Black prisoner and former domestic worker named Eleanor Rush, had been in solitary confinement for six days, and on the seventh day was not fed for over sixteen hours. Rush started yelling for food, to which guards and nurses responded by binding her with a special pair of hand-cuffs called the "iron claw" and silencing her with an improvised gagging mechanism attached to her neck and face. She died of a broken neck thirty minutes later.[16]

Prisoners learned of Rush's death at around 9:00 a.m. the next morn-ing, while on the yard playing softball. They quickly "merged into one large group, yelling and screaming, and pressed into the wire fence at the front gate." About two hundred Black and 150 white women yelled in unison "They killed Eleanor!"; they smashed prison property and hurled broken mirror shards from the cells down upon guards. The disturbance lasted nearly four hours, until guards from the nearby Central Prison arrived and the Prisons Director calmed peo-ple down with a meeting and investi-gation. In fear of future rebellion, the courts surprisingly found a white prison staff member negligent for the death of a poor Black woman, and $3,000 was awarded to Rush's family. The handcuffs used, as well as the practice of gagging, were then made illegal. Despite these

Joan Little (left) celebrates after her acquittal.

concessions, the power structure's point of view was made perfectly clear by the mainstream press: while one paper labeled Rush, "a nuisance at best

15   "Prison Guard Seized in North Carolina," *New York Times*, July 16, 1952.
16   Victoria Law, *Resistance Behind Bars: The Struggles of Incarcerated Women* (Oakland: PM Press, 2009), 215.

and a troublemaker at worst [and] an almost worthless person," another paper simply said, "Her parents should have been sterilized."[17]

On September 22, 1956, eighteen women at the same facility started destroying property in the prison cafeteria, at which point, "five of the women smashed in a glass door to the prison hospital and knocked down a matron" in order to free a friend. These six then sprinted from the room and ultimately scaled a fence to escape. They were later caught by a joint effort of different police agencies and guards from Central Prison.

A decade later, Central Prison itself experienced a massive disturbance. On April 16, 1968, a multiracial group of 500 prisoners sat down in the yard and began a work strike in the yard. According to newspapers, the men were demanding the release of others in solitary, as well as hot lunches; the creation of a grievance committee that could meet with the administration; and an increased pay scale for the many who worked full-time in various industries but were paid a mere ten cents a day. The state corrections commissioner refused to meet any of these demands. The real crux of the issue was not the demands but the assertion of prisoners' collective power; the commissioner admitted changes needed to be made, but that that was "something for the administration to determine—not the inmates."[18]

When the commissioner refused to meet with the men, one prisoner claimed that they would "burn this place down one building at a time" unless he showed up. By nightfall, the prisoners started to make good on the promise, breaking into a supply building and gathering clothes and fabric for starting fires. They also used material from the building to make "torches, spears, clubs, and crude maces." The building was set aflame, and state police and other armed men surrounded the prison and prepared to advance. The prisoners poured gasoline in a long ring along the outside of the southwest yard, and used this massive "wall of fire" to prevent the advance of the guards. According to an account by one guard, "As the officers approached they were met by a wall of fire thrown by about 35–40 prisoners. Fire got on one security dog and one officer.... I saw one officer go down when he was hit by a stick. It appeared that the inmates were going to override the officers."[19]

Prisoners fought against the baton-wielding guards with everything from spears fashioned from long poles to dirt-filled tin cans used as

17 Jim Rankin, "Girl's Death Sparks Riot in Prison Yard," *News and Observer*, August 22, 1954; "Court Says NC Responsible in Death of Woman Prisoner," *News and Observer*, January 12, 1957; and Cahn, *Sexual Reckonings*, 176.
18 "Gunfire Subdues Inmates," *News and Observer*, April 18, 1968.
19 Charles Craven, "Prisoners Formed a Wall of Fire," *News and Observer*, April 18, 1968.

projectiles, and effectively halt-
ed the guards' advance. Around
1:45 am on April 17, when prisoners began to scale the fence to
enter the industrial area of the
facility, the officers opened fire.
Surrounded and armed with no
more than short-range weapons,
it was a disaster for the prisoners:
of the roughly four hundred who
remained in the yard, six were

Women protest and occupy the lawn of NCCCW, Sunday evening, June 15th, 1975

killed and seventy-seven wounded. The media helped the state corrections commissioner to explain away the violence as the prisoners' fault,
and he went one step further, declaring, "By keeping the inmates uncertain as to whether I would appear to bargain with them, we had
bought time which was rapidly running out. But there had never been
the slightest possibility that I would personally negotiate with them.
They had precluded conversation when they demanded it."[20] Unlike the
brutal suppression of prisoners in Attica, New York three years later, this
massacre brought little national attention and few solidarity efforts from
social movements.

Six years later, on August 27, 1974, an individual act of resistance in a
North Carolina jail *did* make national headlines. Joan (pronounced "Jo-
anne") Little, a small Black woman being held in the Beaufort County Jail
for burglary, fought off an attempted rape by a white jailer named Clarence
Alligood, who declared upon entering her cell, "It's time that you be nice to
me 'cause I been nice to you." Other women testified that this was common
at the jail, but Little managed to wrestle away the ice pick Alligood was
holding to her head, and stabbed him eleven times. The jailer bled to death
in the cell with his pants around his ankles, as Little escaped.[21]

The ensuing trial was a national media circus, but also a lightning rod
for antiracist and feminist groups around the country. Ultimately moved
to Raleigh from Beaufort County, the trial attracted large, constant
protests by groups like the Southern Poverty Law Center, the Feminist
Alliance Against Rape, the Rape Crisis Center, the Black Panthers, the

20   Jim Lewis, "Firing on Prisoners Defended in Report," *News and Observer*, July 30, 1968.
21   "Defendant Joan Little's Testimony on August 11–13th, 1975," in the Joan Lit-
     tle trial materials collection, 1975–1976 (#4006), Southern Historical Collection,
     Louis Round Wilson Special Collections Library, University of North Carolina at
     Chapel Hill.

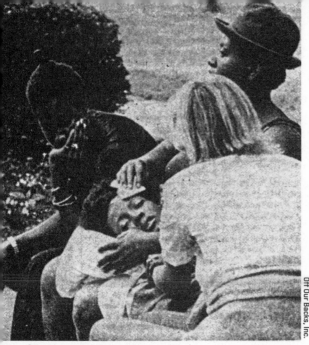

National Organization for Women, the National Black Feminist Organization, and a wide variety of churches and other local organizations.[22]

After the massive wave of support, a courageous testimony by the defendant, and a brilliant legal defense, led by attorney Jerry Paul, in August 1975 Little became the first American woman to ever be acquitted of murdering her rapist. The fact

Several women help a fellow wounded prisoner after the initial confrontation in the gymnasium.

Off Our Backs, Inc.

that this was the murder of a white man by a Black woman, in a state where a judge had recently said, "I don't believe Black women *can* be raped," spoke volumes about the shifting mood of the country and the passionate network of support Little received. The Joan Little trial occurred simultaneously with the 1975 rebellion at NCCCW, just a short drive away, in downtown Raleigh.[23]

A Social Force in the Making

By the late 1960s and early 1970s, then, the South was being dragged kicking and screaming into the social movements and revolts of the period. As discussed earlier, the urban riots that shook northern and western cities like Detroit and Los Angeles were equally a southern phenomenon. Likewise, the politics of Black radicalism spread and grew out of the lived failures and limitations of the region's Civil Rights movement, even as other forms of radical thought and activity—student politics, the antiwar movement, feminism, gay liberation, the Puerto Rican independence struggle, wildcat miner strikes in Appalachia—spread simultaneously.

---

22 J. Reston, "The Joan Little Case," *New York Times Magazine*, April 6, 1975, 38–46.

23 D.L. Chandler, "Joan Little Cleared Of Killing White Sexual Assaulter In Jail on This Day in 1975," *NewsOne* August 15, 2013; "Defense Attorney Jerry Paul's Closing Statement on August 14th, 1975," in the Joan Little Trial Materials Collection.

Each of these distinct but sometimes connected movements had its share of legal battles and political prisoners, and this, along with an obvious ideological affinity with prison struggles, led to the practical necessity of organizing in prison. By criminalizing these movements and placing their members behind bars, the government effectively delivered their ideas and tactics directly to prison populations. Numerous examples of this exchange exist, including Washington State's gay and lesbian antiprison struggles with former George Jackson Brigade members Rita Bo Brown and Ed Mead, and antiauthoritarian Sam Melville's role in the Attica Uprising of September 1971.

It was this last uprising that set the tone for prison struggles ever after, both in the extent of solidarity outside the walls, the cooperation of a self-educated prison majority, and the brutal violence of an administration totally unwilling to negotiate. The uprising at Attica and the massacre of prisoners that followed made that facility the most famous prison in the world; in the words of one penologist, there is simply "Before Attica and After Attica."[24] It is difficult to determine exactly how reference points like Attica were understood on the grounds of NCCCW by 1975, but surely the women there would have heard the name and had an idea of what it represented.

This national atmosphere of revolutionary activity manifested in North Carolina's triangle area in a number of groups and a broader counterculture, which played key roles in supporting the 1975 revolt.[25] At least two groups, the North Carolina Hard Times Prison Project and the Triangle Area Lesbian Feminist Prison Book Project, were involved in sending radical materials into NCCCW as well as communicating with individual prisoners and publishing their writing.[26] A third organization, a prison reform group called Action for Forgotten Women (AFW), was founded a year before the rebellion and played an active role in support and mediation between the administration and the prisoners. Black Panthers were also involved in organizing and speaking at demonstrations outside the prison, though it's unclear the level of personal connection they had with the women on the inside.

---

24 Bert Useem and Peter Kimball, *States of Siege: U.S. Prison Riots, 1971–1986* (New York: Oxford University Press, 1991), 57.

25 The triangle area of North Carolina includes the three distinct cities of Chapel Hill, Durham, and Raleigh, all of which are around 10–15 miles from each other. It was (and is) common for people to work in one city while living in another.

26 The product of some of this work can be found in a large zine titled *Break de Chains of Legalized U$ Slavery*, an incredible resource printed in 1976, which documents in their own words the aspirations, stories, and ideas of many of the women involved in this revolt.

One primary foundation of support for the uprising in June 1975 came from the large, active lesbian and feminist counterculture of the triangle, in particular in Durham. Beginning with a separation from the larger left in the late '60s and early '70s, the area became known for a strong network of women's political and cultural activities. The triangle-wide publication *Feminary*, which started in 1969 in Chapel Hill and became increasingly lesbian-feminist in focus throughout the '70s, exemplified this trend. Well-known author Mab Segrest, an editor for the publication in the late 1970s, described the purpose of *Feminary* as, "To understand what it was to be lesbian ... given the resonance of questions of Southern identity which had denied lesbians openly."[27]

The Triangle Area Lesbian Feminists (TALF), which began as an off-shoot of a gay organization on Duke University's campus in Durham in 1974, also contributed to this trend by hosting dances and meetings, opening a health clinic, and forming communal houses.[28] In one issue of *Feminary*, the group described themselves as

> feminist lesbians, women whose primary loyalty, support, and commitment is to women. Individually and collectively we are exploring all the aspects of our lesbianism. As a collective we all share the responsibility in deciding what TALF activities are. These vary from discussing political and social issues to singing, playing sports together and sharing poetry.[29]

Much of this activity articulated itself along radical/cultural feminist lines, and by the end of the decade Durham boasted one of the strongest lesbian countercultures in the South, including:

> a women's health center, which provided services from abortion to feminist therapy; a rape crisis center; a battered women's shelter; women's studies programs at all three major universities in the area; an alternative medicine center; women-owned

---

27 Risa, "Feminary (Newsletter)," *1970s North Carolina Feminisms*, Duke University, 2011, http://sites.duke.edu/docst110s_01_s2011_bec15/?s=feminary; Mab Segrest, interview by Jennifer Gilbert, February 11, 1993, Durham, NC, tape recording, http://outhistory.org/exhibits/show/nc-lgbt/periodicals/feminary.

28 "Interview with Margie Sved," *1970s North Carolina Feminisms*, http://sites.duke.edu/docst110s_01_s2011_bec15/?s=sved.

29 "Triangle Area Lesbian Feminists." *1970s North Carolina Feminisms*, http://sites.duke.edu/docst110s_01_s2011_bec15/files/2011/04/Screen-shot-2011-04-21-at-4.25.17-PM1.png.

businesses, including an auto mechanic, a bookstore, several self-defense gyms or organizations, printing presses, carpentry companies, restaurants, and snack shops; as well as social and spiritual organizations such as a lesbian twelve-step meeting; Wicca and other women's spirituality groups; and many, many radio shows, much music, films, dance, poetry readings, and other performing arts.[30]

Women prisoners gather on the lawn Monday morning after their overnight sit-in.

By admission of its own participants, the triangle's lesbian community struggled with divisions around race and class, which were often pushed under the rug in favor of essentialist notions of womanhood driven by the cultural and radical feminism of the time. Other more materialist feminists also criticized much of this cultural activity for focusing too strictly on conforming to a certain lifestyle rather than engaging with the social and political conflicts of the day. Nevertheless, the scene was an inspiring experience for large numbers of women, and was undoubtedly a crucial foundation of support and agitation amidst both Joan Little's court case and the revolt at NCCCW.[31]

A lesbian culture developed on the other side of the prison walls as well. According to various studies and interviews, lesbianism was both "widespread and explicit" at NCCCW in the 1970s. Such relationships had always existed to some degree, typically with well-defined roles of butch and femme, but by the 1970s these relationships became more open, explicit, and flexible, with fewer defining categories. In one set of interviews in 1972, women prisoners articulated that they "had learned to overcome their fears of loving women, and how even though most of them (particularly those with children) would probably return to men when

---

30 Kathy Rudy, "Radical Feminism, Lesbian Separatism, and Queer Theory," *Feminist Studies* 27, no. 1 (spring 2001), online at *Les Pantheres Roses*, http://www.lespan-theresroses.org/auto-critique/radicalfeminism-lesbianseparatism-and-queertheory.html.

31 Despite changing notions of gender and a critique of separatism, the queer communities of Durham remain strong, in part due to this foundation of activity laid in the 1970s and '80s.

Police and prison guards from nearby Central Prison amass outside the facility on Monday, June 16.

they returned to the 'free world,' they didn't want their 'special friendships' with women to be denigrated."[32]

It's possible that the communication between lesbian-feminist supporters on the outside played a role in this development. It's also likely that NCCCW's position as the more punitive facility, used to discipline rule-breaking prisoners from other facilities, would have indirectly encouraged the lesbian culture of the prison. One woman interviewed about lesbianism at the minimum-security women's prison at Black Mountain responded, "[It's] definitely not [tolerated here], they do not like homosexuals.... If you get a 23, now, if you get caught in a sex act, you're gone [to Raleigh]."[33] Forming lesbian relationships was prohibited throughout the prison system, and breaking such a rule could get a woman sent to NCCCW.

Sometimes individual relationships between women could branch out and become entire "state families," as the women called them. This could mean individuals seeing themselves as an older brother, daughter, or grandmother, and protecting each other as such. Both prisoners and those on the outside disagree on the role that these families play, whether they are a base for a rebellious comradeship or simply a pale imitation of the

32 Karlene Faith, *Unruly Women: The Politics of Confinement and Resistance* (Vancouver: Press Gang Publishers, 1993).

33 Lori B. Girshick, *No Safe Haven: Stories of Women in Prison* (Boston: Northeastern University Press, 1999), 87.

traditional family.[34] Some argue that the focus on such families reinforces the stereotype that women prisoners merely seek companionship rather than political organization. The relationship between subversion and lesbianism at NCCCW was complicated and is impossible to fully map out, but from later writings by women involved in the revolt, which invoke both radical feminism and a passionate understanding of sisterhood, this culture was clearly a strong social base for the rebellion.

June 1975: NCCCW Explodes

Sunday, June 15

At 5:30 p.m. on Sunday, June 15, 1975, a prisoner from NCCCW made a phone call to members of both Action for Forgotten Women and Triangle Area Lesbian Feminists to request support for a planned sit-in that night in the prison yard. The demonstration was mostly spontaneous despite this warning; presumably word traveled throughout the day through the various social networks of the roughly 430-person population. As tension built and conversations spread from one clique to another, the large tree-shaded prison "campus," nestled alongside Bragg Street, in the unlikely location of a poor, Black neighborhood in southeast Raleigh, remained superficially quiet.[35]

That evening, when the guards announced that it was time to return to the dormitories for 8:00 p.m. lockup, 150 women refused. The prisoners gathered in a circle on the grass of the prison yard, and began staging a large, peaceful sit-in. Individuals arranged benches in a large circle, and used the time and space to meet and discuss their situation.

There were no known plans beyond this initial sit-in. One woman wrote afterward about the beginning of the revolt:

> The protest was spontaneous on our part, contrary to many opinions. It had not been pre-planned or pre-arranged. Unless

---

34 Regardless of how we interpret state families, it is interesting to note that in a range of studies of the phenomenon, the role of husband was found to be almost nonexistent (Girshick, *No Safe Haven*), 90.

35 The urban location of the facility is unique compared to the North Carolina prisons built since the 1970s, which are typically located in remote, rural areas populated by conservative whites. The location played an important role in enabling rowdy demonstrations outside the facility during the rebellion (Mecca Reliance, Marsha Segerberg, and Anne Williams, "Raleigh Women Lose," *Off Our Backs* 5, No. 6 [July 1975]: 26–27).

For four and a half days, activists from various groups and residents from the neighborhood gathered outside the prison to show their support.

someone has been confined and subjected to the cruel environment in which we live, it would be difficult for them to comprehend our reasons for wanting to be recognized as human beings and not as animals in a cage.[36]

The frustration and anger at the facility was broad in scope, not limited strictly to specific policies. Insofar as it makes sense to talk about the anger these protesters felt as separated into individual issues, the grievances the women articulated in their later demands were numerous.

In particular, they focused on medical treatment and the permanent closing of the prison laundry. The women were not just required to do NCCCW's laundry, but that of the *entire* state prison system. This included over thirty-five other facilities, as well as two state tuberculosis sanitariums. A local newspaper article printed years earlier extolled the work programs of NCCCW, pointing with pride to the fact that the laundry was run by a foreman with "a lifetime in the laundering business," who was "always looking for new ways to make the prison budget balance."[37]

36   Anne Willett, "In Our Peaceful Struggle," *Break de Chains of U$ Legalized Slavery* (Durham: North Carolina Hard Times Prison Project, 1976), 3.
37   Suzanne Jones, "Women's Prison, Fashion Center for New and Useful Lives," *Durham*

Balancing the budget apparently included forcing women to work in a 120-degree environment, while handling tuberculosis-infected clothing with no safety equipment. One participant in the revolt wrote of working at the prison laundry:

> When I came here I was in pretty good shape until I was clas-sified to the prison washroom. That's where all my troubles began. I worked there nearly nine months til the germs con-sumed my body. I along with others had to handle infested clothing from sanatoriums, local hospitals, and various insti-tutions along with NCCCW's clothes. We had no protection what-so-ever from any such germs that came in those clothes. And with our bare hands we sorted those clothes because we were forced to. Several complaints were made and nothing was done about it.[38]

The forced, unpaid, and dangerous work at the laundry compound-ed the larger institutionalized medical neglect at the prison. Reports by prisoners of this abuse were well documented, though typically ignored. Nurses would refuse to see or treat a prisoner for any illness if they were not running a fever. Prisoner Edna Barnes, for example, "was forced to have a hysterectomy as a result of minor vaginal infections she [had] had over a period of 3–4 years, and [for] which she was denied treatment by prison officials." Another prisoner, Rosa Harrison, complained repeatedly of pain in her side, but the nurse refused to treat her, claiming she was faking it "to get out of work." Harrison nearly died of a ruptured appen-dix, and ended up in the hospital for eleven weeks. One demand by the prisoners took special issue with the drugging of prisoners, calling for an end to the "indiscriminate dispensing of tranquilizers by staff which make the women passive and submissive."[39]

Racial discrimination was clearly an issue as well. Prisoners demanded that the administration "eliminate or improve the Diagnostic Center, the intake and classification system which results in improper and often unfair placement of prison inmates because of racism and other factors." Related to this was the demand to appoint the acting director Morris Kea, who was Black, to a permanent superintendent position. This demand proved

---

Morning Herald, November 15, 1959.

38   "Open Letter to the People," *Break de Chains of U$ Legalized Slavery*, 28.

39   Marjorie Marsh, "Contradiction," *Break de Chains of U$ Legalized Slavery*, 18; Reli-ance, Segerberg, and Williams. "Raleigh Women Lose," 26–27.

empty, ultimately, as one participant later pointed out that, "Mr. Kea was one Black man standing alone in a white bureaucracy."[40]

The indignity, cruelty, and misery of confinement cannot be summarized by a mere list of grievances, however, and the political critique and aspirations of the women at NCCCW made it clear that they knew their struggle was part of something much larger. Anne Willett, an active participant punished for her role in the revolt, asked "Where are you, my sistas? Join the women's movement now. Become a part of the beautiful army of comrades/sisters such as Harriet Tubman, Sojourner Truth, Assata Shakur, [and] the sistas of the N.K. Koncentration Kamp."[41] Another politically active prisoner named Marjorie Marsh wrote in response to the paltry conciliatory offerings of the prison administration, "We did not ask for a softer bed, a night stand, a locker, etc. We asked for life!"[42]

The sit-in that began around 8:00 p.m. on Sunday, June 15, thus started peacefully but with a deep sense of anger, determination, and solidarity. Around the time that the prisoners initially refused lock-up, 15–20 women involved with AFW and TALF showed up at the front gate of the prison on Bragg Street. While the prisoners arranged blankets and benches in the yard, their supporters prepared to stay overnight on the outside. Deputy Director of Prisons W.L. Kautzky arrived on the scene around midnight in an effort to get the women to end their protest, but he failed. Acting Warden Morris Kea also tried to end the sit-in, but after a group meeting the women refused to be divided, and remained on the lawn. The peaceful yard occupation became a large outdoor assembly, then a campout; some women continued whispered conversations as others went to sleep on the grass or on blankets, surrounded by the bodies of friends, lovers, and comrades nearby.

Monday, June 16

The state didn't let the women sleep for long. Shortly before 5:00 a.m., helmeted guards carrying 3.5-foot batons started arriving from Raleigh's Central Prison. Police were present as well. Deputy Director Kautzky ordered the women to go to the gymnasium, declaring, "This state is run on order. There are beds in the gym. Go there now."[43] Aware of what might happen to them away from the eyes of witnesses, the women refused.

---

40   "Untitled," *Break de Chains of U$ Legalized Slavery*, 4.
41   Ibid., 44.
42   Marsh, "Contradiction," 17.
43   Reliance, Segerberg, and Williams, "Raleigh Women Lose," 26–27.

Within a minute, roughly thirty-five guards advanced on the circle of benches from three directions. Some supporters, who were on the prison grounds but still separated by a fence, yelled, "Lie down! Don't resist!" While some walked to the gym, others ignored these cries and held their ground. According to one witness, "The latter struggled and screamed. Others tried to help and were beaten. Once inside the gym, sounds of breaking glass, screams, and pounding noises could be heard." A prisoner later wrote, "The first blow was struck by the guard to a prisoner while on the front lawn. Others were carried by guards into the auditorium and thrown on top of one another."[44]

Not long after the women were dragged into the gym, a prisoner ran out screaming to the supporters, "They're beating women in there!" She ran back in, and the sounds of broken glass and screams continued to emanate from the building. Fortunately, the first prisoners to enter the gym had found "mop handles, brooms, and concrete blocks." The women fought back, matching the guards' batons with their own janitorial weaponry and breaking concrete into chunks to hurl at the heads of their attackers.[45]

The officers were outnumbered and totally unprepared for this display of resistance, and left the gym in order to barricade the women inside. Angry at the beating, and eager to care for their wounded, the prisoners started banging on the locked doors. Others managed to tear from the floor the metal poles of the gym's volleyball net, which they used as battering rams on the gym entrance. Some smashed the windows of the building in order to escape, and soon the doors gave way and burst open.[46]

While a few carried the wounded outside, the larger group of prisoners chased after the guards and police on the prison lawn. They were still armed with the broom handles, and began throwing rocks and concrete. The uniformed officers were ordered off the property by the prisoners, and retreated under a storm of projectiles. In less than an hour, the women, faced with a potential massacre, had ousted the guards from the property and retaken the prison lawn, just one fence away from a growing crowd of supporters and a poor neighborhood full of potential sympathizers. It was only 6:00 a.m. Those injured from the conflict included both women prisoners, as well as prison guards, police, and one man not in uniform. Three women were hospitalized.

At this point, the women resumed their occupation of the prison lawn, taking the time to care for their wounded and discuss their next step.

44 Ibid.; Willett, "In Our Peaceful Struggle."
45 Willett, "In Our Peaceful Struggle."
46 Reliance, Segerberg, and Anne Williams, "Raleigh Women Lose," 26–27.

Deputy Director Kautzky "appeared to be frightened and at a complete loss to know what to do."[47]

In a pivotal moment, two activists with AFW—Celine Chernier and Brooke Whiting—were allowed by the administration onto the prison lawn to talk to the prisoners, "calming them and persuading them to drop their weapons."[48] They also helped arrange a meeting with the state director of prisons, Ralph Edwards, who soon arrived to take over from overwhelmed Kautzky.

While the women continued their protest on the prison lawn for another five hours, Chernier accompanied four prisoners to the meeting with Edwards. The director agreed to close the prison laundry within ninety days and offered to have an independent team investigate medical conditions, but refused to agree to any of the demands in writing. A second meeting was planned for Thursday. Tired, hungry, wounded, and perhaps satisfied with the promises of change, the women agreed to return to their dormitories.

Tuesday and Wednesday, June 17–18

Despite going back to their cells Monday night, the prisoners refused the next morning to return to their normal routines or work in the laundry, effectively shutting down the facility. According to media reports, the number of active strikers was up to two hundred. The protest was growing. All armed guards pulled from inside the fence the day before remained outside the facility. Having given up their improvised weapons and hard-earned occupation of the outdoor lawn, the strike against prison labor was the remaining way for the women to pressure the administration to hold to its promises.

An uneasy calm descended on the facility, which was increasingly surrounded by media vans, FBI and plainclothes cops, and armed guards. A kind of twenty-four-hour solidarity demonstration surrounded the facility as well, with supporters from feminist and Black Power groups, as well as families from the surrounding neighborhood screaming at the guards and yelling their support for those on the other side of the fence. Prisoners were able to shout to media and occasionally approach the fence to talk with supporters, which helped keep open the lines of communication.

---

47 Willett, "In Our Peaceful Struggle," 5.
48 Reliance, Segerberg, and Anne Williams, "Raleigh Women Lose," 26–27.

As the main women's prison in North Carolina, NCCCW could undoubtedly have housed relatives of the families living in the surrounding low-income neighborhood, and one can imagine the hostility they would have toward the armed guards sent to repress a protest by their own mothers and sisters.[49] The crowd outside became a perfect mirror of the war being fought on the grounds of the prison: small children threw the Black Power salute while riding their bikes, older women with afros screamed into bullhorns, young white women in combat boots with short cropped hair clenched their fists, and husbands and brothers looked on in anger and concern, all while the guards stood nearby, small in number, cautious but also angry and embarrassed at their humiliating defeat the day before.[50]

On Wednesday, several doctors came to the prison offering to treat the wounded and investigate health concerns, but were refused entry by the administration. Director Edwards appeared at the prison to give out a one-page flyer detailing his response to the demands, but also mentioned in a press conference that the laundry "could be fully reopened in an emergency." One newspaper reported the laundry would stay open but at only one-fourth the workload.[51] The prisoners sensed betrayal, and promptly tore up Edwards's flyer in anger.

Cynicism and frustration toward the negotiating process was omnipresent in later writings by prisoners, one of whom wrote, "After the damage had been done, Mr. Edwards made his grand and great appearance. From the very beginning of his purported negotiations he was evasive, could make no decision on his own, and could not even enter the administration building without being surrounded by guards. We held our agreement, but Mr. Edwards was definitely playing games."[52]

Nonetheless, the negotiations accomplished the administration's goal. By encouraging a mediating role on the part of the reform activists in AFW and presenting the appearance of an agreement approached in good faith, the negotiations literally disarmed the prisoners and bought the administration precious time to move more armed guards into the area. Had

---

49   Thirty-eight years later, this sentiment was still present, as reported by participants in a prison solidarity demonstration where family members stood on their lawn cheering or honking their horns in support of the antipolice banners present ("Free All Mothers! A Reportback from the Mother's Day Noise Demo," *Prison Books Collective*, May 14, 2013, http://prisonbooks.info/2013/05/14/free-all-mothers-a-reportback-from-the-mothers-day-noise-demo/).

50   Reliance, Segerberg, and Williams, "Raleigh Women Lose," 26–27.

51   Steve Berg, "Order is Restored at Women's Prison," *News and Observer*, June 21, 1975.

52   Willett, "In Our Peaceful Struggle," 5.

this not happened, the rebellion could have extended to the rest of the facility, and perhaps even beyond the borders of the prison into the highly sympathetic neighborhood surrounding it.

North Carolina Women's Prison Book Project

By Thursday, June 19 over one hundred state police and prison guards had gathered at the prison, and proceeded to sweep protesters off the grounds and enter the facility.

Thursday, June 19

Protests around the facility remained constant throughout the week. On Thursday afternoon, a crowd of one hundred was chanting in support of the ongoing strike, while around two hundred prisoners on the other side of the fence chanted along with them. A second meeting between Edwards, AFW, and the prisoners was expected to take place at 4:30 p.m.

The administration had prepared for this meeting by spreading the lie that AFW had already agreed to Edwards's proposal on the prisoners' behalf. It was a classic ploy to sow division between the women and convince them to end their protest. Possibly the administration already understood that some reform activists saw the prisoners' rebellion in very different terms than the prisoners did themselves. The tactic failed, however, and the prisoners and the women from AFW jointly pressed the state director to keep his word. Edwards in turn denied that he had ever promised to close the laundry. When the women reiterated their demands, Edwards responded by "asking that they write up a proposal." He then left the room, but returned a short time later, drawing a new line in the sand: no proposals would be accepted and the prisoners must accept the officials' offer or else. He ordered AFW to leave. By 7:30 p.m., the negotiations had essentially fallen through.[53]

With Edwards's abrupt about-face and the clock quickly approaching the 8:00 p.m. evening lockup, the writing on the wall was clear: the director had bought all the time he needed, and a clampdown was coming. The AFW activists talked with a Black Panther from Winston-Salem named Larry Little, who soon got on the bullhorn to address the crowd. With his voice echoing down residential Bragg Street and onto the prison grounds, Little screamed, "Basically, the negotiations have broken down.... We've got to start going downtown and rioting. We've got to give Raleigh some hell." Prisoners and protesters cheered in response.[54]

---

53 Reliance, Segerberg, and Williams, "Raleigh Women Lose," 26–27.
54 Paul Horvitz, "Chants Fill Night Around Prison Gates," *News and Observer*, June 20, 1975.

A group of thirty Raleigh police in gas masks soon pushed the pro-testers off the prison property and onto the other side of Bragg Street. Nearly simultaneously, 125 armed guards and police entered the facility. The women who had gathered on the lawn to join the supporters' demon-stration were pushed back into the dormitory buildings. Singing could initially be heard, but soon the sound changed to screams, the smashing of objects, and the breaking of glass. According to one official, the women "began tearing everything apart." The prisoners were actually unable to enter their own cells, as the doors had been locked before they got there; apparently the police had driven them there not for evening lockup but to beat them, away from the prying eyes of media and supporters.[55]

This is exactly what happened. According to one participant, prisoners were "beaten and stomped" and tear-gassed inside the building. Though now on less favorable terrain than the open lawn, and facing larger num-bers of better-prepared guards, the women again fought back. Some guards reported being burned by "caustic acid," while others were cut, bruised, or struck unconscious. Three of the dormitory buildings were "out of con-trol." Ultimately seventeen prisoners and eleven guards had to be carried out on stretchers. In a search of the building the next day, officials found "gasoline and acid," as well as "pitchforks, pick-axes, scissors, dinner forks and knives, hoes, baseball bats and broken bottles."[56]

Prison officials claimed that women were not beaten by guards, but rather that they had been "screaming and fighting among themselves," and even claimed that the injuries of a woman in serious condition were "self-inflicted." The image of the hysterical hair-pulling woman was float-ed to the media, but no explanation was given as to how an inter-prison-er conflict would result in eleven guards leaving on stretchers. Another official, *who had not been physically present* in the dormitories during the conflict, stated he "did not witness any beatings by guards." The media un-critically presented these claims as fact. The prison refused to send many of the women to the hospital, opting instead to treat them at the more private prison infirmary.[57]

During the conflict, the crowd of supporters failed to regain entry or to spark the more generalized disturbance so earnestly suggested on the

55   Reliance, Segerberg, and Williams, "Raleigh Women Lose," 26–27; Berg, "Order is Restored at Women's Prison;" Willett, "In Our Peaceful Struggle," 5.

56   Willett, "In Our Peaceful Struggle," 5; Berg, "Order is Restored at Women's Prison;" Steve Berg, "Prison Violence Leaves 25 Hurt," *News and Observer*, June 20, 1975.

57   Reliance, Segerberg, and Williams, "Raleigh Women Lose," 26–27; Berg, "Order is Restored at Women's Prison."

bullhorn.[58] Had the sidewalk-crowd grown into a force that required more than the thirty police assigned to it, the demonstrators might have been able to pull some of the guards away from the dormitories. As it stood, the crowd looked on in confusion and anguish, unable to know fully what was happening on the inside and unprepared to spread their anger elsewhere.

Retaliation

On the following morning, supporters showed up at the prison to find large numbers of plainclothes armed guards, who quickly pushed them to the other side of the street. Prisoners were soon loaded onto waiting buses; ultimately thirty-four "ringleaders" were transferred to a men's medium security facility in Morganton, nearly three hours west of Raleigh, while some sixty more were put on punitive lock-up in NCCCW's Dormitory C.[59] Another ninety lost certain privileges or were denied parole for their role in the rebellion. All contact with AFW or TALF was officially forbidden at NCCCW, although the women transferred to Morganton were able to stay in touch.[60]

As soon as the rebellion ended, AFW, and specifically Celine Chernier, became the target of a major smear campaign in the media. In classic southern style, the reform activists were labeled "outside agitators" with a "communist element," as the state director attempted to shift blame for the rebellion onto something other than prisoners' self-organization and the abysmal indignity of confinement. It's worth noting that though AFW was playing its dutiful role in disarming prisoners and encouraging negotiations, no such slander appeared in the local press. Only after Edwards had arranged his forces to repress the rebellion, thus allowing him to set

---

58 Shortly before the conflict re-erupted Thursday night, an empty warehouse building was mysteriously burned to the ground six blocks away. Responsibility for the act was never claimed, and it remains unclear if this was a gesture of solidarity intended to distract the police, or just a slumlord making good on his or her insurance policy (Berg, "Prison Violence Leaves 25 Hurt").

59 Reports on the number of women sent to Morganton actually contradict each other, with one claiming thirty-three and another thirty-four. We've relied on the latter report as it comes directly from a letter from a prisoner in Morganton.

60 In our research, the relationship between AFW and TALF remains unclear. It seems likely or at least possible that they shared members, although the prisoners' book put out a year later credits TALF with a publishing and editing role with no mention of AFW; Berg, "Order Is Restored at Women's Prison"; Bessia Marsh and Shirley Moutria, "Letter from Prison," *Off Our Backs* 5, no. 7 (August 1975): 28.

Off Our Backs, Inc.

A spokesperson for Action for Forgotten Women speaks
to the media on Friday, June 20 outside NCCCW.

aside the farce of negotiations, did AFW lose its utility and become a convenient enemy of the state.

On the inside, the guards at NCCCW used the time after the rebellion to exact revenge. While reform activists organized legal action against prison staff, the thirty-four women in Morganton and sixty on lockup at NCCCW fought against their own private hell of isolation and intimidation. Just two months after the riots, on September 29, prisoner Alice Wise observed:

> three male guards going into security (the hole) alone where one woman prisoner was being held. I know there is a State

policy specifying that all guards are supposed to have a matron with them while in the presence of women prisoners. Because the brutality at this camp has been so paramount since our peaceful protest in June of 1975, I became concerned about the prisoner being in the hole alone.[61]

The sixty women in lock-up responded in solidarity by screaming "Pigs! Oink oink!" and singing "We Shall Overcome." The guards left the cell of the sole prisoner, but retaliated against the prisoners' unity by singling out two women and dragging them to solitary confinement as well. According to one of these women, the next day a guard entered her cell, and, "With a wild look in his eyes, pulled out his knife and cut a piece of my [rubber] mattress in the shape of a heart, put his fingers across my lips and told me that I talked too much and I saw too much."[62]

The state's strategy for reasserting control at the facility combined retaliatory threats and solitary confinement with mostly minor changes like the appointment of a new chaplain and a new full-time recreational director, as well as the introduction of some new medical equipment and furniture. The largest change was undoubtedly the shutting down of the prison laundry facility. Despite the failure of negotiations and dialogue, the state director could easily surmise that keeping the workplace open would heighten the likelihood of future rebellions, and quietly shut it down.

Even so, the prisoners were clear on the limited significance of these changes. A year after the riots, one woman told a reporter that the reforms were "just sugar coating to make it look like changes have happened. But that's just on the surface. We still have all the ingredients that brought on the protest." Another woman called the changes "pacifiers."[63]

By June 1976, the majority of the women in solitary had been released back into NCCCW's general population. They maintained contact with their supporters on the outside, and eventually published a small book called *Break de Chains of Legalized U$ Slavery*, which documented in depth their struggle and motivations. Although no major outbreaks of collective resistance broke the surface for some time afterward, the prisoners' solidarity, self-education, and will remained strong. In the words of one riot participant, recorded a year later, "We, sistas/comrades, are the

---

61   Wise, "Untitled."
62   Ibid.
63   "Women's Prison Bears Few Scars from 1975 Riots," *Wilmington Morning Star*, June 16, 1976, 9-A.

carriers of future generations; we are the ones that give birth to human life. Our role must be one of aggression."[64]

Conclusions

The rioting at NCCCW in June 1975 continued a legacy of rebellion that began many years earlier in North Carolina prisons. Possibly due to the role of reform activists and the illusory process of negotiations, a full-fledged facility takeover didn't happen, nor did the rebellion spread to the neighborhood at large or to other facilities. One can certainly judge that, had the prisoners not ignored the peaceful cries of certain activist supporters on the first day, the conflict in the gym could instead have been a one-sided massacre hidden from the public eye. It is a waste of time to look over our shoulders at the past asking "What if?" but insofar as we can ascertain the containment strategy used by the state, we can observe that, by disarming the prisoners and encouraging participation in a pointless negotiation, the activists with AFW aided the broader strategy of the prisoners' enemies. That relations between the prisoners and these supporters remained firm does not change this fact.[65]

The abrupt cease in negotiations at NCCCW on that Thursday reminds us of the words of the state corrections commissioner when he commented on the Central Prison riot seven years earlier: "By keeping the inmates uncertain as to whether I would appear to bargain with them, we had bought time which was rapidly running out. *But there had never been the slightest possibility that I would personally negotiate with them. They had precluded conversation when they demanded it.*" The state's playbook for prison rebellions, which themselves can increasingly be seen to represent social rupture in general, uses dialogue with insurgents merely as a tool with which to mobilize its own material forces, to "catch up to the situation."

Again and again—with Attica, NCCCW, and a dozen others—we are reminded of this fact: dialogue with the state serves the political function

---

64 Willett, "Untitled."
65 In none of the primary sources on this subject—from newspaper articles to editorials, letters, or updates found in various feminist and movement publications—could we find evidence of a vocal critique by prisoners of the role of AFW. It is possible that such a critique was voiced but never printed in any movement documents, and it is also possible that the harsh treatment AFW was already receiving in the mainstream press resulted in a perceived need by some to present a united front against the backlash. Regardless, both AFW members and other observers were clear on the group's role in encouraging prisoners to be peaceful, lay down their arms, and put their faith in negotiation.

of containment, regardless of who initiates it. This does not mean that those in rebellion ought not to articulate specific grievances to each other or to society at large when relevant, or that rebellion without a process of negotiation cannot equally (and even unintentionally) result in changes or an improvement of immediate conditions. The center of gravity is a refusal to engage in dialogue with the state on its terms.

The sisterhood that passed through the fences of NCCCW in 1975 occurred at a kind of crossroads in the history of gendered oppression in the United States. Many of the kinds of authority expressed through the exemplary sterilization program discussed earlier faced new restrictions and challenges starting in the late 1960s. The moral authority of the church was in drastic decline, women started self-defense initiatives to fight back against rapists, mental institutions faced a wave of social criticism demonstrated by films like *One Flew Over the Cuckoo's Nest*, female patients started educating each other and questioning the word of their male doctors, and the male-headed household faced the economic threat of women who were organizing for work and better pay.

One way to view women's incarceration in this period is as an augmentation of these "older" forms of authority that had lost their credibility if not their actual standing.[66] At the same time, the prison rebellion at NCCCW, and its resulting sisterhood, was the consummation of revolt against all the diverse forms of authority that came to bear on the lives of poor women in that period, from the state but also the church, the hospital, the economy, the family, and the diffuse but no less structural forces of white supremacy. Prison struggles may ebb and flow within the rhetoric of

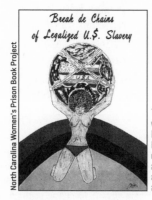

Break de Chains
of Legalized U.S. Slavery

North Carolina Women's Prison Book Project

The following year, prisoners worked with the Triangle Area Lesbian Feminists and the Hard Times Prison Project to document their struggle with a 60-page booklet of firsthand accounts, analysis, poetry, art, and photographs.

---

66 Likewise, the financial "compensation" that North Carolina offered to sterilization victims many decades later was only possible because the state had already moved on to newer, more modern forms of management and discipline.

specific demands and grievances, but it is a mistake to try to understand them strictly through this limited lens. Always the central contest is a more general one between the power of those below with the authority of those above, a struggle for that which can be neither demanded nor given but only seized. The screams of solidarity on the lawn at NCCCW, the joint cries of "Pigs! Oink oink!" in lock-up, the sound of broken glass in the prison gymnasium, and the later silence of the prison laundry are all testaments to the living struggle in the region.

The revolt at NCCCW erupted not just at an intersection of gendered oppression and incarceration but also during a broader explosion in the prison-industrial complex. This growth began first as a conscious reaction to the political radicalism of different sectors of society, but it did not die out in the early 1970s with the decline of these movements. Under the guise of a "war on drugs" and a "war on crime," the United States continued to modernize and militarize its police and prisons. By the mid-1970s the structural impetus for this development was no longer the threat of leftist radicals or urban riots, but rather economic stagnation and a decline in profits.

Prisons themselves became big business, but the reason for the growth of the prison-industrial complex was much broader and more macro-economic in scope than mere lobbyist-interest politics. After World War II, the US dollar officially became the world's dominant currency, and massive profits ensued. Companies could afford to essentially buy off and incorporate certain sectors of the labor movement, but by the 1960s, over-accumulation and economic contraction had begun to occur all over the world. In the United States, the timing for capitalists couldn't have been worse, as the labor market remained tight. Between 1966 and 1973, for example, 40 percent of American workers were involved in strike activity. Along with very real economic crises, represented in part by major events like the OPEC crisis of 1973, a kind of engineered recession came on, as capitalists and politicians sought to lower wages, increase unemployment, and defeat workers' power on the job. The government interventionism of Keynesianism came into question, with the more austerity and laissez-faire-minded ideology of Reaganomics on the horizon.[1]

The pay and power of the American working class(es) has been on the decline more or less ever since. The precarity of a fickle service economy replaced the relative stability offered to many by the manufacturing sector of old, as factories that had first moved to the nonunion South then went overseas. The economy re-centered around service and speculation, and the numbers of the poor and desperate began to grow accordingly, giving rise to entire populations of economically redundant people for whom late-twentieth-century capital had little use other than incarceration. While facilitating this economic transition, the government helped to engineer a massive growth in the prison-industrial complex.

As more and more prisons were built to house the exploding number of the convicted, policing continued to become more militarized.[2] This was

Parenti, *Lockdown America*, 11, 33.

2   It is worth pointing out that, as the domestic police have become militarized, the US military has increasingly taken on the role of global cop, intervening around th

aided with new laws like the Comprehensive Crime Control Act of 1984, which, among an array of get-tough-on crime policies, expanded the state's ability to seize the assets of convicted or accused drug dealers. A semi-private war for profit began, and continues, against communities of color, for which street-level harassment, surveillance, and violence have become constant.[3] Every stash stolen meant a new toy for the cops, and the result has been an unprecedented increase in the power of these blue-clad, quasi-paramilitary urban bullies, who are in fact the direct benefactors of an incredibly profitable and deadly drug trade.

Part of this process is a broader militarization of the entire landscape of poverty, from barbed wire fences and metal detectors at public schools to ID cards and antinarcotics enforcement at public housing. Likewise, social workers and teachers have become mere arms of state discipline and punishment. The state's answer to the "social junk" and "social dynamite" created by late-twentieth-century capitalism, to steal the words of one criminologist, has not just been to create more prisons and more cops, but to attempt to turn every environment into a prison, every citizen into a cop.

The result of these changes with regard to the US prison population is intuitive. Up until the mid-1970s the country's prison population had remained more or less stable, in terms of size, for decades, but by the 1980s that population would grow enormously. Since the NCCCW rebellion in 1975 the rate of US incarceration has increased by a factor of seven: counting only adults, one in one hundred Americans are in jail or prison at this moment. The United States now incarcerates significantly more people per capita than any other country in the world. If the statistics home in on specific demographics, that rate of incarceration is much, much higher: one in three Black men, for example, will go to prison in their lifetime. The racist nature of the system should come as no surprise; decades earlier Nixon's chief of staff wrote in his diary, "You have to face the facts that the whole

world, less with the goal of winning a war or seizing territory than with the explicitly stated aim of preserving certain kinds of economic and political relations.

3   A perfect example of the kind of military operation that grew common was Operation Ready-Rock, a massive raid of the entire 100 block of North Graham Street in Chapel Hill, North Carolina, in 1990, which saw forty-five camo-clad cops armed with automatic assault rifles comb the area. Whites were courteously allowed to leave the block while over one hundred Blacks were searched. The police search warrant stated, "We believe there are no innocent people at this place." The search netted thirteen minor arrests for drug possession. (Parenti, *Lockdown America*, 11.) Twenty-one years later, an equivalent force was used just a few blocks away to evict the occupation

oblem is really the Blacks. The key is to devise a system that recognizes this without appearing to."[4]

Prisoners haven't taken these developments lying down. Even in the absence of any widely recognized social movement against prisons on the outside, the prison system has been constantly struck with riots and rebellions since the mid-1970s. The sometimes bloody and senseless interprisoner brutality of the prison riots in New Mexico in 1980 and Michigan in 1981 represent one version of this, but equally relevant are the prison takeovers in West Virginia in 1986; the prison takeovers by Cuban immigrants in Atlanta, Georgia, and Talladega, Alabama, in 1987; the simultaneous protests at sixteen federal prisons over a congressional decision to keep disproportionately punitive sentencing for crack cocaine in 1995; the riots by North Carolina and Texas prisoners over conditions in private prisons in 1995 and 1996; the riot at a youth facility in Raleigh, North Carolina, during New Year's Eve 2001; the coordinated labor strikes at Georgia facilities in 2010; the repeated wave of mass hunger strikes in California prisons in 2011–2013; and a labor strike at three Alabama facilities in January 2014.[5] Many of these examples share a relatively "apolitical" character, in the sense that they were unconnected to known social movements on the outside at the time, and as such often resembled the demandless but potent riots that hit urban centers in the same periods.[6]

Prison, then—along with the entire world of police, judges, courts, state-appointed psychiatrists, social workers, probation officers, and guards—has gone from being a temporary state of exception to a permanent one. As both a physical place and a constant looming threat, this suspension-of-life is increasingly experienced simply as a fact of life. It is important also to understand the ways in which this reality is territorialized. There are more and more neighborhoods where everyone has at least one friend or family member on the inside, and where attitudes toward the

Adam Liptak, "US Prison Population Dwarfs That of Other Nations," *The New York Times*, April 23, 2008; H.R. Haldeman, *The Haldeman Diaries: Inside the Nixon White House* (New York: G.P. Putnam's Sons, 1994), 53, quoted in Parenti, *Lockdown America* (our italics).

5 Michael Hames-Garcia, *Fugitive Thought: Prison Movements, Race, and the Meaning of Justice* (Minneapolis: University of Minnesota Press, 2004), 253; Useem and Kimball, *States of Siege*, 161–197; Bert Useem, Camille Camp, and George Camp, *Resolution of Prison Riots: Strategies and Policies* (New York: Oxford University Press, 1996).

6 Some of these protests articulated clear demands, while others did not. All, however, resemble to some degree the "spontaneous" riots that were happening on the outside in both their participants as well as their social distance from professional movement

police are universally hostile and antagonistic. This phenomenon is certainly racialized, but also cannot be understood strictly on those terms; nearly every anticop riot or prison rebellion of the recent past has involved significant numbers of white as well as Black and Brown participants.

The social ruptures of twenty-first-century America are almost exclusively playing out at this territorial intersection of race, poverty, and punishment. The street and prison have become the "workplaces" of old, with the warden and cop playing their role as boss and manager. The nationally resonant names of the Jena 6, Troy Davis, Trayvon Martin, and Michael Brown coincide with the small, local riots that break out every time a cop murders another kid, whether that place is Oakland, Brooklyn, or Durham. In the global theater, entire countries have erupted in social antagonism and insurrection, not because of a general strike or a "social movement," but due to a single act of physical violence by one cop against one poor teenager's body. Forms of organization and decision making, social networks and communication, cultures and traditions of resistance, ethics of care and solidarity have all been important factors in these moments, but the *political* of demands and parties is increasingly treated as a mere obstacle to be overcome.

"Our age not only does not have a very sharp eye for the almost imperceptible intrusions of grace, it no longer has much feeling for the nature of the violences which precede and follow them."

—Flannery O'Connor,
Mystery and Manners: Occasional Prose

"To articulate the past historically does not mean to recognize it 'the way it really was'…It means to seize hold of a memory as it flashes up at a moment of danger."

—Walter Benjamin, *Theses on the Philosophy of History*

"As insurrection becomes the common situation, time will begin to contract."

—Institute for Experimental Freedom,
Between Predicates, War

CONCLUSION:

Preliminary Notes for an Anarchist Historiography of the American South

At various times in the writing of this book, friends and comrades have asked us why we would spend so much time on a project so abstracted from our current affairs. In our milieu—where far more emphasis has been placed on contemporary theory, analysis, and, above all, action—history seems a strange choice. One simple response is that we want to share the inspiration we've found from these moments that have typically been relegated to the shadows. But our desire to tell these stories goes well beyond yearning to share the stories of those who have been marginalized or disappeared from the pages of textbooks. Such an aim by itself would represent little more than an effort to correct the record, a task that is as impossible as it is misdirected. History is not "the past" but our own relationship to that past; it is not a mass of data to be entered and processed but an infinite set of revolutionary possibilities, which arise again to communicate themselves during every new outburst of struggle and conflict. The insurgents of these pages accompany us to our battle-fields like the *sluagh* of the Scottish highlands, those ghosts of the dead that fought alongside the living, hoping for a final redemption.[1]

This history has been written upon *and is* our bodies, our conversations, our families, our colloquial expressions and gestures. It lives in every place of social life from the field to the factory to the bedroom to the bus stop. The many stereotypes and archetypes of the American South—the

---

1   On the *sluagh*: "The spirits fly about in great crowds like starlings, up and down the face of the world, and come back to the scenes of their earthly transgressions. They fight battles in the air as men do on earth. They may be heard and seen on clear, frosty nights, advancing and retreating, retreating and advancing against one another;" Anonymous, *Contradictionary* (Eugene: Crimethinc, 2013), 265.

passive-aggressive Southern belle, the loyal Uncle Tom, the dangerous Black male, the lazy southern worker, the racist hick, the no-good white trash, the millenarian evangelist, the benevolent white liberal, the Indian who passes as white, the rebellious tomboy—are, in all their truth and lies, part of this social inheritance, and these subjectivities themselves invite and navigate different kinds of power, management, and resistance.

Even our perception of time itself is shaped by our relationship to this past. We refer not merely to the mythology of the Faulknerian tale, situated in a southern land that time forgot, but about our own struggles as well. As more than evidenced in these pages, revolt in the American South has often appeared as a kind of messianic or millenarian break with time, seeing itself less as a step toward some inevitable future than as an attempt—as Walter Benjamin said in *Theses on the Philosophy of History*—to "blast open the continuum of history."[2] Perhaps all revolt carries with it this character; certainly our own emphasis has been on these struggles as ruptures rather than objective phases, appropriately taking place in a region that has resisted the ideal of progress from countless divergent and contradictory directions. Many southerners carry this antagonistic relationship with time alongside us, eschewing progressive ideals and fighting as much to finally carry out the deeds of an "oppressed past" than for any specific future ideal.[3]

This history is not merely the inheritance of southerners, either; the history of revolt and insurrection in the American South is the history of the country, and even hemisphere, as a whole. The conflicts that played out in these swamps, forests, farms and cities have had ramifications far beyond their own territorial borders.[4] In these events and in this region we see (in part) the invention of whiteness, and in rebellion against that construct, the oppositional pan-African identity of Blackness. We also see a legacy of tactics—barn burning, the occupation of wilderness areas as a

---

2   Benjamin, "Theses on the Philosophy of History," 262.

3   Our relationship to time, in the context of capitalist work—but also the entirety of life itself—can hardly be taken for granted. We are reminded of an anecdote from nineteenth-century France: In July 1830, a revolution broke out that ultimately replaced the French king. On the first night of fighting, rebels simultaneously and independently fired on clock towers throughout Paris. One observer-poet wrote, "As though irritated with time itself, [they] fired at the dials to stop the day" (Benjamin, "Theses on the Philosophy of History," 262).

4   To even speak of these borders is difficult if not impossible, as they refer as much to a heterogeneous cultural and historical inheritance as any territorial delineation, semi-humorous arguments about what constitutes the South (Texas, southern Florida, Arkansas?) notwithstanding.

staging ground for attack, the mass liberation of prisoners, the dissolution of the activist protest into the demandless riot—that remains as relevant as ever. Crucially, there also exists in this history a countertradition to the narrative of progress exemplified by former slaves' refusal of labor contracts, push-backs against northern industrialization, and a generalized disinterest in traditional forms of labor organizing.

In the preceding pages we have tried to mostly limit ourselves to immediate interpretation, and even here we can only begin to lay out a few more abstracted analyses about the region—its waves of rebellion, and the strategies for repression and management used by those in power—that might speak to our own times. In particular we hope to interrogate the possibility of a specifically anarchist historiography, as a counter to the Leftist and progressive conceptions of history that have so vastly dominated our understanding (or lack thereof) of these events.

Contemplating the South as a Region

One way to understand the early southeastern region lies within a colonial/anticolonialist framework, positing the area as one large resource colony existing for the benefit of a foreign ruling class. Technically all of the original colonies could be understood in this way, but patterns of agricultural production and labor exploitation made this especially true for the southern colonies, with many areas like low-country Georgia closer resembling the mass sugar production of the Caribbean than the small homesteads of New England. After the Revolutionary War this colonial relationship shifted, as northern capitalists gained massive influence over (and owed their very existence to) the cotton, indigo, rice, sugar, and tobacco plantations of the slave-holding South.

Stretched too far, of course, this anti/colonial framework breaks down. The early southern ruling class of planters and politicians consisted of more than just puppets for northern or European interests, and revolt against their regimes of exploitation and control targeted the plantation system directly, rather than taking any kind of nationalist orientation toward foreign exploiters. The colonial framework does lend to a useful observation, though, in that throughout the history of revolt in the South, at least up to the mid-twentieth century, uprisings against the established order typically had to contend with both a local or regional ruling class, as well as a "foreign" one. The two major wars fought on this country's soil were both fought between interests competing, in large part, to determine how best to exploit the land and people of this region. In much the same way that a colonizing country will refine its strategies of repression among the colonized before importing those strategies back home, methods of control have often been pioneered here before being exported elsewhere.[5] At the same time, strategies of repression have been brought here under the guise of modernization and progress when the local methods failed.

In this sense, the region's dispossessed have forever had to articulate their resistance simultaneously against multiple, competing visions of exploitation and social control. Seen first in the early American elites and British imperialism, and later in northern industrialists and southern planters, the ruling classes have had overlapping but conflicting interests. Marooned laborers, former slaves resisting the new regimes of Reconstruction, and miners fighting the convict lease all revolted in a context of local and foreign ruling-class tension, often playing these internal conflicts against each other to advance their own cause. One of the consequences of the northern-southern, dual ruling class was the hybrid system of discipline and control that developed first after the Civil War. Certain structures of law and order imposed from the North joined with the traditions of vigilantism and private discipline inherited from the plantation system, all of which were directly injected into new forms of policing and incarceration that continue to this day.

The political and cultural tensions of North and South continued well into the Civil Rights and Black Power eras. It was during this time that the Black and white liberal political classes' framework of citizenship and rights functioned to finally bring the South into the nation. The urban riots of the late 1960s and '70s in part reflected this shift; while they had to confront a specifically southern Civil Rights model of recuperation, the riots outlasted this model and were ultimately of a generic, national, or even international character. A slightly adjusted photograph from the riots in Atlanta could easily be from another city or time; by 1980 a riot in Miami *was* São Paolo, Mexico City, Paris, Johannesburg, Los Angeles.[6]

These territorial tensions between the South and the rest of the country over economy, race, and culture also point to the fact that the resource and

---

5   Broad examples like the invention of whiteness itself, as well as specific ones like the Freedmen's Bureau or the media narrative of the "outside agitator," could equally serve here, as could the various modes of prison labor experimented with in this region before it was exported nationally.

6   These urban anticop riots speak to us immediately because they have become general, and have become so because, despite regionally unique dynamics of race, ethnicity, class, and gender, the broad role of police under democracy is everywhere, functionally, the same.

labor extraction that defined early southern development was an essential part of the process of primitive accumulation that created American capitalism as a whole. The US and international economies simply could not have developed without the influx of resources and labor brought by the brutal violence of planters, sheriffs, merchants, politicians, and industrialists in the Southeast. Any conception of American capitalism that ignores this violence is utterly bankrupt.

This history forces us to question the classical understanding of primitive accumulation as a one-time historical moment. As Silvia Federici elucidates in her own writing on the European witch-hunts, it is not a singular historical period that makes the world safe for capital to inhabit, but a constantly unfolding process of structural development, changing social norms, and new methods of policing, social control, and population management. The guerilla war of the maroons in the Tidewater region of North Carolina and Virginia waged on for over 150 years, as racial and gender norms became almost unrecognizable from what they had once been, and as the land literally changed shape to fit the needs of industrialists five hundred miles away. When the smoke cleared, state and capital continued their war of accumulation via the new social and legal norms of Reconstruction, along with the rewriting of territorial and property boundaries to fit industrialists' needs. A few years later, the convict lease and the quasi-feudalism of sharecropping arose to solve labor problems for capital that it could not solve with classically understood labor contracts and wages.

Many of the traditional understandings of a developed, modern capitalist economy do not fit well here; what one sees is something more like the original sin of primitive accumulation stretched timelessly on into infinity. The violent forms of dispossession and dehumanization that we are told characterize capital's earliest stage simply never end. Like a field that must be constantly weeded else it re-wild, making the world safe for capitalism is not a one-time event but a constantly renewing process of dispossession, physical displacement, and the destruction or cooptation of noncapitalist spiritual and social norms. In the South, as everywhere, this process has been as much social and political as economic; it refers equally to the continuous consolidation of state power, the ongoing entrenchment and transformation of social hierarchies, alienation from the land and self, and attacks upon earlier, persisting forms of social and ecological cohesion.

Race, Violence, and Democracy

Perhaps no topic better characterizes the South than that of race, specifically the white supremacy that emerged in the first century of colonization and has continued to develop and shift with the needs of the society that it has come to define. The ongoing consolidation of state power and wealth could not have happened without this ingenious social hierarchy, this intricate mix of social norms and structures, initially beaten into the consciousness of the indigenous, the colonized, the criminal, the indentured, the indebted, and the chained, and then written in blood on the bodies of millions of Black slaves for over two hundred years. The paranoia and obsession with which early planters and politicians racialized legal codes and divisions of labor speaks to this development as part of a process of primitive (and ongoing) accumulation, and every revolt since has had to deal head on with this meeting of violence and the racialized subject.

It is at this intersection of violence and race that we really get to the heart of the matter. In its genesis, white supremacy imposed divisions of labor and social alienation upon nonwhite subjects with a brutality of biblical proportions, with the violence directed at the Black body, as Frank Wilderson describes, "open ended, gratuitous, without reason or constraint." Those who would risk extending solidarity across racial boundaries would find themselves the recipient of exemplary violence in order to instill fear of constant consequence for this treason.[7] Ever after, *meaningful cross-racial affinity can only be found in moments of revolutionary violence.* This is not a new idea nor is it a proposal: it has simply always required a violent rupture for white, Black, Brown, and Native rebels to actually find themselves side by side in true affinity.[8] The long history of maroon rebellion along the Atlantic and Gulf Coasts, early slave rebellions alongside

---

7   As Frank Wilderson writes, "Blackness cannot be disimbricated from slavery, in the way that Irishness can be disimbricated from colonial rule or in the way that labor can be delinked from capital." Thus, even in situations of multiracial transcendence, the history of slavery challenges both Marxist and humanist notions that we should fight side by side because either we face similar "conditions" or because "we are all human." Frank B. Wilderson III, *The Black Liberation Army and The Paradox of Political Engagement* (Ill-Will Editions, 2014), 27.

8   Some might object to this assertion, perhaps posing the Civil Rights Movement of the 1950s as a counterexample, but we would strongly disagree. Meaningful affinity cannot include a situation where the most privileged actors withdraw their support as soon as the situation gets out of their control, which unfortunately describes the majority of white (and Black) liberal activity in the 1950s and '60s, and continues to define that of many "allies" today. A better example of real cross-racial affinity from the mid-twentieth century might be the actions of guerillas like Sam Melville, the United Freedom Front, David Gilbert, or the George Jackson Brigade.

indentured servants, the banditry of the Lowry gang, the stockade wars in Tennessee, early labor battles and later prison riots, and the increasingly multiracial character of the urban anticop riot, all speak to this reality.[9] It's an uncomfortable reality, but it stares us clearly in the face: everywhere race and violence are inseparable. Our resistance is no different. The baptism of blood and skin that gave birth to our current misery will also be our horrible salvation. We will dip our heads in this river again and again until we reach the other shore.

Anticolonial thinker Frantz Fanon considered this intersection of race and violence not just in "political" and revolutionary terms but also in personal, psychological ones: "At the individual level, violence is a cleansing force. It rids the colonized of their inferiority complex, of their passive and despairing attitude. It emboldens them, and restores their self-confidence."[10] Combine this with the words of the "Rebel" from a tragedy by the Martinican poet Aimé Césaire, himself an important influence on Fanon, just before his character kills the Master: "There is not in the world one single poor lynched bastard, one poor tortured man, in whom I am not also murdered and humiliated."[11] This is not merely a token expression of solidarity—it is a statement on the psycho-affective elements of memory, racialized violence, and identity.

It is no coincidence that this violence of the colonized that Fanon describes has had an immediate and messianic quality. It is not the gradual approach of a future, better world that drives it, but a fervent need to redeem the past, and in doing so exit this world immediately and totally. Many of the uprisings illustrated in this book show this explicitly, reflecting struggles that are of an incendiary and revolutionary character without being necessarily oriented toward any articulated political program or utopia. That cross-racial affinity has at times been created in these moments of violence, without any progressive political vision and in the most white supremacist region in the world, suggests that violence often brings forth an immediate possibility for new social relations.[12] This opening starts to

---

9   Obviously this is not to say that the reverse is necessarily true; that violence of any kind automatically creates the conditions to break down racial hierarchies.

10   Frantz Fanon, *The Wretched of the Earth* (New York : Grove Press, 1963), 51.

11   Ibid., 45.

12   We understand "violence" in this case not just to indicate the moment the blow lands, but the entire context in which a social body erupts and normality ceases to go unquestioned. In this sense, many kinds of revolt, some with traits that would hardly be judged physically destructive, could fit the category of a "violent," convulsive rupture with the status quo. Relatedly, it is worth noting that it is ultimately our enemies who retain the power to define what is violent. *Any* act that threatens to destabilize their

close when time restarts, when the old normality is allowed to return or a new normal is forcibly imposed, but the possibility remains with us ever after. This is *our* accumulation.

Throughout the history of this country, race can be understood by the relation of nonwhite subjects to regimes of discipline and punishment. This is done in order to realize a social hierarchy in which whiteness is maintained as a nonracialized, civil subjectivity. In this sense, the problem of race and violence leads us directly to the defining feature of democracy, its function as an adaptive system of management and social control. In particular, at two key moments of crisis—Reconstruction and later the tumultuous 1960s—systems of power in the United States were saved by a democratic integration (or the promise thereof) of the Black subject into the state apparatus. The South was at the center of both of these conflicts, and while multiple rebellions in these periods violently transcended the boundaries set by the framework of rights and citizenship, democracy ultimately succeeded in augmenting but maintaining social relations.

Contrary to the traditional formula of Popular Fronts and antifascist groups worldwide, in our understanding it was not a reversion to fascism that saved our enemies in their moments of crisis, but democracy and its varied practices of self-policing. The Freedmen's Bureau and its contracts, the ballot and its representatives, the lure of citizenship and its eventual expression in the White Hats of Tampa—these are what is offered to us by democracy. This is not to deny the fascist character of some of America's organized white supremacists, and their supporting role in these moments of crisis, but to draw attention to the primary structures the state has and will continue to use to maintain power.[13] This observation will only prove to be more true with time, as our entire world, from social media and tax-payer-funded CCTV to community policing and do-gooder vigilantism, is increasingly defined by a self-professed, citizen-ist horizontalism. The atomized death of civil society has allowed for its ghoulish reanimation as a neighborhood watch group.

To somehow claim that the structures used in these moments of crisis were not "real" democracy, or that "direct" democracy might offer us something fundamentally distinct from this state-guaranteed trap of rights

---

power is likely to be labeled as such.

13   As an organization with pre-industrial roots that emphasized conservatism, Protestantism, and the preservation of democracy, even the KKK would hardly fit the traditional image of a fascist organization. These nuances are important, as they help draw out the fact that white supremacy's greatest ally in this country has been democracy, not fascism.

and contracts, is delusional. If we were to believe that democracy is something altogether different than these forces of repression and recuperation, then at best the term loses all meaning and ought to be dispensed with altogether. The social control of democracy and the violence of the state are inextricable; even outside of state structures, one can see that direct democracy in social movements results in the same kinds of management, coercion, and betrayal, which ultimately feeds the energy of these movements back into state structures.

The nature of democracy's institutions is not changed by the fact that some oppressed people have been convinced to fight for inclusion in them. That many Black people have indeed died in struggling for the right to vote does not change the function of the ballot as an apparatus of management and control, any more than the historic sacrifices of many rank-and-file workers would make trade unions something other than a tool for brokering false peace between workers and bosses. As Ashanti Alston has argued, in this land the law and other related structures were put in place to preserve the original hierarchies of seventeenth-century colonization. When we use these channels to try to make change, we are forever like Sisyphus, once again "bringing ourselves back to the original conquest" as the rock rolls back down the hill.[14]

Rejecting a History of Progress

Despite the fact that so many social struggles in the South have powerfully transcended (or were betrayed by) the democratic form, many of them have nonetheless come to be understood by historians as merely attempts to extend processes of democratization and thus secure greater privileges within the framework of state and capital. It is true that some of the prominent members and ideologues of the historical moments in question articulated themselves with the rhetoric of democracy and rights, often and in large part because explicitly revolutionary ideologies have been hard to come by in much of the history of the South. The same could be said with a selective glance at many insurrections occurring around the world today. However, to not look beyond these leaders' words to the more diverse substance of the rebellions themselves is to totally miss the point. To see the assertion of civil rights in a mass expropriation and communization of plantation land, or to see only a

---

14   Ashanti Alston, "Turtle Island, the African and the U.S. of Amnesia: Recovering Self-Determination Through Penile & Penal Abolition," speech given at University of North Carolina, September 5, 2014.

union-based reformism when striking women destroy city infrastructure is not just bad politics, it is bad history.

Yet these progressive narratives, which point with their certainty to some distant future, and see the advance of democracy in every revolt, comprise the vast majority of texts on southern social movements. This could be a Marxian dialectic that has every meaningful struggle pointing down the road to State Socialism, or the more subtle but equally false ideal of a liberalism that aims toward an end of history, a society of rational but atomized individuals governed by the equal opportunity exploiter of a nonracist democratic state.[15] Despite their differences, these frameworks hold in common a progressivism whereby the protagonists and their actions are never allowed to act outside of pre-formulized processes. "Freedom," in this view, can only be understood as the gradually obtained synthesis of a specific kind of development, never an immediate expression or result of the revolt itself. In their gradualism, both kinds of progressivism affirm state power and reflect authoritarian interpretations of social movements.

Likewise, such a progressive approach tends to see history as a series of causes and effects, dumped onto a blank, universal slate with little immediate or urgent connection to our own. As Benjamin summarizes in his own critique of progressivism, "The concept of the historical progress of mankind cannot be sundered from the concept of its progression through a homogenous, empty time."[16] For the anarchist, history comes into itself only in that moment when time *ceases* to be empty, when it is filled with a "revolutionary chance" and "pregnant with tensions" that link directly with our own. To adopt this perspective one must necessarily break with the gradualist perspective that siphons revolutionary activity into forms of management for human progress.

In all the insurrections and struggles of this book, a clear contrast lies between the immediacy of the insurrections themselves—both in the forms of life that they created and the tactics that they used—and the gradualist, progressive shading posthumously applied to them. Take for example the writing of Marxist historian Eugene Genovese, who interprets

---

15   We're dispensing with the nicety that authoritarian Marxists ever actually intended to see the state wither away into a libertarian communism. For humorous (but substantive) support of this argument, we would direct the reader to the sarcastic, curt response by Frederick Engels, a factory owner himself, to an anarchist worker arguing that workers could and should run their workplaces without bosses, titled "Versus the Anarchists" (*Marx-Engels Reader*).

16   Benjamin, "Theses on the Philosophy of History," 261.

the revolt of slaves and maroons as blending "easily into the message of the Revolutionary War." Genovese selectively quotes Frederick Douglass in saying that "the Constitution is a glorious liberty document," and thus portrays the militant efforts of former slaves as in line with the democratizing effects of capitalist-engineered Reconstruction.[17] The historian thus argues that these rebellions were a continuation of the bourgeois revolutions of the age, rather than a violent challenge to them.[18] This bizarre reading is an attempt to legitimize slave rebellions by inserting them into a set of Enlightenment-era currents already deemed acceptable, but a skilled historian ought to recognize the irony and subtle cynicism of the language with which an adept movement demagogue like Douglass speaks to his enemies. Genovese is certainly sympathetic to the slaves' cause, but in addition to being historically inaccurate, his view does a huge disservice to those rebels of history as well as to those who would follow in their footsteps.

We see a similar blindness in the otherwise brilliant work of W.E.B. Du Bois, in his assertions that the former slaves who refused to work for their new northern masters were merely protesting certain conditions rather than asserting an autonomous desire to be done with such work altogether. The mass takeover of plantation land, for the sake not of industrial production but rather destruction, and the autonomous communities of the maroons, are both inconvenient to a Marxist orthodoxy that declares such laborers have not yet passed through the necessary phase of development to make communism, and so these things are simply *not seen*.

Such a perspective also remains committed without reflection to an *industrial* vision of resistance, one that is incapable of even considering the possibility that many laborers might choose to destroy capital's modes of work and life rather than just appropriate them. Certainly there were former slaves of many persuasions, some who eagerly desired to try their hand at paid labor and monocultural agrarian capitalism. To ignore the variety of inspiring and forceful counterexamples to this attitude, however, paralyzes us and robs us of the critical insights necessary to push further. We lose sight of the deeper substance of conflicts that might have offered a real way out, those tensions that communicate

---

17   Such claims appear particularly ridiculous in light of the fact that a large number of the slaves and maroons who took part in the Revolutionary War fought on the British side.

18   Eugene D. Genovese, *From Rebellion to Revolution: Afro-American Slave Revolts in the Making of the Modern World* (New Orleans: Louisiana State University Press, 1979), 132–133.

themselves to our current struggles and thus offer the only real meaning in studying history.

The contrast between the self-directed activity of rebellious slaves and laborers and the progressive interpretation of them becomes particularly apparent in the Reconstruction era, that time when northern modes of production and social control were imported on the backs of a victorious, "emancipatory" Union Army. From a progressive standpoint, for a group of former slaves to rebel against a Union-backed regime, *after* victory in the Civil War, makes no sense, and consequently these historical moments have been largely forgotten.

To the extent that struggle in this period is even discussed, it tends to be a narrative of the victimization of newly freed slaves by former Confederates attempting to hold on to their power, or highlights the attempts to hastily erect a Black political class. But as the histories of the Ogeechee Insurrection and the Lowry Wars both indicate, much of the rebellion of this time focused directly on undermining the new economic and political regimes being imported by northern capital. These communities had already freed themselves and in many places captured large swaths of land and even arms. The power vacuum of the late 1860s South thus presented the perfect opportunity to create a totally new world in an immediate sense. The tactics that these insurgents used—land occupations, the community arming itself, the creation of totally new cultural and religious forms, the mass destruction of plantation property, a refusal to participate in courts or labor contracts, a refusal to orient agriculture around cash crops—reflect this immediate and utopian orientation. It is impossible to understand these actions in the narrow context of individuals asserting their newly attained "political rights," but this is precisely how many progressive historians have attempted to understand this period.

It should be said that the work of Du Bois, as well as the incredible research of slave revolt done by Herbert Aptheker, crucially succeeded in resituating the demise of slavery as the result of Black rebellion itself, and thereby shattered the myth that "Lincoln freed the slaves." We would add to this understanding that the resistance that occurred after the war, in its broad scope and willingness to attack northern authorities as well as southern ones, suggests a reexamination of the substance and intent of those same slave communities' revolt *during* slavery. In other words, the implication is not only that Black slaves and maroons catalyzed the end of the Confederacy and the plantation system, but that perhaps the notions of freedom that motivated them to do so were very,

very different from the ones projected onto them years later by northern scholars and politicians.

Likewise, the tactics used by former slaves are equally a reminder that many laborers in the South did not experience the new world of paid work and labor contracts as fundamentally different from slavery or bonded servitude. Often this "new" form of labor led to workers being coerced into working the same jobs for the same masters—hardly the fundamental ethical break projected onto such changes a century and a half later by economists and other proponents of "free labor."

This points forward to the ways in which historians dealing with the subject of labor revolts in the South have been troubled, both by the region's relative ambivalence toward unionism and by unions' relative ambivalence toward the region. As books like Louis Adamic's *Dynamite* make startlingly clear, the history of labor has classically been treated as mostly synonymous with the history of trade unions. In a region with little unionism but high levels of class violence, this is an obvious problem, and as a result, non-union-based proletarian revolt in the South has often been simply ignored. This omission carries a particular racial dynamic as well because rebellious Black laborers, both pre- and post-emancipation, were often excluded from union membership, and in any case typically had little use for the trade-union model in their specific positions of work and bondage. In seeing the union as the sole reflection of proletarian struggle, scholars have effectively whitened the history of class war in this country.

Related to this has been the "uneven" economic development of the South, and its adoption of a wide range of "nontraditional" or nonclassical means to meet its labor needs, such as slavery, the convict lease, and sharecropping. Consequently, when large labor insurrections have occurred in the southern states, they have often been overlooked or seen as irrelevant to struggles elsewhere. The battle over the convict lease in Tennessee fit this pattern perfectly, receiving only a tiny fraction of the attention paid to the simultaneous strike by steelworkers in Homestead, Pennsylvania. Even though the Tennesseans' struggle proceeded from, originated with, and was organized by unionized miners, it was relatively independent from any national union bureaucracy, and it stemmed as much from the cohesive and tight-knit daily life of rural Appalachia as it did from official union structures. Its tactics set it apart awkwardly as well: what could the burning of stockades and the mass liberation of prisoners have to say about workplace struggle over wages or union recognition? The answer seems clear enough to us now, but for many at the time the response was silence and dismissal.

Little attention has been paid to the strike in Elizabethton, Tennessee, for perhaps similar reasons, even though it helped to catalyze a massive series of union-directed strikes in towns like Gastonia and Marion, where Communist Party workers, male organizers, and union bureaucrats played a greater role. In general, labor historians have an easier and more comfortable time telling the story of strikes with clear demands and mediating institutions. When the primary driving force is age-old kinship networks rather than unions, or the tactics go far beyond a strike to involve the destruction of city infrastructure or mass theft, the story can be more difficult to tell, and its implications more dangerous. Often the most basic forms of workplace resistance in this region—laziness, arson, sabotage—have gone entirely unnoticed or unconsidered as forms of intelligent rebellion.

The progressive narrative of southern resistance continues on into the 1960s and '70s with the museum-like glossy veneer of Civil Rights painted over the multitude of riots and organizing that challenged this model. Activists of the time simultaneously invisibilized and demonized those rebels whose actions challenged their regionalized narrative of nonviolence and rights. Historians who retroactively project onto these riots a similarly simplified narrative of "the Black struggle against racism" suffer from the same myopia. Even some state communists, who ought to at least recognize the nascent anticapitalism of the emerging ghetto riot, have seen this as merely a rights-oriented phase in their larger dialectic.[19]

The Left as a whole has had a particularly difficult time understanding the meaning and importance of the "nonpolitical" urban riots that were so clearly part of the living legacy of the post–Civil Rights period. These riots continued to happen across the country long after the movement organizations of that period had faded or become wholly institutionalized, but little attention has been given to the urban revolts of the 1970s and 1980s as a collective phenomenon. Consequentially, when the Rodney King riots broke out in Los Angeles and across the country in 1992, few had anything insightful to say or contribute beyond the typically stale and hollow calls for "justice" and against "police brutality." With few exceptions, the riot itself was portrayed by the Left as an unfortunate warning rather than

---

19   There were, on the contrary, a variety of more antiauthoritarian Marxists who had interesting things to say about this growing phenomenon, including Guy Debord's piece on the Watts riots and the Chicago Surrealist Group's take on the 1992 uprising in Los Angeles.

an inspiring rebellion that in itself had something meaningful to contribute to revolutionary practice and theory. These riots, and so many others since, often made no specific demands, had no single, politically legible constituency, and spoke primarily of destruction, the elimination of police from certain territories, and the mass expropriation of goods. What could the progressive historian possibly have expressed, other than apologies and confusion, about a struggle that articulates so much but asks the state for nothing? This is the dynamic of struggle that we now inhabit. A perspective that does not at least try to understand and find inspiration in the history of "illegible" rebellion will hardly be able to understand the present.

An Anarchist Historiography?

We are not suggesting the simple substitution of a singular "anarchist" narrative, as if such a thing could even exist, for a progressive one. Any historical narrative, taken as singular and omnipotent, threatens to "swallow everything it does not crush."[20] Framed another way, any writing of history, but in particular one that prioritizes a specific narrative approach, forces the writer to dismiss or set aside the infinite diversity of human actions in favor of those that fit a specific set of processes and constraints.

The solution to this problem cannot be to write history without analysis or interpretation. Doing so only reinforces the myth of the objective scholar and the inevitability of the world as it already exists, yet again committing the historicists' error of filling inconsequential data into an empty, linear timeline. Despite our caution toward any singular narrative, we have found it necessary to criticize head-on this narrative of progress with counterexamples that clearly demonstrate the substance of something deeper and more fundamental. While none of the insurrections or rebellions in this book represent a final break with the systems they attacked, their struggles express to us an inspiring urgency. In particular, we take inspiration from the participants' absolute refusal to wait, from their gestures toward an immediate and lived freedom with those comrades, friends, and family present.

Taken together as part of a larger and more thorough history, one might position these moments in any number of processes and narratives, as we have done at times in order to better understand their larger context. The tactical and strategic wisdom (and failures) of these insurrections

---

20 Anonymous, "The Strangest Prayer Vigil We've Ever Seen," http://prisonbooks.info/2013/12/21/durham-nc-the-strangest-prayer-vigil-weve-ever-seen/.

themselves pushed the state and capital to adapt its own structures, and in doing so, these crises can be articulated in retrospect as contributing to certain periods or phases of development. But we insist that these insurrections are best appreciated on their own terms as explosions out of the continuum of history rather than as inevitable confirmations of it.

Despite all the examples of legitimacy, patience, and submission, in every period of social life there have also been struggles that transcended the society in which they arose. The fundamental and immediate nature of these revolts, however incomplete, is what attracts us to them and drives us to find similar elements in our own struggles that could serve to fuel a more total break. In this desperate and forceful drive to redeem in the present all the missed possibilities of the past, history takes on meaning, not as an empty mass of data that points inevitably toward some future social peace, but as the potential for a total rupture with time itself. Our history must conjure the idea that utopia, communism, anarchy, freedom, the wild—whatever words we choose to give this yet unknowable ideal— are always possible, right now in the immediate present.

In addition to crediting these insurrections with their own transcendental force, we would emphasize that to resist adopting a singular historical narrative means refusing to portray history's struggles as determined solely by any singular category or structure of oppression, or by any one protagonist. This drives us to question the relationship of such categories to each other and to the whole. We would suggest, for example, that race, in its inherent violence, could be reframed from a question of identity and belonging *to a method of government.* This is not to simplify the problem of race along lines of a one-dimensional economic determinism—i.e., to say that racism is simply a tool by which "capitalists divide the workers"— but rather to complicate the problem so as to approach it in a more total light. With a little more introspection all these categories of structure and oppression—race, gender, sexuality, economy, state, among others—start to collapse into each other. For example, labor can be understood as a question of gender and social reproduction, capitalism's development as a process of state consolidation, race as a function of policing and democratic management, resource extraction and ecological destruction as practices of government and social control. Though in this book we have often been forced to do so in a kind of rhetorical shorthand, in our world today it is increasingly difficult to talk about any of these systems cogently as distinct phenomena, because they have all grown so fluidly into each other.

In avoiding a singular historical narrative, the anarchist project is not to collapse this vast matrix of oppressions and systems into a single question of "the state," in the way the vulgar Marxist does with economics, for example. Rather, the project is *to see this totality for itself and attack it as such.* This totality of oppression can never be fully grasped, but the horror of its vision drives us forward. It is in the sense of this totality that we have continued to phrase the struggles discussed in this book, along with our own, as that of social war. This term proves useful not simply because all existent definitions of class and class war have turned stale, but because this concept implies the total integration of these systems with each other and into every aspect of our lives, from the micro to the macro, the personal to the "political," the mundane to the monumental.[21] This war is ongoing and general, whether that fact is articulated "politically" or not.

Past and Future
The struggles and rebellions of the southeastern United States weigh on our hearts and minds, inspirational and suffocating and unknowable all at once; a history at once of bitter defeat and recuperation and also beautiful, determined acts of defiance and courage. But memory is an elusive space, within which constant conflicts of ownership occur, and our attempts to research and explore these acts are limited.

> For those of us who live without elders, books may be necessary for us to recover our histories, but history cannot live on paper. It must live in the streets, in the earth, and be constantly nourished. Like any other living being, history dies without nourishment. How can we hope to carry around a thousand years of history in our tiny little heads? We must take these

---

21 We also reiterate this combative understanding partly as a counter to the explanation of anarchism as centrally being "against hierarchy." While of course we must reject the pyramid schemes of the world around us, to see our struggle strictly in such terms, in this increasingly democratic, horizontalist world, is to set ourselves up for failure. We are reminded of the success of 1990s do-it-yourself counterculture in laying the groundwork for our current hell of tech startups and obsession with "local." The ways we choose to explain the anarchist project must tear the masks off of our enemies' faces, and to do so our explanations must undermine rather than confirm these enemies' rhetorical mythology. In the days of our grandparents, this mythology spoke of rights and economic democracy; now it speaks of breaking down barriers, participatory structures, voluntarism, and horizontal networks. In such a world, to speak of being "against hierarchy" is, at best, a bland nonstarter; at worst it is a self-betrayal in the making.

stories out of the archives, out of our skulls, and plant them in the world around us, in the change of the seasons, in the places where they occurred. By making use of this larger mind, we can remember much more.[22]

More important than any text is memory as lived experience: the feeling of walking on ground where we remember a slave revolt or an out-of-control mill strike, the smell of gunpowder or of a salve made by a grandparent, the field trip with new friends to all the spots in the land we belong to where our struggle has unfolded, the assembly or the feast where we have sat a hundred times before and know we will sit a thousand times more.

This lived memory implies also our fleeting glimpses of a different world. History, as memory, as experience, is both impossible and meaningless without these visions. Messianic and millenarian, hopeful and hopeless, beautiful and creative, horrible and destructive, impossible and realized, dogged and partial, immediate and total, individual and desperate, collective and inspired, our visions haunt us like dreams of a different past, yearning for redemption. This redemption offers up a new field of social life, full of new possibilities. The historical force of resistance, constantly defeated but resilient across time and space, might resolutely transform into the unknown substance of life we have always known was possible. The necessarily negative character of revolt might give way to authentically new forms of community, kinship, play, work, learning, and decision making. Freedom may finally lose the bitter taste of a cynical word without substance, and those who came before us may finally rest in peace.

---

22   Llev Zlodey and Jason Radegas, *Here at the Center of the World in Revolt*, (Anonymous, 2014), 148.

BIBLIOGRAPHY

An Introduction

Agee, James and Walker Evans. *Let Us Now Praise Famous Men*. Boston: Houghton Mifflin, 1988.

Benjamin, Walter. "Theses on the Philosophy of History." In *Illuminations*, edited by Hannah Arendt, 253–264. New York: Schocken Books, 1969.

Federici, Silvia. *Caliban and the Witch: Women, the Body, and Primitive Accumulation*. Brooklyn: Autonomedia, 2004.

Foucault, Michel. *Discipline and Punish: The Birth of the Prison*. New York: Vintage Books, 1979.

Mann, Sally. *Deep South*. New York: Bulfinch Press, 2005.

Chapter 1: A Subtle Yet Restless Fire

"Acts of the Assembly of Albemarle Rattified and Confirmed by the Proprietors the 20th Jan 1669 (–70)." Colonial and State Records of North Carolina (CSRNC), vol. 1: 183–184.

Allen, Theodore W. *The Invention of the White Race*. New York: Verso, 2012.

Aptheker, Herbert. *American Negro Slave Revolts*. New York: International Publishers, 1943.

———. "Maroons Within the Present Limits of the United States." In *Maroon Societies: Rebel Slave Communities in the Americas*, edited by Richard Price. Garden City, NY: Anchor Books, 1973.

The Boston Gazette and the Country Journal, June 18, 1792. In Leaming, Hugo P. *Hidden Americans: Maroons of Virginia and the Carolinas*. New York: Garland Publishing, 1995.

Byrd, William. "William Byrd's Diary," *Africans in America*, edited by Louis B. Wright and Marion Tinling. http://www.pbs.org/wgbh/aia/part1/1h283t.html.

———. *William Byrd's Histories of the Dividing Line Betwixt Virginia and North Carolina*. Raleigh: North Carolina Historical Commission, 1929.

Cheek, William F. *Black Resistance Before the Civil War*. Beverly Hills: Glencoe Press, 1970.

Genovese, Eugene D. *From Rebellion to Revolution: Afro-American Slave Revolts in the Making of the Modern World*. New Orleans: Louisiana State University Press,1979.

Federici, Silvia. *Caliban and the Witch: Women, the Body, and Primitive Accumulation*. Brooklyn: Autonomedia, 2004.

Hawks, Francis L. *History of North Carolina*, 2 vols. Fayetteville, NC: E.J. Hale and Son, 1858.

Leaming, Hugo P. *Hidden Americans: Maroons of Virginia and the Carolinas*. New York: Garland Publishing, 1995.

Linebaugh, Peter. "Jubilating, or How the Atlantic Working Class Used the Biblical Jubilee Against Capitalism, to Some Success," *New Enclosures: Midnight Notes* 10 (1990): 94.

"Lord Culpeper to Lords of Trade and Plantations, December 12, 1681." In *Calendar State Papers, Colonial Series*, 155. HM Public Record Office: 1898.

Marx, Karl. "Volume One: Capital." In *The Marx-Engels Reader*, edited by Robert C. Tucker. New York: W.W. Norton, 1978.

Merchant, Carolyn. *The Death of Nature: Women, Ecology, and the Scientific Revolution*. New York: HarperCollins, 1980.

Mullin, Gerald W. *Flight and Rebellion: Slave Resistance in Eighteenth-Century Virginia*. New York: Oxford University Press, 1972.

O'Donnell, William James, Jr. *The Maroons of the Great Dismal Swamp*. Chapel Hill: The University of North Carolina at Chapel Hill, 1993.

Olsen, Jack. "The Cursed Swamp." *Sports Illustrated*, November 26, 1962, 68.

Parent, Anthony S. Jr. *Foul Means: The Formation of a Slave Society in Virginia, 1660–1740*. Chapel Hill: University of North Carolina Press, 1996.

Richmond Daily Examiner, January 14, 1864. in Aptheker, Herbert. *American Negro Slave Revolts*. New York: International Publishers, 1943.

Rediker, Marcus and Peter Linebaugh. "The Many Headed Hydra." In

Gone to Croatan: Origins of North American Dropout Culture, edited by Ron Sakolsky and James Koehnline, 129–160. Brooklyn: Autonomedia, 1993.

Shoatz, Russell "Maroon." *Maroon the Implacable: The Collected Writings of Russell Maroon Shoatz*, edited by Fred Ho and Quincy Saul. Oakland: PM Press, 2013.

Stowe, Harriet Beecher. *Dred: A Tale of the Great Dismal Swamp*. New York: Penguin Books, 1856.

Tidwell, John. "Maroons: North America's Hidden History." August 26, 2002. http://www.freewebs.com/midnightsea/maroons.pdf

"Virginia Proclamation (July 24th, 1711)." In *CRNC*, vol. 1, 776.

Chapter 2: Ogeechee Til Death

"A Letter from President Lincoln.; Reply to Horace Greeley. Slavery and the Union The Restoration of the Union the Paramount Object." Published August 24, 1862. *New York Times*. http://www.nytimes.com/1862/08/24/news/letter-president-lincoln-reply-horace-greeley-slavery-union-restoration-union.html.

Bell, Karen. "'The Ogeechee Troubles': Federal Land Restoration and the 'Lived Realities' of Temporary Proprietors, 1865–1868." *The Georgia Historical Quarterly* 85 (2001): 375–397.

Benjamin, Walter. "Theses on the Philosophy of History." In *Illuminations*, edited by Hannah Arendt, 253–264. New York: Schocken Books, 1969.

"Bessie Jones." National Endowment for the Arts biography: http://arts.gov/honors/heritage/fellows/bessie-jones.

Clifton, James M. "Twilight Comes to the Rice Kingdom: Postbellum Rice Culture on the South Atlantic Coast." *The Georgia Historical Quarterly* 62 (1978):146–154.

Du Bois, W.E.B. *Black Reconstruction in America 1860–1880*. New York: Simon and Schuster, 1935.

———. "John Brown." In *The Oxford W.E.B. Du Bois Reader*, edited by Eric J. Sundquist, 258–259. New York: Oxford University Press.

"Ella Thomas, Augusta, 1868." In *Standing upon the Mouth of a Volcano: New South Georgia, A Documentary History*. edited by Mills Lane, 73–79. Savannah: Beehive Press, 1993. Original diary entries taken from the Ella Gertrude Clanton Thomas papers 1848–1978 in the David M. Rubenstein Rare Book & Manuscript Library at Duke University.

Foner, Eric. *A Short History of Reconstruction.* New York: Harper Perennial, 1990.

———. *Nothing But Freedom: Emancipation and Its Legacy.* Baton Rouge: Louisiana State University Press, 2007.

"Frances Leigh, St. Simon's Island, 1866–68." In *Standing upon the Mouth of a Volcano: New South Georgia, A Documentary History,* edited by Mills Lane, 63–73. Savannah: Beehive Press, 1993. Originally published in Frances Butler Leigh, *Ten Years on a Georgia Plantation Since the War* (London, 1833).

"John H. Kennaway, 1865." In *Standing upon the Mouth of a Volcano: New South Georgia, A Documentary* History, edited by Mills Lane, 3–7. Savannah: Beehive Press, 1993. Originally published in John H. Kennaway, *On Sherman's Track or the South after the War* (London, 1867): 105–163.

Linebaugh, Peter. "Jubilating, or How the Atlantic Working Class Used the Biblical Jubilee Against Capitalism, to Some Success," *New Enclosures: Midnight Notes* 10 (1990): 84–98.

Lockley, Timothy James. *Maroon Communities in South Carolina: A Documentary Record.* Columbia: University of South Carolina Press, 2009.

Marx, Karl. *Capital: A Critique of Political Economy.* New York: The Modern Library, 1906: 834.

"The Ogeechee Insurrection, 1868–69." In *Standing upon the Mouth of a Volcano: New South Georgia; A Documentary History,* edited by Mills Lane, 79–89. Savannah: Beehive Press, 1993. Originally published in the *Savannah Morning News* between December 23, 1868 and January 8, 1869.

Stewart, Mart A. "Rice, Water, and Power: Landscapes of Domination and Resistance in the Lowcountry, 1790–1880." *Environmental History Review* 15 (1991): 47–64.

Williams, Eric. *Capitalism and Slavery.* Chapel Hill: University of North Carolina Press, 2004.

Chapter 3: The Lowry Wars

Dial, Adolph L. and David K. Eliades. *The Only Land I Know: A History of the Lumbee Indians.* San Francisco: Indian Historian Press, 1975.

Evans, W. McKee. *To Die Game: The Story of the Lowry Band, Indian Guerrillas of Reconstruction.* Baton Rouge: Louisiana State University Press, 1971.

Genovese, Eugene. *From Rebellion to Revolution: Afro-American Slave Revolts in the Making of the Modern World*. Baton Rouge: Louisiana State University Press, 1979.

Lumberton *Robesonian*, January 20, 1958. In Dial, Adolph L. and David K. Eliades. *The Only Land I Know: A History of the Lumbee Indians*. San Francisco: Indian Historian Press, 1975.

Newsweek, LI, January 27, 1958, 27. In Dial, Adolph L. and David K. Eliades. *The Only Land I Know: A History of the Lumbee Indians*. San Francisco: Indian Historian Press, 1975.

Norment, Mary C. *The Lowrie History, As Acted in Part by Henry Berry Lowrie, the Great North Carolina Bandit. With Biographical Sketches of His Associates. Being a Complete History of the Modern Robber Band in the County of Robeson and State of North Carolina*. Wilmington: Daily Journal Printer, 1875.

Townsend, George Alfred. *The Swamp Outlaws: or, The North Carolina Bandits; Being a Complete History of the Modern Rob Roys and Robin Hoods*. New York: Robert M. DeWitt, 1872.

Weekly Journal, Wilmington, September 24, 1869. In Evans, W. McKee. *To Die Game: The Story of the Lowry Band, Indian Guerrillas of Reconstruction*. Baton Rouge: Louisiana State University Press, 1971.

Wilmington *North Carolinian*, February 15, 1865. In Evans, W. McKee. *To Die Game: The Story of the Lowry Band, Indian Guerrillas of Reconstruction*. Baton Rouge: Louisiana State University Press, 1971.

Wilmington *Star*, August 18, 1871. In Evans, W. McKee. *To Die Game: The Story of the Lowry Band, Indian Guerrillas of Reconstruction*. Baton Rouge: Louisiana State University Press, 1971.

Chapter 4: The Stockade Stood Burning

Daniel, Pete. "The Tennessee Convict Wars." *Tennessee Historical Quarterly* 3 (Fall 1975): 273–292.

Kaspar, Johann. *We Demand Nothing*. Everywhere: The Institute for Experimental Freedom, 2009.

Lichtenstein, Alex. *Twice the Work of Free Labor: The Political Economy of Convict Labor in the New South*. New York: Verso, 1996.

Oshinsky, David. *Worse Than Slavery: Parchman Farm and the Ordeal of Jim Crow Justice*. New York: The Free Press, 1996.

Shapiro, Karin A. *A New South Rebellion*. Chapel Hill: University of North Carolina Press, 1998.

Chapter 5: Wild Hearts in the Southern Mills

Adams, David. "Internal Military Intervention in the United States." *Journal of Peace Research* 32 (May 1995): 197–211.

Associated Press. "President of the Rayon Companies Commits Suicide." *Kentucky New Era*, October 1, 1929.

Bernstein, Irving. *The Lean Years: A History of the American Worker 1920–1933*. Boston: Houghton Mifflin, 1960.

Cole, Robert. Interview by Jacquelyn Hall, May 10, 1981. Interview number H-0311 in the Southern Oral History Program Collection *(#4007)*, Southern Historical Collection, The Louis Round Wilson Special Collections Library, University of North Carolina at Chapel Hill.

Edens, Bessie. Interview by Mary Frederickson, August 14, 1979. Interview number H-0313 in the Southern Oral History Program Collection *(#4007)*, Southern Historical Collection, The Louis Round Wilson Special Collections Library, University of North Carolina at Chapel Hill.

Galliher, Christine and Dave Galliher. Interview by Jacquelyn Hall, August 8, 1979. Interview number H-0314 in the Southern Oral History Program Collection *(#4007)*, Southern Historical Collection, The Louis Round Wilson Special Collections Library, University of North Carolina at Chapel Hill.

Hall, Jacquelyn Dowd. "Disorderly Women: Gender and Labor Militancy in the Appalachian South." In *Half Sisters of History: Southern Women and the American Past*, edited by Catherine Clinton, 180–223. Durham: Duke University Press, 1994.

Hall, Jacquelyn Dowd, James Leloudis, Robert Korstad, Mary Murphy, Lu Ann Jones, and Christopher B. Daly. *Like a Family: The Making of a Southern Cotton Mill World*. Chapel Hill: University of North Carolina Press, 1987.

Salmond, John A. *Gastonia, 1929: The Story of the Loray Mill Strike*. Chapel Hill: University of North Carolina Press, 1995.

Selby, John G. "'Better to Starve in the Shade than in the Factory': Labor Protest in High Point, North Carolina, in the Early 1930s." *NC Historical Review* 64 (1987): 43–64.

Smith, Albert C. "'Southern Violence' Reconsidered: Arson as Protest in Black-Belt Georgia, 1865–1910." *The Journal of Southern History* 51 (1985): 527–564.

Tippett, Tom. *When Southern Labor Stirs*. Huntington: Appalachian Movement Press, 1972.

Whalen, Robert Weldon. *"Like Fire in Broom Straw": Southern Journalism and the Textile Strikes of 1929–1931.* Westport: Greenwood Press, 2001.

Chapter 6: From Rebel to Citizen and Back Again

Agamben, Giorgio. *Means Without Ends: Notes on Politics.* Minneapolis: University of Minnesota Press, 2000.

Alston, Ashanti. "Black Anarchism." http://prisonbookscollective.files. wordpress.com/2011/03/Blacktotal.pdf.

Anderson, Carol (Emory Associate Professor of African American Studies), Emory University. Podcast Video, March 13, 2012. http://news. emory.edu/stories/2012/03/hidden_history_of_civil_rights_movement_tennessee_riot/campus.html.

Bains, Lee E. "Birmingham 1963: Confrontations over Civil Rights." *Birmingham, Alabama, 1956–1963: The Black Struggle for Civil Rights.* Brooklyn: Carlson Publishing, 1989.

Bender, Don. "The Atlanta Riots." *Mennonite Central Committee News Service,* September 30, 1966. http://www.mcusa-archives.org/plowshares/atlanta/9.30.1966.html

Blauner, Robert. "Internal Colonialism and Ghetto Revolt." *The Black Revolt: The Civil Rights Movement, Ghetto Uprisings, and Separatism.* Englewood Cliffs, NJ: Prentice-Hall, 1971.

Booker, Washington. Interview by Willoughby Anderson. November 17, 1991, http://dc.lib.unc.edu/cdm/ref/collection/sohp/id/8091.

The Chicago Surrealist Group. "Three Days That Shook the New World Order." *Race Traitor* 2 (1993).

"A Disgrace before God: Striking Black Sanitation Workers vs. Black Officialdom in 1977 Atlanta." http://libcom.org/library/disgrace -god-striking-Black-sanitation-workers-vs-Black-officialdom -1977-atlanta.

Ervin, Lorenzo Komboa. "Black People Have a Right to Rebel." *How Fast It All Blows Up: Some Lessons from the 2001 Cincinnati Riots.* St. Louis: One Thousand Emotions, 2001.

Eskew, Glenn T. *Review Essay: Civil Rights History in Louisville and Kentucky.* http://filsonhistorical.org/wp-content/uploads/2013/02/OVH_ WINTER_10.pdf.

"Freedom Now." *Time,* May 17, 1963. http://cgi.cnn.com/ALLPOLI-TICS/1996/analysis/back.time/9605/15/.

Harmon, David Andrew. *Beneath the Image of the Civil Rights Movement and Race Relations: Atlanta, Georgia, 1946–1981.* New York: Garland Publishing, 1996.

Harris, Daryl B. *The Logic of Black Urban Rebellions: Challenging the Dynamics of White Domination in Miami.* London: Praeger, 1999.

Hornsby, Alton, Jr. *Black Power in Dixie: A Political History of African Americans in Atlanta.* Gainesville: University Press of Florida, 2009.

It's About Time. "Black Panther Party Pieces of History 1966–1969," *It's About Time.* http://www.itsabouttimebpp.com/chapter_history/bpp_pieces_of_history.html

Kaspar, Johann. *We Demand Nothing.* Everywhere: The Institute for Experimental Freedom, 2009.

K'Meyer, Tracy. *Civil Rights in the Gateway to the South.* Lexington: University Press of Kentucky, 2009.

———. "Empowerment, Consciousness, Defense: The Diverse Meanings of the Black Power Movement in Louisville, Kentucky." In *Neighborhood Rebels: Black Power at the Local Level,* edited by Peniel E. Joseph. New York: Palgrave MacMillan, 2010.

Machado, Joey. "The 1967 Central Park Riots in Tampa." http://jam1592.blogspot.com/2008/02/sample-3-1967-central-park-riots-in.html.

McCartin, Joseph A. "'Fire the Hell Out of Them': Sanitation Workers' Struggles and the Normalization of the Striker Replacement Strategy in the 1970s." *Labour: Studies in Working-Class History of the Americas* 2, no. 3 (2005). Oberschall, Anthony. "The Los Angeles Riot of August 1965." In *The Black Revolt: The Civil Rights Movement, Ghetto Uprisings, and the Separatism,* edited by James A. Geschwender. Englewood Cliffs, NJ: Prentice-Hall, 1971. 264–284.

"Police-Community Relations in Tampa: An Update." *United States Commission on Civil Rights.* Florida Advisory Committee.

Report of the National Advisory Commission on Civil Disorders. New York: Bantam, 1968.

Tyson, Timothy. "On Robert F. Williams." University of Wisconsin-Madison, reprinted in "I Will Not Crawl" (NC Piece Corps, Chapel Hill, 2009).

———. "Robert F. Williams, 'Black Power;' and the Roots of the African American Freedom Struggle." *The Journal of American History* 85, no. 2 (1998): 540.

Van West, Carroll. "Columbia Race Riot, 1946," http://tennesseeencyclopedia.net/entry.php?rec=296.

Widell Robert W., Jr. "The Power Belongs to Us and We Belong to the

Revolutionary Age: The Alabama Black Liberation Front and the Long Reach of the Black Panther Party." In *Liberated Territory: Untold Local Perspectives on the Black Panther Party*, edited by Yohuru Williams and Jama Lazerow, 136–180. Durham: Duke University Press, 2008.

Williams, Robert F. *Negroes with Guns*. Detroit: Wayne State University Press, 1998.

Zinn, Howard. *A People's History of the United States*. New York: Harper-Collins, 2003.

Chapter 7: "We Asked for Life!"

Bakst, Daren. *North Carolina's Forced Sterilization Program*. Raleigh: John Locke Foundation, 2011.

Break de Chains of U$ Legalized Slavery. Durham: North Carolina Hard Times Prison Project, 1976.

Foucault, Michel. *Discipline and Punish: The Birth of the Prison*. New York: Vintage Books, 1979.

Girshick, Lori B. *No Safe Haven: Stories of Women in Prison*. Boston: Northeastern University Press, 1999.

Hames-Garcia, Michael. *Fugitive Thought: Prison Movements, Race, and the Meaning of Justice*. Minneapolis: University of Minnesota Press, 2004.

Law, Victoria. *Resistance Behind Bars: The Struggles of Incarcerated Women*. Oakland: PM Press, 2009.

Parenti, Christian. *Lockdown America: Police and Prisons in the Age of Crisis*. New York: Verso, 1999.

Stuart, Susan. "Now Have You Ever Seen Justice?," *Break de Chains of U$ Legalized Slavery*. Durham: North Carolina Hard Times Prison Project, 1976.

Useem, Bert, Camille Camp, and George Camp. *Resolution of Prison Riots: Strategies and Policies*. New York: Oxford University Press, 1996.

Useem, Bert and Peter Kimball. *States of Siege: U.S. Prison Riots, 1971–1986*. New York: Oxford University Press, 1991.

Wittig, Monique. *Les Guerilleres*. New York: The Viking Press, 1969.

Conclusion: Preliminary Notes for an Anarchist Historiography of the American South

Anonymous. *Between Predicates, War: Theses on Contemporary Struggle*, United States: Institute for Experimental Freedom, 2013.

Benjamin, Walter. "Theses on the Philosophy of History." In *Illuminations*, edited by Hannah Arendt, 253–264. New York: Schocken Books, 1969.

O'Connor, Flannery. *Mystery and Manners: Occasional Prose.* New York: Farrar Straus, and Giroux, 1969.

Wilderson, Frank B. "The Black Liberation Army and The Paradox of Political Engagement." Ill-Will Editions, 2014.

INDEX

Support **AK Press!**

AK Press is one of the world's largest and most productive anarchist publishing houses. We're entirely worker-run & democratically managed. We operate without a corporate structure—no boss, no managers, no bullshit. We publish close to twenty books every year, and distribute thousands of other titles published by other like-minded independent presses and projects from around the globe.

The Friends of AK program is a way that you can directly contribute to the continued existence of AK Press, and ensure that we're able to keep publishing great books just like this one! Friends pay $25 a month directly into our publishing account ($30 for Canada, $35 for international), and receive a copy of every book AK Press publishes for the duration of their membership! Friends also receive a discount on anything they order from our website or buy at a table: 50% on AK titles, and 20% on everything else. We've also added a new Friends of AK ebook program: $15 a month gets you an electronic copy of every book we publish for the duration of your membership. Combine it with a print subscription, too!

There's great stuff in the works—so sign up now to become a Friend of AK Press, and let the presses roll!

Won't you be our friend? Email friendsofak@akpress.org for more info, or visit the Friends of AK Press website: www.akpress.org/programs/friendsofak